Teaching the Reformations

Special Issue Editor
Christopher Metress

MDPI • Basel • Beijing • Wuhan • Barcelona • Belgrade

Special Issue Editor
Christopher Metress
Samford University
USA

Editorial Office
MDPI AG
St. Alban-Anlage 66
Basel, Switzerland

This edition is a reprint of the Special Issue published online in the open access journal *Religions* (ISSN 2077-1444) in 2017 (available at: http://www.mdpi.com/journal/religions/special_issues/reformations).

For citation purposes, cite each article independently as indicated on the article page online and as indicated below:

Author 1; Author 2. Article title. *Journal Name.* **Year**. *Article number*, page range.

First Edition 2017

ISBN 978-3-03842-522-9 (Pbk)
ISBN 978-3-03842-523-6 (PDF)

Table of Contents

List of Contributors

J. Caleb Clanton is University Research Professor and professor of philosophy at Lipscomb University, and he holds an adjoint appointment in engineering management at Vanderbilt University. His research centers on issues in philosophy of religion, moral philosophy, and the history of philosophy. He is the author or editor of several books, including most recently *Philosophy of Religion in the Classical American Tradition* (University of Tennessee Press, 2017).

Rachel B. Griffis is an assistant professor in the Language and Literature Department at Sterling College, where she teaches writing and literature courses. She also serves as Director for the Integration of Faith and Learning. Her scholarly interests include colonial and nineteenth century American literature, women writers, religion and literature, and Christian teaching and learning. She has two publications about Christianity and teaching: one is a book chapter titled "Vocation is Something that Happens to You: Freedom, Education, and the American Literary Tradition," which will appear in *Christian Faith and University Life: Stewards of the Academy*, and the other is an article for *International Journal of Christianity and Education* titled, "Self-Knowledge and Character Formation: Teaching to Students' Weaknesses."

Christopher A. Hill is an associate professor of English at the University of Tennessee at Martin, where he teaches sixteenth and seventeenth century English literature. He holds degrees from Samford University and the University of North Carolina at Chapel Hill. His research is focused on the intersections of rhetoric and religious thought in the prose and poetry of the Tudor and Stuart periods in English literature, and has published essays on George Herbert's poetry and on the Martin Marprelate Controversy.

R. Ward Holder is a historical theologian and professor of theology at Saint Anselm College. Across his career, he has examined the era of the Reformations, the work of John Calvin, political theology, and how various faith communities ground their truth claims. Among other works, he has authored *John Calvin and the Grounding of Interpretation: Calvin's First Commentaries* (Brill, 2006), *and Crisis and Renewal: The Era of the Reformations* (Westminster John Knox, 2009), and he has edited *Reformation Readings of Romans*, with Kathy Ehrensperger (T. & T. Clark 2008), *A Companion to Paul in the Reformation* (Brill, 2009), *The Westminster Handbook to Theologies of the Reformation* (Westminster John Knox, 2011), and *Calvin and Luther: The Continuing Relationship* (Vandenhoeck & Ruprecht, 2013). His current work focuses on Calvin's use of the theological tradition as a source for his own doctrinal formulations.

John MacInnis serves as associate professor of music and Music Department Co-Chair at Dordt College, in Sioux Center, Iowa. His teaching duties include Music History, Music Theory, World Music, and contributing arts courses to the college's CORE curriculum. As an organist and pianist, he enjoys learning new literature and collaborating with other musicians.

Beth McGinnis is assistant professor of musicology at Samford University, where she teaches courses in music history and piano. She is organist at Vestavia Hills Baptist Church, accompanist for the Alabama Symphony Orchestra Chorus, and a yoga instructor at the YMCA.

Scott McGinnis is associate professor of religion at Samford University, where he teaches courses in theology and history. He regularly teaches general education courses as well as the Western Intellectual History sequence in the University Fellows Program. He serves as Samford's faculty representative to the Lilly Fellows Program in Humanities and the Arts, and he is the co-editor of *Teaching Augustine*, selected papers from the inaugural 2014 TCIT conference on "Augustine Across the Curriculum."

Bruce McNair is associate professor of history at Campbell University. He teaches Western Civilization survey courses, as well as upper level courses on European history ranging from Ancient Greece and Rome to Modern Europe. His primary areas of interest are the Italian Renaissance, the Reformation, and Medieval Philosophy.

G. Sujin Pak served as Associate Dean of Academic Programs at Duke Divinity School from 2012-15 and is a faculty member in the history of Christianity at Duke Divinity School. She specializes in the history of Christianity in late medieval and early modern Europe. Her teaching, research and writing focus upon the theology of the Protestant reformers, the Protestant Reformation and the Jews, women and the Reformation, and the history of biblical interpretation. Professor Pak is the author of *The Judaizing Calvin: Sixteenth-Century Debates over the Messianic Psalms* (Oxford, 2010) and several articles in journals such as *Church History, Reformation & Renaissance Review, Church History and Religious Culture,* and *Calvin Theological Journal.* Her current research project studies the shifting views of prophecy and uses of Old Testament prophecy in the Reformation era.

Josh Reeves is assistant professor in Science and Religion in the philosophy department at Samford University. He is a graduate of Cambridge University and Boston University and completed a postdoctoral position in the Heyendaal Program for Theology and Science at Radboud University in the Netherlands. He is co-author of *A Little Book for New Scientists* and has published articles in journals such as *Zygon,* the *Journal of Religion,* and *Theology and Science.*

Aaron M. Schubert is a PhD student in Theological Studies at Dallas Theological Seminary. He received his BA in History from Hillsdale College, and his Masters of Theology also from Dallas Theological Seminary. His Master's thesis argued for the importance of the doctrine of Divine Simplicity for contemporary theology. His research interests include Patristic hermeneutics and Augustinian theology.

About the Guest Editor

Christopher Metress is University Professor and a Wilton H. Bunch Fellow at Samford University, where he teaches courses in literature, film, and western intellectual history. He has published more than 100 essays and reviews in such journals as *Studies in the Novel, African American Review, English Literature in Transition: 1880-1920,* and *Southern Quarterly,* and his most recent books include *Memory, Invention, and Delivery: Transmitting and Transforming Liberal Arts Education for the Future* (co-edited with Richard Dagger and Scott Lee, 2016) and *Teaching Augustine* (co-edited with Samford colleague Scott McGinnis, 2016). He is one of the founders of the Teaching the Christian Intellectual Tradition project and has co-chaired both national conferences.

Preface to the TCIT Series

The role of the humanities in university curricula has been the topic of much national debate, with politicians predicting the imminent demise of liberal learning, a fate feared by some and perhaps welcomed by others. Even if one stops short of such apocalyptic scenarios, core and general education courses that promote a humanities-based liberal arts education are under tremendous pressure to justify themselves in an environment where dollars are tight and professionalization is all the rage. Concurrently, humanities departments feel a similar push, urged by their administrations to pitch their disciplines more for the skills they develop than the dispositions they cultivate, or the questions they inspire. In this context, it is more important than ever that liberal arts courses not only be taught, but taught well.

In support of teaching excellence in the liberal arts, Samford University hosted its inaugural Teaching the Christian Intellectual Tradition (TCIT) Conference, the first in a series of biennial gatherings designed to explore ways for non-specialists to teach the Christian intellectual tradition more effectively in undergraduate core and general education courses. In October 2014, more than fifty scholars from across the disciplines gathered in Birmingham for "Augustine Across the Curriculum." To share the findings of this conference with a larger audience, the organizers of TCIT partnered with *Religions* to publish *Teaching Augustine*, a special issue of selected papers that later appeared as a similarly titled print volume. This partnership continues with the publication of a second special issue and printed volume on *Teaching the Reformations*, the focus of the 2016 conference.

TCIT conferences are committed to the liberal arts as both a foundation for and a unifying force of degree programs across the university, and we assume that general education and core courses are the key locations where this integrative learning will take place. This strategy, however, faces several difficult challenges. For instance, core courses at institutions similar to Samford often draw faculty who are asked to teach outside of their disciplines and areas of expertise. Specialists in Romanticism find themselves pondering with their students Luther's theology of justification in the context of the late medieval church; theologians struggle to offer historically informed readings of post-colonial fiction; and Latin American historians edge their way cautiously into the foreign world of the drawing rooms of English nobility. The challenge can be daunting, particularly for younger faculty. Having emerged recently from specialized graduate training, they are now called upon to teach, and teach well, texts they may not have read since their undergraduate years, or ever.

A somewhat different problem emerges in general education courses. Here, faculty move more comfortably within their own disciplines. However, professional training and disciplinary pressures often marginalize the great works of the Christian intellectual tradition, resulting in general education courses that, whether by intention or benign neglect, fail to draw to upon the rich insights of that tradition. What emerges are survey or introductory courses that perpetuate the notion that the concerns and positions of the faithful have no place in the disciplines. Finally, for those faculty fully committed to the Christian intellectual tradition, there remains the further challenge of finding a way to promote a creative, constructive, and critical engagement with that tradition without lapsing into either hagiography or shallow presentism. Just as simply teaching the humanities is not enough, teaching the Christian intellectual tradition is not enough. It must be taught well, and that means creatively and critically, with a mind toward how that tradition, through its own long and contested engagement with the deepest questions, enriches every discipline and, by extension, every curriculum.

The TCIT conferences are designed to address these challenges in academic professional training by providing venues for non-specialists to gather and exchange ideas and strategies for engaging in productive classroom discussions of key writers and, ultimately, the fundamental questions of human existence and flourishing: Who are we? Why are we here? How does one live purposefully and morally with others? Given that such questions transcend any university degree program or discipline, and given that the Christian intellectual tradition provides an array of influential answers to these questions, it is appropriate that such discussions both within and across the disciplines be made available to all. It is with this intent that the following volume is offered.

Christopher Metress
Special Issue and Series Editor

Editorial

Teaching the Reformations—Introduction

Christopher Metress

Samford University, 800 Lakeshore Drive, Birmingham, AL 35229, USA; cpmetres@samford.edu

Received: 9 June 2017; Accepted: 12 June 2017; Published: 29 June 2017

Abstract: This introduction to the Special Issue "Teaching the Reformations" summarizes the volume's essays and discusses the conference at which they were presented.

Keywords: Reformations; Martin Luther; John Calvin; Protestantism; Catholicism; humanities; the liberal arts; pedagogy; core and general education curricula

In October 2014, Samford University hosted its inaugural biennial conference on "Teaching the Christian Intellectual Tradition." Drawing more than fifty scholars from thirty-plus universities, and supported by a generous grant from the Lilly Fellows Program in the Humanities and the Arts, "Augustine Across the Curriculum" was designed to help non-specialists teach the writings of Augustine more effectively in undergraduate core and general education classes. Anchored by plenary addresses from Peter Iver Kaufman and Kristen Deede Johnson, a selection of conference papers was published in a special issue of *Religions* in spring 2015, helping to disseminate the interdisciplinary insights of "Augustine Across the Curriculum" to a wider international audience. Building upon the energy and partnerships established at this conference, Samford developed a companion initiative: a biennial "Teaching the Christian Intellectual Tradition Summer Institute." Led by faculty from the University Fellows Program, this week-long residential seminar met in June 2015 and focused on "Teaching Dante's *Commedia*," with more than a dozen faculty from the fields of history, classics, English, philosophy, and theology engaged in a close reading of Dante's masterpiece. Both biennial initiatives—the conference and the summer institute—flow from a common conviction that Samford shares with many universities and colleges across the country: in this era of intense competition for resources, when the liberal arts are increasingly valued (or devalued) in terms of the "skills" and "measurable outcomes" they produce, it is more important than ever to support institutions and faculty committed to teaching the Christian Intellectual Tradition, and teaching it well.

The papers gathered in this special issue represent the work of "Teaching the Reformations," the 2016 follow-up to "Augustine Across the Curriculum." As Eamon Duffy has recently noted, 31 October 1517 marks "the fifth centenary of one of the few precisely datable historical events that can be said to have changed the world forever" (Duffy 2016). Of course, that precisely datable event is not complemented by a precisely understood theological, political, and cultural legacy, and the challenges of teaching that rich and contested legacy to today's undergraduates was the focus of the 2016 conference. In the conference's opening plenary address, which also serves as the opening essay to this collection, R. Ward Holder reminds teachers of the Christian Intellectual Tradition to resist convenient narratives about the Reformations. In "The Reformers and Tradition: Seeing the Roots of a Problem" (Holder 2017), Holder acknowledges how, when faced with the theological and ecclesiological complexities of the era and limited time to explore them, faculty "will trot out a number of old chestnuts, because as we have found, the old ideas got to be old ideas because people liked them and could remember them." Among these chestnuts, "We will talk about the three Reformation solas—*sola fide*, *sola gratia*, and *sola scriptura*. We will impress (or bore) our students by explaining the meaning of the ablatives and how that gives just the right amount of nuance to these formulae." Moreover, "We will turn to the 17th century for a description of the Reformation—Ecclesia

Reformata, Semper Reformanda—and consider that this was trying to capture a dynamism that sought to argue with the classicism of medieval Catholicism." Finally, "At some point we will arrive at the difference between scripture and tradition" because, "although we know it not to be nuanced, we see great explanatory powers in bumper-sticker history." Challenging "tradition vs. scripture" as a manner of distinguishing Protestants from Catholics during the early modern period, Holder's essay argues instead for teaching undergraduates about how Reform movements exist on a "continuum of continuity with the medieval inheritance," manifesting "genealogical and influential links across the eras." Alert to how these movements negotiated the traditions they inherited from the patristic fathers and the medieval church, Holder pays special attention to Luther and Calvin, noting that their selective and intentional engagement with these traditions was not only a hallmark of their reforms but also, perhaps, a key to the survival and expansion of the new traditions they established (as opposed to, say, the Anabaptists, whose more thorough rejection of tradition put them at odds with the temporal realms of their day, making it much more difficult for their message to grow and spread.) Teaching these reform movements along a "continuum of continuity" with earlier church traditions relies on distinguishing carefully between "Traditions" (capital T) and "traditions" (small t). Borrowing this distinction from Yves Congar, Holder urges us to see "traditions" as "those habits of mind and pieces of received wisdom that the church constantly passes down to the next generation," against "Traditions," the "power of the Church, based on a conveniently oral source, to proclaim authority in a manner it saw fit." For the Reformers, it was "Tradition" that was the problem, while "traditions," which represented the "inheritance of the prior fifteen centuries," were "the common birthright of Christians across Europe" and, rightly understood, were available to all. Clarifying this distinction has a threefold benefit. First, it "is simply better history": access to fifteen centuries of church tradition "generally stood various reforming movements in good stead," and to "argue otherwise involves historians in an attempt to bend history to justify doctrine." Second, this distinction creates "a better typology of reform movements than some we presently use," one which has "the increased value of being able to place all of the large ecclesiastical and ecclesiological reform movements of the era together" along a more nuanced continuum. Finally, this deeper understanding of the Reformers and tradition helps students to understand themselves better as "historically-situated" subjects who are living, like the Reformers were, in a "stream of tradition that helps to define them." By examining what the Reformers did with "their mental and emotional inheritance," our students not only come to know the Reformers better, but they also grasp more deeply their "own efforts at making progress on understanding the human condition."

In the conference's other plenary address, G. Sujin Pak also asks us to reconsider the Reformers as historically-situated subjects. In "The Protestant Reformers and the Jews: Excavating Contexts, Unearthing Logic" (Pak 2017), Pak highlights the important task of understanding how Luther and Calvin developed their views of and teachings about Jews and Judaism within particular immediate contexts and specific theological frameworks. Acknowledging that this topic is "both ethical and personal ... because it involves actual persons and actual bodies," Pak nonetheless warns us against the "temptation to move immediately to ethical judgments" about the views held by Luther and Calvin. Instead, we must seize upon this fraught topic as an "opportunity for critical self-reflection," embracing the "historian's task" to "unearth the logic that drives any given person or group, regardless of the moral judgments one might feel compelled to make." When we do so, we not only help undergraduates to understand better the "wider historical and intellectual landscapes" within which Luther and Calvin operated, but we also help our students to draw implications for the present about what Christian faithfulness might look like in response to "the other" in light of the long and troubled history between Christian and Jews. Noting that relations between Christians and Jews were always in flux—cycling through times of "peaceful coexistence" and "intellectual collaboration" against moments of "outright persecution"—Pak establishes that, for Christians, the "key point of tension" in their history with the Jews was the fact that "the vast majority of Jews, to whom the promises of the Old Testament were made, rejected Jesus Christ and the promised Messiah," a rejection that "threatened to undermine the legitimacy of the Christian faith." On this point of tension, then, the Reformers introduced nothing new to the history of Christian-Jewish relations, operating within a "prior tradition of Christian anti-Jewish teachings and actions." While this context does not excuse the Reformers, it is a "a point that should [not] ... be lost upon us," particularly in light of the secondary literature on Luther, some of which presents him "as the father of anti-Semitism, drawing a direct line from Luther to the Third Reich." Perhaps because Calvin did not, like Luther, write treatises devoted specifically to the Jews or Judaism, his legacy is more ambiguous, with some scholars treating him as a "firm antagonist" of the Jews, yet others haling him "as one of the least anti-Judaic figures of his time." Although Pak is attuned to the many socio-cultural contexts that contributed to how both men viewed Jews and Judaism, she places at the heart of her analysis the "centrality of biblical interpretation" and the Reformers' defense of Scripture's perspicuity. For Luther, Jews and Judaism were "a central concern ... across his lifetime," and his anti-Semitism developed in large part because he was defending a theological framework that rested on a "christological exegesis of the Old Testament and key reformational teachings that he genuinely believed were the perspicuous content of Scripture." For Calvin, a theological framework was also at work in the development of his ideas about Judaism: because of his strong affirmation of the unity of the covenant, Calvin "read Jews of the Old Testament as participants in God's eternal covenant"; thus, the rejection of Christ by contemporary Jews threatened to "endanger the very exegetical principles that Calvin maintained for the preservation of the perspicuity of Scripture." In the end, Pak, like Holder, would have faculty and students draw lessons from this deeper understanding of a historically-situated Reformations. For Holder, that lesson goes to our own "situated-ness" as agents in a stream of inherited traditions that are always defining us. For Pak, that lesson goes to the heart of Christian identity in a pluralist world. Called always to proclaim and defend the faith, Christians would do well to remember the history of Christian-Jewish relations, and particularly the examples of Luther and Calvin, which can "demonstrate what can happen when Christians care more about the content of their defense than whether their method is ethical and faithful." An ethical and faithful defense of the teachings of Scripture would not, in light of this history, be any less convicted; rather, such a defense would keep in mind always the difference between "to convert" and "to witness," and in doing so recall that we must "let God do what God may with that witness," holding to our convictions "in a manner consistent with the belief in a God who would die on a cross and take the sin and violence of the world onto God's very own Self, precisely to end all violence and oppression." This kind of Christian witness would draw deeply from a historical understanding of our fallen nature, resting upon a "profound humility" that is necessary for "negotiating truth communally with an openness to the image of God even in the 'other.'"

Complementing these plenary addresses, this special issue also contains eight additional essays, each one selected for how well it enriches the ways in which a key text, issue, or controversy from the Reformations can be introduced into the classroom. The first four essays cluster around Luther and Calvin, building upon the insights of the two plenaries while introducing new points of entry, and the final four essays expand beyond these two major figures to introduce new writers, as well as new hermeneutical and disciplinary issues. In "Martin Luther and Lucas Cranach Teaching the Lord's Prayer" (McNair 2017) Bruce McNair examines how, in a diverse set of writings and sermons on the Prayer spanning a twenty-year period, Luther found "new ways to express his most fundamental theological principles, such as justification by faith alone, the alien and proper work of God, the corruption of the will and the hiddenness of God." Particularly helpful to understanding this developing expression of principles are the Cranach woodcuts that Luther included in the *Large Catechism* of 1529. Intended to reinforce specific interpretations of the Prayer in the *Large Catechism*, Cranach's woodcuts "also reflect the ways in which ... [Luther's] interpretations of the Prayer changed as the historical context changed," thus helping students to see that "Luther's reforms were not static" and his teachings were responsive to political and historical developments. Moving systematically through six of the Prayer's seven petitions, and exploring how each of these six petitions are addressed in the *Large Catechism* as well also other seminal works (beginning with *An Exposition on the Lord's Prayer for Simple Layman* [1517] and concluding with *A Simple Way to Pray* [1535]), McNair provides a helpful way of tracing the development of Luther's core theological principles, principles that Luther wanted to make "easily accessible to an audience of laypeople" and yet pertinent to specific historical circumstances (such as "the economic and social problems of the mid 1520s and the failure both of Protestant unity and reconciliation with the Catholics by the 1530s").

For Beth and Scott McGinnis, teaching Luther presents a different challenge. Like Pak, they are interested in Luther's writings on Jews and Judaism, and they too call for a historically-informed approach. Acknowledging that using "morally or otherwise offensive materials in the classroom has the potential to degrade the learning environment or even produce harm if not carefully managed" (McGinnis and McGinnis 2017), the McGinnises urge professors to approach Luther's anti-Semitism as an "opportunity for constructive dialogue." To create this dialogue, they place Luther's writings alongside two works by Johann Sebastian Bach, arguing that a proper contextualization of Luther and Bach within their historical moments can teach students to appreciate the ethical issues and insights raised by historical study. For instance, how do we address Luther's shift from *That Jesus Christ Was Born a Jew* (1523)—where he expresses a "welcoming attitude toward Jews"—to the "thoroughgoing hostility" of *On the Jews and Their Lies* (1543)—which "stands as one of the most explicit anti-Semitic statements of the Reformation era, a period that had no lack of vitriol." One way to do so is through a historically-informed reading that can account for Luther's shift as "one of style, not substance." Believing in 1543 that he was living in the last days, Luther "saw the enemies of Christ coalescing around him: the Jews joined papists, Turks, Anabaptists, and others as those who impeded the spread of the gospel and thus exposed themselves to the final, wrathful judgment of God." From Luther's perspective, then, the Jews' "evangelical moment seemed to have passed, and he channeled what he believed was the divine disgust, using the most vituperative language he had at hand." Additionally, professors can place Luther's anti-Semitism against "the larger backdrop of processes by which societies established boundaries and maintained social control through the identification of the 'Other.'" What these historically-informed readings cannot do, however, is "consider the weight of these texts as they come into our own age and classrooms" where students "encounter texts and ideas and understand them through their own interpretative contexts, and crucially, they do so in the presence of other students who may or may not share their context." This challenge is made clear in the McGinnises' discussion of Bach's *St. John Passion*, a 1724 work composed on a libretto from Luther's translation of John's Gospel, a translation which "specifically identifies the people who taunt Jesus and cry out for his crucifixion not as the 'crowd' or 'mob' but as the 'Jews.'" Exploring contemporary objections to the performance of the *St. John Passion*, as well as the role of historically-informed approaches to this work in Bach criticism, the McGinnises make a strong case for a two-fold approach to teaching potentially offensive materials: first, faculty must provide a proper historical context for understanding these materials and, second, they must clear a "space for students to consider and address the ethical questions that arise from the study of such works." Students "inevitably make moral judgments," and "bringing those judgments into the discourse of the classroom is the hard work of education, not without risk, but rich with potential benefits for all."

In "John Calvin and John Locke on the *Sensus Divinitatis* and Innatism" (Clanton 2017), J. Caleb Clanton outlines an exemplary strategy for teachers who want to place the concerns of the Reformers in dialogue with the larger Western Intellectual Tradition. Noting that "Reformed thinkers have long disagreed about whether knowledge of God's nature and existence can be or need be acquired inferentially," Clanton concludes that "they have nonetheless traditionally coalesced around the thought that some sense or awareness of God is naturally implanted or innate in human beings," a position rooted firmly in Calvin's influential discussion of the *sensus divinitatis* in the opening book of *The Institutes of the Christian Religion*. Juxtaposing Calvin's "treatment of the naturally implanted awareness of God" with John Locke's polemic against innatism in Book I of *An Essay concerning*

Human Understanding, Clanton situates the *Institutes* among "the great canonical texts ... [of the] early modern period" and helps students to see some of the larger epistemological issues at stake for the Reformers, drawing their theological concerns into a more comprehensive interdisciplinary conversation. Moving systemically through the most helpful passages in Calvin and Locke (chapters 1–6 of Book I of the *Institutes*, as well as chapters 2 and 4 of Book I of the *Essay*), Clanton does not argue that Locke is responding directly to Calvin's *Institute*; rather, it is Clanton's contention that "reading Calvin in tension with Locke helps shed light on both thinkers, as it provides a useful framework for undergraduates to explore the limits of Calvin's treatment of the *sensus divinitatis*, as well as the limits of Locke's rejection of innatism." Moreover, such an approach has "the historical pay-off of introducing students to two of the most towering Protestant figures of the Christian intellectual tradition," as well as setting "the stage for a philosophical and theological inquiry of ongoing significance": "Are we born blank slates, for example, and are all the contents of our minds derived of some sort of prior experience? Can we have knowledge of God's existence, and if so, *by what means*? Can belief in God be properly basic? How should we interpret key passages in Romans 1 and 2? And so on." Clanton is careful to acknowledge that scholars disagree as to the nature of Calvin's innatism (is it more *occurrent* or *dispositional*?), and he understands that students will want to be told clearly "whether Locke's polemic against innatism, in the end, poses a fatal threat to Calvin's treatment of the *sensus*." However, in this essay so attuned to effective teaching strategies, Clanton rightly concludes that "It remains, as it always does, for students to wrestle with these issues for themselves."

John MacInnis's "Teaching Music in the Reformed/Calvinist Tradition: Sphere Sovereignty and the Arts" (MacInnis 2017) provides a fitting conclusion to the group of essays in this collection that cluster around Luther and Calvin. Like the McGinnises and Clanton, MacInnis wants us to place these Reformers in dialogue with post-Reformation texts and issues. In particular, he shares strategies for engaging students in a Reformed/Calvinistic vision of the arts generally, and music specifically. Grounding this vision of the arts in a series of lectures delivered by Abraham Kuyper in 1898, MacInnis asks his students at Dordt College, a confessional Calvinist institution, to form "their own opinions and to develop insights for living productively and faithfully as musicians and people invested in musical cultural, wherever God may call them." In a team-taught core curriculum class populated by students from across the disciplines, MacInnis structures his allotted eighteen class periods around topics his students find most relevant: "music for films, television, and interactive media, popular music, and church music." In addition to emphasizing such topics as "musical meaning and intertextual relationships, the craft of making music, musical form, and music's functions in various settings," he must also "keep clear for students the intent of the class and its purpose within the college's core curriculum." To do this, he repeatedly foregrounds the question, "Are we able to discern and articulate what God intends art and music to be in this good world, here and now?" This major question is complemented by two subsidiary questions: "(1) What does God intend for art and music in my life personally?; (2) What should be the place of the specialized artist in my community?" Essential to these questions is the concept of "sphere sovereignty," which is "rooted in John Calvin's own distinguishing between the powers of the church and the state, both free to assert appropriate authority within their own spheres." According to MacInnis, sphere sovereignty should develop in students a "respect for diversity"—and thereby a respect for the field of "aesthetics"—because it requires them to acknowledge that "different arenas of human endeavor deserve space to do their work well" and "that care must be taken to preserve the integrity of each sphere ... [so] that no sphere may impose its principles upon another ... for they all exist directly under the rule of God." Admitting that there are "different perspectives" in the Reformed tradition when it comes to specifying creational laws for artists, MacInnis does assert that, generally speaking, the tradition is "resolute in affirming our rootedness in the material world, the physical universe in which we are called to action and accountability," and that, therefore, "artistic endeavor in this tradition is often a wrestling with material reality and our extraordinary existence as physical beings *coram deo*, 'before the face of God,' rather than a striving after an otherworldly, immaterial ideal." To bring this idea home,

MacInnis concludes with a song cycle entitled *The God of Material Things*, composed by recent Dordt graduate Jonathan Posthuma, a work that helps his students to embrace "the comprehensive vision [of the arts] articulated in the Reformed/Calvinist tradition, a vision that allows believers to be faithfully engaged in every field of human endeavor because it presupposes that Christ is concerned with it all, even music."

The final four essays in this collection take the concerns of the conference in multiple and fruitful directions, appealing to faculty who teach across the liberal arts in disciplines as varied as theology, literature, and the sciences. In "Dirk Philips' Letter and Spirit: An Anabaptist Contribution to Reformation Hermeneutics" (Schubert 2017), Aaron Schubert brings attention to a lesser-known figure who deserves greater recognition, one who "provides perhaps the most systematic explication of an Anabaptist hermeneutic of the Scriptures." According to Schubert, Philips' *Enchiridion* offers students a clear view of this hermeneutic at work, as Philips "reads all of Scripture to center on Christ and the Church, a reading established in the dichotomy of the letter and the Spirit of the text through a hermeneutic of obedience." For Philips, Scripture "can be read for the meaning of the letter, as presented in the Old Testament, and the meaning of the Spirit, as presented in the New Testament." The "meaning of the letter" represents "the historical reading," taking the "events portrayed in the Old Testament as historical events recorded by men through the work of the Holy Spirit." However, this reading for the meaning of the letter alone is "insufficient" because it "sees the types and figures without perceiving their object, the shadow but not the person" behind the Old Testament, who is Christ. According to Philips, because "all things are changed in Christ and are transfigured and made new by him, that is, changed from the letter to the Spirit," a "letter reading" of the Old Testament, while not incorrect, is not what brings life to Scripture. Instead, as Schubert notes, what brings life is found only "in the Spirit reading," one that "sees the symbolic and figurative reality of the Old Testament pointing forward to Christ and the Church." For Philips, this "guiding hermeneutic allowed for both concrete, literal interpretations [of Scripture] as well as spiritual allegorizing, as long as the former were interpretations of the New Testament and the latter of the Old." Reading Scripture in the letter of the Spirit is not, of course, the work of man but of the Holy Spirit, for only the Spirit can reveal how the figures of the Old Testament symbolize the reality of God's full revelation, and not just human opinions about that revelation. However, as Schubert carefully notes, this position "merely raises a new question for many students": "How can one know what is taught by the Holy Spirit and what is human opinion, either in one's own reading or in the teaching of others?" Philips' answer to this is a "hermeneutic of obedience," in which the "origin of an interpretation, human or divine, is evidenced the person's life." For Philips, "the obedient life, which is also the work of the Spirit, is inseparable from a right understanding of the Word of God, which must be understood spiritually, not merely in its letter . . . .[and therefore] obedience is a necessary prerequisite to understanding." As Schubert concludes, this hermeneutic, in "which the life of the interpreter plays a key role in validating his interpretation," will be "unfamiliar to most students"; therefore, by recovering it, we introduce students to a "significant, if often forgotten, contribution of the Anabaptist theologians to the study of the Reformation and to later evangelical and pietistic movements."

For Christopher A. Hill, the forgotten legacy that needs recovering is the theological and ecclesiastical pamphlet warfare that erupted in Reformation England after the publication of Fields and Wilcox's 1572 *Admonition to Parliament*. In "Spenser's Blatant Beast: The Thousand Tongues of Elizabethan Religious Polemic" (Hill 2017), Hill focuses on the final two books of the 1596 edition of Edmund Spenser's *Faerie Queene*. These two books are dominated by the presence of the Blatant Beast, a "formidable adversary" who, in Hill's reading, "represents the worst excesses of [the] caustic and satirical rhetoric" that characterized these disputes, in particular the Martin Marprelate pamphlets and the flood of anti-Marprelate pamphlets that emerged between 1589 and 1591. Acknowledging that the 1596 Second Part of *The Faerie Queene* appeared "far too late to serve as a direct intervention into the specific controversy to which it seems to refer," Hill argues that "the discursive and rhetorical concerns highlighted by the brief Martinist pamphlet warfare are very much on Spenser's mind";

thus, teachers of Elizabethan history and culture "can profitably use Spenser's allegorical method" to draw links between the excesses of the Blatant Beast and "the burgeoning market for cheaply printed religious polemic." Like many of his contemporaries, Spenser believed these polemics did more to regenerate themselves and their own rhetorical excesses than they managed to resolve disputes. Alerting students to Spenser's "heavily allegorized presentation of polemic and pamphleteering in the figure of the Blatant Beast—and the travails of the Knights of Justice and of Courtesy in bringing the beast to heel"—can help to illustrate not only the degradation of this public discourse but also "Spenser's call for the timely application of 'well guided speech' as the solution to these reckless disputes." For Spenser, "immoderate language," no matter the theological or doctrinal motivation behind it, "forecloses the possibility of any meaningful resolution" to such disputes, and the "repeated use of harsh invective, satire, and mockery can only break the communal bonds that make a church possible in any sense, regardless of the particularities of theological controversy." Ultimately, it is the "social virtue of courtesy," represented by Calidore, that Spenser champions. As a "combination of so many other virtues," courtesy necessarily generates "moderate and apt speech," providing a remedy to "profitably counter and even overcome the grievous proliferation of vain and destructive speech" that prevented the church from becoming one body.

In "Reformation Leads to Self-Reliance: The Protestantism of Transcendentalism" (Griffis 2017), Rachel B. Griffis also demonstrates the value of using literary works to teach the complex and expansive legacy of the Reformations. According to Griffis, nineteenth century American literature "reflects the far-reaching effects of the sixteenth century European Reformation, which distantly yet significantly inspired the literature of the United States to function as a moral voice in the lives of the people." Through figures such as William Ellery Channing and Ralph Waldo Emerson, who "idealized literature as the conduit for the values and concepts of individualism, freedom, and self-government," early American literature became a "powerful agent for Protestantism," finding its "best expression [in] . . . contemporary iterations of self-reliance." Beginning with Channing's and Emerson's readings of John Milton, Griffis shows how a distinct literary tradition developed by combining "Protestant-inflected ideals" with "American principles." In particular, Channing and Emerson interpreted Milton as "an apostle of freedom," an interpretation that complemented their "high view of human nature, . . . [which] they believed had its roots in the Protestant cause, but had been obstructed by Calvinism in America." Moreover, for Emerson, "perhaps the most studied and influential of the transcendentalists," the Protestant Reformation and the American Revolution were "steps in the path to self-reliance, the ultimate form of human freedom." It is not surprising, then, that having embraced this view of the promise of the Reformation, "many American writers in the nineteenth century viewed themselves as stewards of Protestantism in the New World and not necessarily apostates who sought to liberate others from religion." This sense of stewardship led, in turn, to a growing emphasis in the latter half of the nineteenth century on a "right of private judgment" in both the sacred and secular spheres, a logical development of our nation's "Emersonian Protestantism" of self-reliance. Attuned to how this vision continues to shape American cultural and intellectual life, Griffis concludes by reminding us how this fully-internalized legacy of self-reliance presents pedagogical challenges, particularly when faculty want to introduce students to a different kind of "moral language." In an environment that encourages students, when they interrogate texts, to above all else "arrive at their own interpretations and thus their own beliefs," teachers will necessarily have a difficult time communicating "with their students about . . . moral traditions to which they may be indocile."

In the collection's final essay, Josh A. Reeves broadens the conversation beyond the disciplines and legacies previously addressed. In "How Not to Link the Reformation and Science: Reflections on Brad Gregory's *The Unintended Reformation*"(Reeves 2017), Reeves focuses on Gregory's opening chapter, offering two critiques of its thesis about the Reformation's influence on modern secular science. While acknowledging that *The Unintended Reformation* is a "work of enormous scope and scholarship" and makes a profound case for "why we all, secular and religious alike, should study the Christian intellectual tradition," Reeves takes issue with Gregory's argument that "the real blame for the rise of secular science lies with [the influence of] medieval philosophy" on the Reformers, in particular the influence of Duns Scotus and William of Ockham. For instance, according to Gregory, Scotus rejected Aquinas's "analogical metaphysics of creaturely participation in God," paving the way for an "'antisacramental' view of nature, because the natural and supernatural cannot be active at the same time in the same event." By bringing God "down to the same ontological order as the created world," Scotus made it easier "to exclude God from explanations of the natural world." The Reformers "inherited from Scotus these inferior metaphysical beliefs about God," and when the "intractable theological disputes of the Reformation" proved to be "unsolvable theological disagreements," these inferior metaphysical beliefs began to have "toxic effects." In the end, "Unable to conceive of God as working through natural causes, disenchantment became the only option when empirical science was unable to discover God's action in the world." Unfortunately, Reeves claims, the "real difficulty with Gregory's narrative is how little historical evidence he gives for it." Lacking primary sources to back up its claims, and ignoring historical studies that refute the widespread influence of Scotus' metaphysics on Reformed orthodox thought, Gregory's argument simply "repackages a traditional Catholic metanarrative which blames Christianity's problems on a deviation from the metaphysical scheme of Thomas Aquinas." Moreover, according to Reeves, Gregory never makes it clear why a "mechanistic philosophy of nature should be equated with excluding God from the natural world," ignoring the fact that "many ... early advocates [of this philosophy] had strong theological reasons for supporting it." Finally, Gregory is "overly optimistic" that Thomist metaphysics "could have resolved the major tension between science and Christianity, or could have headed off the rise of naturalism." Because *The Unintended Reformation* is "a deeply pessimistic book, attributing most of modern ills to the Reformation," Gregory is unwilling to consider "a more positive account of the way Christianity encouraged the rise of science," such as the fact that the "Reformers' literalism denied the symbolic capacity of objects to refer beyond themselves, which became a necessary ingredient of the Scientific Revolution," or the way that "Reformed presuppositions can also be detected in the advocacy of experimental approaches to natural knowledge, where persons like [Francis] Bacon and Robert Boyle argued that the effects of original sin required a cautious, experimental approach to nature." In a fitting conclusion to both his essay and to this special issue, Reeves reminds us that as "inheritors and teachers of the Christian intellectual tradition," we are stewards of a rich legacy, one we are not only called to teach, but to teach well, and faithfully. The challenge, of course, is that the legacy we have inherited is as contested as it is rich, making our calling more difficult, but all the more important. It is my hope that the essays in this collection can offer some insights, and perhaps some inspiration, as we continue to take up the challenge.

Acknowledgments: The author expresses appreciation to the following individuals who assisted with the preparation of this volume: Karl Aho (Tarleton State University), Charlotte Brammer (Samford University), Caleb Clanton (David Lipscomb University), Walker Cosgrove (Dordt College), Peter Dykema (Arkansas Tech University), Steven Epley (Samford University), Rosemary Fisk (Samford University), Maria Poggi Johnson (University of Scranton), Peter Iver Kaufman (University of Richmond), Beth McGinnis (Samford University), Scott McGinnis (Samford University), Matt Moser (Loyola University Maryland), Jonathan Murphy (Texas A&M International University), Robert Olsen (University of Mobile), Bridget Rose (Samford University), Ken Roxburgh (Samford University), Dennis Sansom (Samford University), Bradley Sickler (University of Northwestern, St. Paul), Timothy Sutton (Samford University), and Bryan Whitfield (Mercer University).

Conflicts of Interest: The author declares no conflict of interest.

References

Clanton, J. Caleb. 2017. John Calvin and John Locke on the *Sensus Divinitatis* and Innatism. *Religions* 8: article 27. [CrossRef]

Duffy, Eamon. 2016. The End of Christendom. *First Things: A Journal of Religion and Public Life* no. 267: 51–57.

Griffis, Rachel B. 2017. Reformation Leads to Self-Reliance: The Protestantism of Transcendentalism. *Religions* 8: article 30. [CrossRef]

Hill, Christopher A. 2017. Spenser's Blatant Beast: The Thousand Tongues of Elizabethan Religious Polemic. *Religions* 8: article 55. [CrossRef]

Holder, R. Ward. 2017. The Reformers and Tradition: Seeing the Roots of the Problem. *Religions* 8: article 105. [CrossRef]

MacInnis, John. 2017. Teaching Music in the Reformed/Calvinist Tradition: Sphere Sovereignty and the Arts. *Religions* 8: article 51. [CrossRef]

McGinnis, Beth, and Scott McGinnis. 2017. Luther, Bach, and the Jews: The Place of Objectionable Texts in the Classroom. *Religions* 8: article 53. [CrossRef]

McNair, Bruce. 2017. Martin Luther and Lucas Cranach Teaching the Lord's Prayer. *Religions* 8: article 63. [CrossRef]

Pak, G. Sujin. 2017. The Protestant Reformers and the Jews: Excavating Contexts, Unearthing Logic. *Religions* 8: article 72. [CrossRef]

Reeves, Josh A. 2017. How Not to Link the Reformation and Science: Reflections on Brad Gregory's *The Unintended Reformation*. *Religions* 8: article 83. [CrossRef]

Schubert, Aaron. 2017. Dirk Philips' Letter and Spirit: An Anabaptist Contribution to Reformation Hermeneutics. *Religions* 8: article 41. [CrossRef]

Article

The Reformers and Tradition: Seeing the Roots of the Problem

R. Ward Holder

Theology Department, Saint Anselm College, Manchester, NH 03102, USA; wholder@anselm.edu

Academic Editor: Christopher Metress

Received: 10 February 2017; Accepted: 15 May 2017; Published: 31 May 2017

Abstract: Challenges the ideal of scripture vs. tradition as a manner of separating Protestants from Catholics in the early modern period, to argue instead that historians should be setting out a continuum of continuity with the medieval inheritance, and considering our typologies of the Reform movements against that. Then, as we teach the Christian Intellectual Tradition, we can see both genealogical and influential links across the eras, and present a better picture of what was going on in the Era of the Reformations, and through that, come to a greater understanding of the human condition.

Keywords: scripture; tradition; Reformation(s); Reformers; Protestant; Catholic; radical; Martin Luther; John Calvin

---

In 1517, on the Vigil of All Saints Day, Martin Luther posted his 95 Theses on the door of the church in Wittenberg, and changed history forever. Actually, many of these facts can be challenged—Luther may or may not have posted the 95 Theses, for instance. But for teaching the Christian Intellectual Tradition, this is truly one of those "red letter days." That's why all early modernists worth their salt are going to spend the remainder of this year and next talking about how their research throws particularly bright light on Martin Luther, and the Reformation. Early modern or Reformation scholarship is going to be all Luther, all the time, for the remainder of 2016 and 2017.

In doing so, we will trot out a number of old chestnuts, because as we have found, the old ideas got to be old ideas because people liked them and could remember them. We will talk about the three Reformation solas—*sola fide*, *sola gratia*, and *sola scriptura* (Vanhoozer 2016).[1] We will impress (or bore) our students by explaining the meaning of the ablatives and how that gives just the right amount of nuance to these formulae. We will turn to the 17th century for a description of the Reformation—Ecclesia Reformata, Semper Reformanda—and consider that this was trying to capture a dynamism that sought to argue with the classicism of medieval Catholicism (Benedict 2002).

At some point we will arrive at the difference between scripture and tradition. Again, we will trot out this commonplace because although we know it not to be nuanced, we see great explanatory powers in bumper-sticker history. And if it's not nuanced, it's also not wholly wrong, we tell ourselves. It is easy to find Luther or Calvin deriding the use of tradition. For instance, in his dedicatory letter to Pope Leo X that introduced *The Freedom of the Christian*, Luther claimed that he would only accept that which came from clear reason and the word of God (Luther 1962). Similarly, Calvin wrote, "Let this be a firm principle: No other word is to be held as the Word of God, and given place as such in the church,

---

[1] Kevin Vanhoozer is bringing out a book, *Biblical Authority after Babel: Retrieving the Solas in the Spirit of Mere Protestant Christianity*. Grand Rapids: Brazos Press, 2016, that concentrates on the traditional "sola" statements.

than what is contained first in the Law and the Prophets, then in the writings of the apostles; and the only authorized way of teaching in the church is by the prescription and standard of his Word."[2]

But it's not only Protestants of various stripes who have clung to the idea of scripture and tradition as a mnemonic device for understanding the two sides of the Reformation struggles. Fr. George Tavard, in his *Holy Writ and Holy Church*, sought to argue that the two were inseparable, while always accepting that these two divisions illustrated the sides of Reformation faith (Tavard 1959).

But surely things have changed: hasn't the aim of modern pedagogy and historiography pointed toward greater sophisitication? Well, perhaps. There have been studies that look at the Protestant Reformers' use of the tradition. All too frequently, these are simply laundry lists of the material that Reformers used from patristic sources. Out of that, we get brilliant studies that feature terms like "use of," or even more simply, "and": "Luther's use of the fathers," "Calvin and Augustine," etc. But actually, things have not changed that much. In these recent studies, it is still possible to find scholars holding on to the idea that Reformers simply read the scriptures as the basic method of preaching, commenting upon scripture, and construction of theological works. An extraordinary example was published only a few years ago that found all of the Reformers were bound by the pure teachings of the Scriptures. The author found the Reformation to have been an extraordinarily biblical event.

> The Protestant Reformation was a revolution in the original scientific sense of that word: the return of a body in orbit to its original position. It was never the desire of Luther to start a new church from scratch. He and the other reformers who followed in his tracks wanted to re-form the one, holy, catholic and apostolic church on the basis of the Word of God and to do so by returning to the historic faith of the early church as they found it set forth in the pure teachings of the Scriptures. This led to a fundamental reorientation in Christian theology. Luther's re-discovery of justification by faith alone, Zwingli's insistence on the clarity and certainty of the Bible, Calvin's emphasis on the glory and sovereignty of God[,] and the Anabaptist quest for a true visible church all found expression in numerous new confessions, catechisms, commentaries, liturgies, hymns, martyrologies and church orders. Like a great earthquake that continues to generate seismic aftereffects long after the first shock is over, the Reformation set in motion a revolution in religious life the effects of which are still being felt half a millenium later. (George 2011)

While this is an extraordinary example of a tendency from which modern historiographical directions have attempted to part company, it demonstrates that this tendency still exists. For some, the issue is simply that the Reformers rediscovered the pure Bible. That tendency worked on both sides of the Protestant and Catholic divide. While Protestants could smugly claim to hold to the purity of the scriptural witness, Catholics could look down their noses at a renegade band that refused to admit the ways that they had been formed by tradition, and pretended to be the church.

Historiographically, this was helpful. Academics, and American academics in particular, pretend to love freedom. We proclaim in a variety of ways that the search for truth must be unhindered and unchained by any extraneous constraints, and any pre-conceived notions. That's what we say. But in point of fact, that kind of scholarship, which always begins with a blank slate, is extraordinarily difficult. There is nothing more terrifying to a working scholar than a blank piece of paper, or in this age, a truly blank Google doc. So we use those principles and axioms we believe either to have been long proven, or so self-evident that their truth lies beyond proof. One such is the division between scripture and tradition, an important marker for setting out the division between Protestants and Catholics in the time of the Reformations.

---

2   (Calvin 1960; Calvin 1895). CO 2.850. "Esto igitur hoc firmum axioma, non aliud habendum esse Dei verbum cui detur in ecclesia locus, quam quod lege primum et prophetis, deinde scriptis apostolicis continetur, nec alium esse rite docendi in ecclesia modum nisi ex eius verbi praescripto et norma."

But ... does that historical theory really capture the essence of the moment? Did the Reformers really innovate a new religion that avoided all traditional material culture and traditional belief and practice? If so, why did they argue amongst themselves about the proper degree of departure from Rome? So, in this effort at thinking about our pedagogy, I want to challenge the ideal of scripture vs. tradition as a manner of separating Protestants from Catholics, to argue instead that what we should be doing is setting out a continuum of continuity with the medieval inheritance, and considering our typologies of the Reform movements against that.[3] Then, as we teach the Christian Intellectual Tradition, we can see both genealogical and influential links across the eras and, I hope, present a better picture of what was going on in the Era of the Reformations and, through that, come to a greater understanding of the human condition.

1. The Era of the Reformations, Re-Envisioned

The old theory of the Reformations is that after a long period of deep darkness, in which Catholicism's lust for power had nearly drowned all true piety God sent an apostle, Martin Luther, to wake the church from darkness, and to shine the glorious light of the gospel on these corruptions through a dependence on the Holy Scriptures. This was an extraordinarily Protestant and not very historically accurate picture. But my point is not to examine the Roman Catholic and Protestant confessional historiographical divide again, but to examine this theory. If it was only the light of the gospel, why use non-scriptural traditional materials? Further, how did the Protestant Reformers' use the traditions that came to them from the medieval church?

2. Winners Accepted Traditions, if Not Tradition

In the Reformations, winners accepted traditions, if they did not wholly embrace Tradition. Speaking about winners and losers in the Reformations is crude, harkens too much to an us-vs.-them mentality we're supposed to have conquered, and doesn't allow for the sophisticated view of the Reformations that is so in vogue. But anyone who doesn't believe that there were winners and losers in the period of the Reformations is either ill-informed, or blind. The Peasant's War had losers, mostly lords and castles in the early period, followed by serious losses by the peasant bands. Dying in battle makes you a loser, surviving a battle makes you either a winner, or someone who still has a chance to become a winner. Zwingli lost the Second Battle of Kappel in 1531. The victorious Catholics took his body, burned it, and mixed the ashes with dung so as to keep it from being made into relics. This showed an astonishing lack of understanding of Protestant spirituality, but it also showed that they won. The anti-reform party lost in Münster, and then the followers of Jan of Leiden lost, and were horribly slaughtered. Huguenots lost in the St. Bartholomew's Day Massacre in 1572, and it was such a great loss that the Vatican struck a memorial medal. The English won against the Spanish Armada in 1588, and were able to maintain Elizabeth I on the throne, and their brand of middle way Protestantism in their realm. Protestants under Henry of Navarre won several battles against the forces of the Catholic League, a fact that no doubt helped set the stage for the promulgation of the Edict of Nantes in 1598, and to a great degree settled the French Wars of Religion.

Obviously, I've been speaking about military losses—which would be capped spectacularly in the Thirty Year's War that began near the centennial of Luther's 95 Theses. But the boundaries between the intellectual and physical worlds are always at best semi-permeable. Catholic forces lost the Disputation at Zurich, as well as the Second Disputation at Zurich. Catholic voices lost the battle for the religion of Geneva, and so were forced to convert or immigrate. Oecolampadius lost to Eck at the Disputation of Baden, and the quest for a united evangelical Switzerland was badly damaged. Conrad Grebel and

---

[3] The literature investigating and supporting the thesis of continuity of the reform movements with the medieval world is vast. Significant volumes would include Oberman (1966); Oberman (1989), see especially Oberman (1994), see especially his discussion of the medieval mystical heritage, pp. 2–12 and (Cameron 1991), see his discussion of tradition, p. 89ff.

his band lost the argument with the Zurich city fathers, and were forced to flee. Catholic preachers dominated the streets of Paris, and excited the crowds to view the Huguenots with fear and disgust. From Wittenberg to Prague, from Lausanne to Edinburgh, arguments were made about what was the true Christian religion.

There is no doubt that there were winners and losers in the period of the Reformations. What remains to be seen is what useful divisions we can make between those groupings. My point is that for Protestants, winning—and the consequent survival as a confessional group—was related to accepting a significant number of traditions, though generally not the theory or theology of Tradition. Those Protestant movements that thrived, that grew numerically, that took over territories, were those movements that avoided a radical primitivism in their return to the sources, and instead accepted the historical nature of the Christian witness and their own place in the passing down of Christianity from earlier to later generations. One example might suffice. Every school child who learns a date for the beginning of the Reformation learns 1517. There are a host of other possibilities—Steven Ozment even pushed the era of reform back to the mid-thirteenth century! (Ozment 1981). But again and again we return to Luther's posting of the 95 Theses on the door of the church in Wittenberg, whether he did so or not!

However, in the 95 Theses, Luther never suggested that the church did not have the power he sought to bridle. As Reformation documents go, it was thoroughly medieval. Luther sought to clarify, as in Thesis 20, where he stated, "Therefore the pope, in speaking of the plenary remission of all penalties, does not mean 'all' in the strict sense, but only those imposed by himself." (Dillenberger 1962, p. 492) Luther posted this in a church where the prince himself maintained an enormous collection of relics, and one of the reasons that prince did not allow the plenary indulgence to be preached in his realm was that he did not want the competition with his own relics. Traditional religion was everywhere in Wittenberg!

Perhaps a second example can help. Everyone who has studied the Reformations knows that Martin Luther said something like "Here I stand, I can do no other," before the Emperor Charles V, stating that he could not be moved without scripture's witness. Luther was kidnapped soon after that interview, and was secreted away to the Wartburg, a castle in Thuringia near the town of Eisenach. He had thundered at the pope that it was far past time to reform the church and the church's doctrines according to the plain sense of scripture. It's a stirring portrait, and we love it as much for the heroic character as for what it tells us about the history of the Reformations.

But during Luther's absence, things went awry in Wittenberg. Luther had himself convinced his senior colleague, Andreas Bodenstein von Karlstadt, to join the evangelical camp. In Luther's absence from Wittenberg, Karlstadt was able to take matters in his own hands, and he argued that, in removing error, tardiness was a sin. He pushed for a radical reformation of the worship that, he argued, was based on the scriptures. At Christmas, Karlstadt administered the Lord's Supper dressed in peasant's clothing, asking that he be called "Brother Andy," and giving both the bread and wine to the people. He denied the efficacy of images, and even called for their abolition from the churches in Wittenberg. All of these reforms, Karlstadt claimed, were scripturally based.

Wittenberg was in an uproar. Luther's prince, the Elector Frederick the Wise, was furious. Luther hurried back from the Wartburg and, after a brief time, preached a set of sermons, the Invocavit Sermons, that quelled the turbulence and brought peace back to Wittenberg. Our histories laud both the power of the preached word, and consider an important note on the shared role of the church and the prince to provide for the people. But it was Karlstadt who claimed to be following scripture! The plain sense arguments at the very least seem to support him. Jesus said, "All of you, drink of it."[4] The Decalogue rejected religious iconography, but only of those things that walk on the earth, or fly in the air, or swim in the water.[5] That breadth impacted all religious iconography. Jesus instructed his

---

[4] Matthew 26.27.
[5] Exodus 20.4.

disciples that they should not care about what they wore.[6] All of Karlstadt's innovations or reforms were scripturally based.

But Karlstadt was the loser, and Luther the winner. We don't go visit our Scandinavian friends at the Evangelical Karlstadtian Church of America, or the stricter Karlstadtian Church, Missouri Synod. The Lutheran confession continued precisely because Luther found a meaningful compromise with the liturgical, doctrinal, and pastoral traditions that he inherited. If that is the case, then we must revise our grasp of the era of the Reformations, or the early modern period, on the grounds of far more continuity than change, on far more shared religion than prophetic jeremiad.

So, I will try to make my case on by examining two positive cases, that of Martin Luther and Lutherans after him, and of John Calvin. I'll add to that a negative case, that of the Anabaptist group around Conrad Grebel, the supporters of the Schleitheim Brotherly Union. It's also important to note what I'm trying to illustrate and what I'm not. By pointing out those confessions and movements that thrived in the sixteenth and seventeenth centuries, I am making an intellectual historian's judgment, not that of a theologian. I am in no way arguing that Lutherans or Calvinists or Anglicans were better Christians. That's a different argument for a different day. What I'm trying to ascertain is whether their shared survival and expansion can be correlated to a particular historical choice that, while not accidental in the sense of human willing, is absolutely accidental in an Aristotelian sense.

3. Martin Luther and Lutheran Tradition

Martin Luther stood before Charles V and said, "Unless I am convinced by the testimony of the Scriptures or by clear reason (for I do not trust either in the pope or in councils alone, since it is well known that they have often erred and contradicted themselves), I am bound by the Scriptures I have quoted and my conscience is captive to the Word of God. I cannot and will not recant anything, since it is neither safe nor right to go against conscience. Here I stand, I can do no other. May God help me. Amen." (Brecht 1985–1993). It's a scene almost made for a heroic epic or movie. It's heroic, and it fits the crusading piety of a religious hero that many still want to believe. But does it accurately describe Luther's work? In his attacks on the peasants and the Jews, Luther ignored the scriptural prohibitions on violence in the New Testament.[7] *Against the Robbing and Murdering Hordes of Peasants* was harsh, inspired by Luther's personal trip into Thuringia, where he viewed firsthand the depredations of the rebels (Luther 1955–1986; Luther 1883–2002). This treatise encouraged all who would come upon them to "smite, slay, and stab" the rebels.[8] In his *An Open Letter on the Harsh Book against the Peasants* in August of that same year, Luther did not attempt to apologize for his vehemence, only to explain it.[9] His 1543 treatise *The Jews and their Lies* continued this strain[10]. In it, Luther advised that the synagogues should be burned, Jewish houses be destroyed, Jewish holy books be confiscated, rabbis forbidden to teach, Jews be prohibited from the safe passage on public roads, the occupation of money-lending be denied to Jews, and Jews be forced to do manual labor for their livings. Luther had given up on converting Jews by kind words, and wanted to force conversions by making life impossible for members of this minority religion, paying no attention to scriptural demands to take care of the neighbor, even one of a hated religion.[11] We can say that Luther was a man of his time, but that is simply another way of saying that he accepted the ecclesiastical and cultural traditions he inherited. A more sympathetic reading of Luther might argue that he read the Sermon on the Mount as a personal

---

6 Matthew 6.28.
7 Matthew 26.52; Matthew 5.44; etc.
8 LW 46.50. WA 18.359.
9 LW 46.57–86. WA 18.384–401.
10 LW 47.121–306. Roland Bainton opined that it was unfortunate that Luther had not died before writing the treatise (Bainton 1950). A modern example comes from James McNutt, who even in the midst of setting forth the plain facts about Luther's anti-semitism, seeks to find threads in Luther's theology from which a compensatory ecumenical theology could be built. See (McNutt 2011).
11 Luke 10.25–37.

rather than corporate ethic, following a tradition that stretched back at least to Augustine. But that observation merely supports the thesis from a different angle, as it demonstrates Luther's formation in and acceptance of a persecuting culture.

After Luther's death, the tendency toward adoption of the traditions of medieval Christianity only strengthened. A good example is the struggle between Lutherans and Calvinists in the Palatinate. The disastrous Schmalkaldic War, and the consequent Augsburg and Leipzig Interims, demonstrated the fissures that existed within the formerly solid appearance of the edifice of Lutheranism. It was that divided German evangelical world into which Calvinism originally entered, through the flights of refugees who settled in Aachen, Metz, Trier, Emden and Bremen, in the 1560s (Brady, Jr. 2009, p. 252). Various princes accepted the faith, converting frequently, though not always, from Lutheranism. This movement is sometimes called the Second German Reformation, and it peaked in the early 1590s.[12] Moreover, according to Thomas A. Brady, "The faith presented itself to the German lands as not a new faith but an enhancement and extension of Luther's reformation. Luther's heirs thought differently" (Brady, Jr. 2009, p. 253). Moreover, "Lutherans gagged at the Calvinist requirement of leavened bread in the Lord's Supper; Calvinists fumed at Lutherans' attachment to so many rags and tags of defeated 'popery'" (Brady, Jr. 2009, p. 254). This struggle did not stop at expressions of discontent with the religious habits of the other confessions. Power struggles for control of territories could and did result in the loss of ministerial positions, banishment, and even the loss of life (Jürgens 2013). Reformed thinkers viewed the Lutheran belief in the local presence in the Lord's Supper, the exorcism rite in the baptismal service, church art, liturgical vestments, and a church calendar that retained the Marian festivals as examples of papal religion that had been retained, and needed to be purified away (Nischan 2000). Notably, the Calvinist arguments depended upon the priority of scripture over tradition. But Lutheran belief and cult was a popular movement that had been well established, and one that depended upon a continuity with the liturgical and doctrinal traditions of the medieval church.

4. John Calvin and Tradition

While a great amount of effort has been spent on whether Calvin was the progenitor of that which came after him—Protestant scholasticism—far less has effort has been expended on Calvin's relationship to the antecedent tradition, especially the traditions of the medieval church. But Calvin's engagement with the Christian tradition was rich, a career-spanning effort that saw significant change. While we cannot trace every bit of that, some examples can suffice. For instance, Calvin used the tradition in his biblical interpretive work. He used the patristic sources not just as sparring partners, but as authoritative guides to the true interpretations (Holder 2006). While he did not slavishly follow the interpretations of his authorities, neither did he set them aside lightly. Frequently, the questions that he chose to answer in his commentaries were those that the tradition of commenting had set as important (Thompson 2007; Steinmetz 1990; Steinmetz 1991). Calvin used the tradition in his systematic doctrinal work. At times, Calvin added citations from the fathers and medievals that did not even add to his case, or to the argument. Unless we wish to argue that he was acting like a Ph.D. candidate, scurrying along and putting in a footnote to every possible source to prove that he had read it, the most likely reason for Calvin engaging in such a practice was to add theological authority to his own work (Holder 2009). This was the argument from authority, a normal facet of medieval theological dialectic. Calvin regularly sought the imprimatur of his favorite orthodox theologians, including Augustine, Ambrose, Chrysostom, and Bernard.

But Calvin's engagement with the orthodox doctrinal tradition did not end there. Beyond the framework and the development of his thought, Calvin even went so far as to use the theological

---

[12] But see, Klueting (2004)—which argues that the term "second Reformation" is worse than unhelpful.

tradition for the substance of his doctrine.[13] A fascinating instance comes from Calvin's consideration of infant baptism. It appeared in the midst of a full-throated attack on the power of tradition that Calvin published in 1549, the Adultero-German Interim.[14] This was Calvin's response to the Augsburg Interim of 1548, and Calvin's attack upon it was as devastating as that of any Lutheran. But Calvin included an interesting side-note in his destruction of the Roman model of unwritten traditions. He noted that his opponents adduced "a plausible example in the Baptism of Infants; but as there is no fiction too gross or childish to be vended in the Papacy under the name of Tradition, whosoever has not the caution to keep out of this trap, voluntarily entangles himself in all kinds of superstition."[15] What attracts our attention is what Calvin gave up—the Romanists have a plausible example in pedobaptism as coming from the tradition of the church. They argued this on the basis of the lack of specific New Testament scriptural witness to any instance of infant baptism. Calvin, after introducing the issue of tradition, would argue that all sacraments were founded on the scripture, and that all the ancients knew that infant baptism was licit, ignoring the counter examples in Tertullian and Gregory of Nazianzus.[16] One wonders why he mentioned it at all.

The careful observer can see that Calvin immersed himself in the Church's theological tradition, setting the framework for his argumentation, and framing the questions that Calvin believed had to be answered, either in exegeting a passage of scripture, or in considering the impact of a particular doctrine in a theological or pastoral complex. Finally, the tradition sometimes was the substance of Calvin's argument—and a part of his mind was aware of both the possibilities and dangers that lay therein. But there can be no doubt that Calvin formed his reforms through a selective intentional engagement with and harvest from the medieval and early traditions.

5. The Anabaptists and Medieval Tradition

The list of those who engaged the medieval tradition only extends further. Anglicanism became impossible to understand without the concept of a via media. Doctrinal constructs that had been forged on the anvils of councils and conflicts were not abandoned, whether there was "adequate" scriptural support for them or not, prescinding at all times from settling the question of what "adequate" scriptural support would be, and who served as the arbitrator who determined that the canon had been reached.

One ill-defined group that certainly did not meet the standard of being traditional enough was the Anabaptists. This loose conglomeration of spiritual leaders, primitivist theorists, and dedicated followers never gained large numerical following. George Huntston Williams' system of dividing the Protestant camps into magisterial Reformers and radical Reformers avoided the question of what held Anabaptists together with Spiritualists and Anti-Trinitarians, and saw a common purpose in their rejection of working with the organs of the early modern state or realm. But our typology may fit them even better.

By 1525, the Swiss Brethren had already attempted to interest Huldrych Zwingli in their more thoroughgoing reform based on pure biblical models. Failing that, and under suspicion from the Zurich city council, on 21 January 1525, George Blaurock was baptized by Conrad Grebel in Zurich. He was a close friend of the first Anabaptist martyr, Felix Manz, who was executed by drowning in

---

13 Randall Zachman has seen this in Calvin's expanding use of the laying on of hands in ordination services (Zachman 2007). Zachman argues for what he termed an " ... increasing catholicity in the development of Calvin's theology." (p. 437) While Zachman's analysis was concentrating upon Calvin's expanding use of visual symbols, I believe that my own analysis of an increasing dependence on the orthodox theological tradition is a parallel development.

14 Published in 1549, CO 7.545–686. Interim Adultero-Germanum: Cui Adiecta Est Vera Christianae Pacificationis Et Ecclesiae Reformandae Ratio.

15 CO 7.614. "Plausibile quidem exemplum adducunt in baptismo parvulorum, sed quum nullum sit tam crassum aut puerile commentum, quod non traditionis nomine venditetur in papatu, omni superstitionum genere ultro se implicat, quisquis ab hac captione sibi non cavet."

16 Tertullian, De Baptismo, 18, and Gregory of Nazianzus, Or. 40, De Baptismo.

the Limmat on 5 January 1527. The Anabaptists sought a biblical primitivism previously unseen in the era of the Reformations. The confession they would write in 1527, The Schleitheim Brotherly Union, that Calvin, Zwingli, Oecolampadius, Haller and other reported as representative of Anabaptism, sought to argue that its roots in scripture and against the practices of the pope and libertines were what freed people to serve Christ.[17]

The various Anabaptist groups never reached the numerical strength of the Lutheran, Reformed, or Anglican bodies. It was unthinkable that they could ever be a state church, so the process of growth by birth in a region was foreclosed to them. Further, they took the fact of their numerical inferiority as a mark of the truth of their confession. Anna Jansz, on the way to her own execution by drowning in 1539, instructed her son through her will, that said, in part, "I urge you, my son, submit to the yoke of Christ; endure it willingly; for it is a great honour and joy. Do not follow the majority of the people, but when you hear about a poor, simple, repudiated handful of men and woman cast out of the world, join them. Do not be ashamed to confess your faith. Do not fear the majority of the people. It is better to let go of your life than deviate from the truth."[18] In a parallel that has always puzzled me, much like Socrates, Jansz identified the majority with trouble. Perhaps the shared experience of being executed makes connections that historians have a difficult time tracing.

If there is a group in the early modern period that fulfills the dictum scripture vs. tradition, it would be the Anabaptists. Their strict communitarian religion demanded rejection of the sword and infant baptism, because of the text of the New Testament.[19] This put them at odds with the temporal realms of their day, and the fusion of the sacred and secular which was so much a part of the early modern world. This so horrified Holy Roman Empire that, at the Diet of Speyer in 1529, one of the few topics on which Lutherans and Catholics could agree was the necessity of executing Anabaptists.

6. Getting to the Roots of the Problem

So I've argued for an eschewal of the tried and true scripture vs. tradition formulation in favor of seeing the various reforming groups on a continuum of engagement and acceptance with the shared inheritance of the medieval and patristic tradition.[20] Obviously, there will be outliers, the various groups of Anabaptists and Radicals being the paradigmatic examples. But they will serve as either the example of what happened when one took things too far, or as the exception that proves the rule, or the illustration of the fixed boundary. But that leaves a significant hole in my theory. Historiographically, if this is as clear as I'm arguing, why have so many thinkers before taken the other tack?[21] And the obvious answer is, because the Reformers said so. Luther attacked tradition. Calvin attacked tradition. Cranmer, Knox, Karlstadt, Melanchthon, Beza, Musculus, Bucer, and Oecolampadius attacked tradition. All did so in order to place Christian doctrine and practice upon the clear foundation of the written word of the scriptures.

But do we have to accept what they said at face value? What if their categorical denial of the power of tradition was actually relative and contextually fraught? The great exponent of the Church's tradition in the twentieth century has been Yves Congar, who argued that throughout history there was a theological source, the apostolic deposit, that was uniquely recognized and wielded by the magisterium, and especially the pope. Congar would go so far as to approve of Pope Pius

---

[17] See Yoder's introduction to Schleitheim in (Sattler 1973).

[18] Quoted in (Haude 2000).

[19] Schleitheim, paragraphs 1 & 6. in (Sattler 1973).

[20] Recent analysts have continuted to assert an acceptance of the thesis of the early modern period's continuity with the prior medieval tradition. Some examples are Terpstra (2015), depends upon the models of the medieval from R. I. Moore, Benedict Anderson, and Guido Ruggiero. (Wiesner-Hanks 2008), states bluntly that " . . . in many aspects of life, continuities outweighed change." (p. 9). Thomas A. Brady, Jr., orients his study by beginning with the medieval inheritance, whether canonical, cultural, or imagined (Brady, Jr. 2009).

[21] See (among others), (Walker 1985, p. 428; Smith 1930, p. 279; Bainton 1952, p. 42; Ozment 1975, pp. 148ff; Eire 2016, p. 173; Matheson 2007, pp. 275–76; MacCulloch 2004, pp. 97–98; Wandel 2011, pp. 112–13; Lindberg 2010, p. 82; Dickens et al. 1985, p. 36; Cameron 1991, pp. 139ff; Hillerbrand 2007, pp. 52–53).

IX's statement that he was the tradition. This argument, in its early form, was defended by John Driedo, Melchior Cano, Nicholas of Cusa, and Alphonsus de Castro. This was the "tradition" that the Reformers sought to tame, and that which Congar would call "Tradition—capital T."

But in the modern age, we speak of Tradition and traditions. To borrow Congar's useful delineation, "traditions" (small t) are those habits of mind and pieces of received wisdom that the church constantly passes down to the next generation; "Tradition" (capital T) is the power of the Church, based on a conveniently oral source, to proclaim authority in the manner it saw fit. The inheritance of the prior fifteen centuries, the Reformers argued both implicitly and explicitly, was the common birthright of Christians across Europe, and did not belong to the Church any more than it belonged to the prince, or any of the ranks of society. To say otherwise was to suggest that history was not available to all, but that it was malleable at the desire of a privileged few.

The Reformers sought to deny Tradition, while accepting and controlling traditions. They had their detractors, from the left in the Anabaptists who attempted to recreate the church of the New Testament and in heretics like Miguel de Servet who argued on the basis of the New Testament texts that the trinity simply could not be found in the world of the early church. They had their detractors as well on the right, with Catholics asking, "Where was your church before Luther?" But as creators of institutions, access to fifteen centuries of traditions generally stood the various reforming movements in good stead, though there was always the question of what was enough.

So, why is that important to us as teachers of the Christian Intellectual Tradition? First, considering the reforming movements of the early modern period as being on a continuum of engagement with the inherited traditions, rather than dropping tradition for the purity of scripture, is simply better history. From Luther to Zwingli to Calvin to Cranmer to Vermigli to Knox to Ursinus to whomever, time and again we see practices and doctrines being accepted from the medieval heritage. To give a particular case, Lutheran doctrine on the presence of Christ in the eucharist stayed so close to the medieval heritage that, in the twentieth century, Karl Rahner declared that both confessions accepted the unambiguous words of Scripture concerning the real presence (Rahner 1961). The Reformers took over traditions, and to argue otherwise involves historians in an attempt to bend history to justify doctrine.

Second, this insight might create a better typology of reform movements than some we presently use. The magisterial-Radical typology raises the church's relationship to the state to the zenith of importance. But very few thinkers in the sixteenth century believed that their church was under the thumb of the prince, and many princes bemoaned that very fact. A different typology that considers continuity with received traditions as the gauge to be measured might have the increased value of being able to place all of the large ecclesiastical and ecclesiological reform movements of the era together, and rate them on a continuum, helping us to understand them better.

Finally, it is worthwhile in this postmodern age to consider not only our objects of study, but ourselves as the analysts. In 1960, Hans-Georg Gadamer published the first edition of his *Truth and Method*, and the world of hermeneutics would never be the same. While it has enjoyed significance in a number of fields, for our purposes today it is enough to say that it has shifted the modern notion of tradition. Gadamer argued that all people have a historically-effected consciousness (*wirkungsgeschichtliches Bewußtsein*); thus, all people are living in a historical stream of tradition that helps to define them. This description of historically-situated existence nicely parallels what I'm describing in the argument for Reformers engaging "tradition." All the Reformers, whether Lutheran, Catholic, Reformed, Radical or Anglican, received the Christian Intellectual Tradition of fifteen centuries, along with traditions of worship, piety, and a sense of how those complexes fit together with the rest of society. By examining what they did with their mental and emotional inheritance, we will go much further in our understanding of them, and in our own efforts at making progress on understanding the human condition. As scholars, but even more so as teachers of the Christian Intellectual Tradition, that is a worthy goal.

Conflicts of Interest: The authors declare no conflict of interest.

References

Bainton, Roland. 1950. *Here I Stand: A Life of Martin Luther*. Nashville: Abingdon Press, p. 379.

Bainton, Roland. 1952. *The Reformation of the Sixteenth Century*. Boston: Beacon Press.

Benedict, Philip. 2002. *Christ's Churches Purely Reformed*. New Haven: Yale University Press.

Brady, Jr., Thomas A. 2009. *German Histories in the Age of the Reformations, 1400–1650*. Cambridge: Cambridge University Press.

Brecht, Martin. 1985–1993. *Martin Luther*. Translated by James L. Schaaf. Philadelphia: Fortress Press, p. 460.

Calvin, John. 1960. *Institutes of the Christian Religion*. 2 Vols. Translated by Ford Lewis Battles. Edited by John T. McNeill. Philadelphia: Westminster Press, p. viii.8.

Calvin, John. 1895. *Opera Quae Supersunt Omnia*. 59 Vols. Edited by Wilhelm Baum, Edward Cunitz and Edward Reuss. Brunswick: Schwetschke and Sons.

Cameron, Euan. 1991. *The European Reformation*. Oxford: Oxford University Press.

Dickens, Arthur Geoffrey, John M. Tonkin, and Kenneth Powell. 1985. *The Reformation in Historical Thought*. Cambridge: Harvard University Press.

Dillenberger, John. 1962. *Martin Luther: Selections From His Writings*. New York: Doubleday, p. 492.

Eire, Carlos M. N. 2016. *Reformations: The Early Modern World 1450–1650*. New Haven: Yale University Press.

George, Timothy. 2011. *Reading Scripture with the Reformers*. Grand Rapids: IVP Academic, pp. 17–18.

Haude, Sigrun. 2000. Anabaptism. In *The Reformation World*. Edited by Andrew Pettegree. London: Routledge, p. 237.

Hillerbrand, Hans J. 2007. *The Division of Christendom: Christianity in the Sixteenth Century*. Louisville: Westminster John Knox Press.

Holder, R. Ward. 2006. *John Calvin and the Grounding of Interpretation: Calvin's First Commentaries*. Leiden: Brill, pp. 111–24.

Holder, R. Ward. 2009. Calvin and Tradition: Tracing Expansion, Locating Development, Suggesting Authority. *Toronto Journal of Theology* 25: 215–26. [CrossRef]

Jürgens, Henning P. 2013. Intra-Ptorestant Conflicts in 16th Century Poland and Prussia—The Case of Benedict Morgenstern. In *Calvin and Luther: The Continuing Relationship*. Edited by R. Ward Holder. Göttingen: Vandenhoeck & Ruprecht, pp. 143–64.

Klueting, Harm. 2004. Problems of the Term and Concept 'Second Reformation': Memories of a 1980s Debate. In *Confessionalization in Europe, 1555-1700: Essays in Honor and Memory of Bodo Nischan*. Edited by John M. Headley, Hans J. Hillerbrand and Anthony J. Papalas. Burlington: Ashgate, pp. 39–49.

Lindberg, Carter. 2010. *The European Reformations*, 2nd ed. Malden: Wiley-Blackwell.

Luther, Martin. 1883–2002. *D. Martin Luthers Werke: Kritische Gesamtausgabe*. 69 Vols. Weimar: Hermann Böhlau, vol. 18, pp. 357–61.

Luther, Martin. 1955–1986. *Luther's Works*, American Edition. Edited by Jaroslav Pelikan and Helmut Lehmann. Philadelphia and St. Louis: Concordia, vol. 46, pp. 45–56.

Luther, Martin. 1962. Freedom of a Christian. In *Martin Luther: Selections from his Writings*. Edited by John Dillenberger. Garden City: Anchor Books, p. 50.

MacCulloch, Diarmaid. 2004. *The Reformation*. New York: Viking.

Matheson, Peter, ed. 2007. Reformation Christianity. In *A People's History of the Church*. Minneapolis: Fortress.

McNutt, James. 2011. Luther and the Jews Revisited: Reflections on a Thought Let Slip. *Currents in Theology and Mission* 38: 40–47.

Nischan, Bodo. 2000. Germany after 1550. In *The Reformation World*. Edited by Andrew Pettegree. London: Routledge, p. 402.

Heiko Oberman, ed. 1966. *Forerunners of the Reformation: The Shape of Late Medieval Thought*. New York: Holt, Rinehart and Winston.

Oberman, Heiko. 1989. *Luther: Man between God and the Devil*. Translated by Eileen Walliser-Schwarzbart. New Haven: Yale University Press.

Oberman, Heiko. 1994. The Longed-For Reformation; Dennis Tamburello. In *Union with Christ: John Calvin and the Mysticism of St. Bernard*. Louisville: Westminster John Knox Press.

Ozment, Steven. 1975. *The Reformation in the Cities: The Appeal of Protestantism to Sixteenth-Century Germany and Switzerland*. New Haven: Yale University Press.

Ozment, Steven. 1981. *The Age of Reform, 1250–1550: An Intellectual and Religious History of Late Medieval and Reformation Europe*. New Haven: Yale University Press.

Rahner, Karl. 1961. *Theological Investigations*. 21 Vols. Baltimore: Helicon Press, vol. 4, pp. 287–311.

Sattler, Michael. 1973. *The Legacy of Michael Sattler*. John H. Yoder, trans. and ed. Scottdale: Herald Press, pp. 32–34.

Smith, Preserved. 1930. *A History of Modern Culture*. New York: Henry Holt.

Steinmetz, David. 1990. Calvin and the Patristic Exegesis of Paul. In *The Bible in the 16th Century*. Edited by David Steinmetz. Durham: Duke University Press, pp. 100–18.

Steinmetz, David. 1991. Calvin among the Thomists: Exegesis of Romans. In *Biblical Hermeneutics in Historical Perspective*. Edited by Mark Burrows and Paul Rorem. Grand Rapids: Eerdmans, pp. 198–214.

Tavard, George. 1959. *Holy Writ or Holy Church: The Crisis of the Protestant Reformation*. London: Burns and Oates.

Terpstra, Nicholas. 2015. *Religious Refugees in the Early Modern World: An Alternative History of the Reformation*. Cambridge: Cambridge University Press.

Thompson, John. 2007. *Reading the Bible with the Dead: What You Can Learn from the History of Exegesis that You Can't Learn from Exegesis Alone*. Grand Rapids: Eerdmans.

Vanhoozer, Kevin. 2016. *Biblical Authority after Babel: Retrieving the Solas in the Spirit of Mere Protestant Christianity*. Grand Rapids: Brazos Press.

Walker, Williston. 1985. *A History of the Christian Church*, 4th ed. New York: Scribners.

Wandel, Lee Palmer. 2011. *The Reformation: Towards a New History*. Cambridge: Cambridge University Press.

Wiesner-Hanks, Merry. 2008. *Women and Gender in Early Modern Europe*, 3rd ed. Cambridge: Cambridge University Press.

Zachman, Randall. 2007. *Image and Word in the Theology of John Calvin*. South Bend: University of Notre Dame Press, pp. 313–17.

Article

The Protestant Reformers and the Jews: Excavating Contexts, Unearthing Logic

G. Sujin Pak

History, Duke Divinity School, Durham, NC 27708, USA; spak@div.duke.edu

Academic Editor: Christopher Metress
Received: 26 December 2016; Accepted: 31 March 2017; Published: 20 April 2017

Abstract: This article highlights the important initial tasks of excavating the pertinent contexts of the sixteenth-century Protestant reformers and discerning what is at stake for them (i.e., "unearthing logic") in order to analyze their views of and teachings about Jews and Judaism. Pertinent contexts include the immediate contexts to which Luther and Calvin responded (e.g., Jewish "blasphemy" and/or Christian Hebraism), as well as attending to the significant theological frameworks in which they each operated. Equally important is activity of sifting through the discrepancies in the secondary literature's depictions of Luther and Calvin's place in the history of Christian-Jewish relations. The article highlights biblical interpretation—particularly the defense of Scripture's perspicuity—as the distinctive locus of the reformers' angst concerning Jews and Judaism. In conclusion, the author offers some lessons from church history for discerning what Christian faithfulness might look like in response to this troubling history.

Keywords: Luther; Calvin; reformers; Jews; Judaism; anti-Semitism; Jewish-Christian relations; biblical interpretation; Scripture; context; perspicuity; Christian Hebraism

1. Introduction

The topic of the Protestant reformers and the Jews is both an ethical and personal topic because it involves actual persons and actual bodies, as well as real consequences for those persons and bodies. Yet the temptation to move immediately to ethical judgments too often succumbs to the temptation of mere dismissal and fails to seize the opportunity for critical self-reflection. Such difficult topics reveal the key strengths of the historian's task, for it is incumbent on the historian to unearth the logic that drives any given person or group, regardless of the moral judgments one might feel compelled to make. In order to do this well, the historian must identify and excavate the pertinent contexts necessary to understand a subject both in its original setting and in its wider historical and intellectual landscapes. Only then can one more judiciously draw implications for then and now. We begin with this act of excavation—with a focus on Martin Luther and John Calvin—in order to unearth aspects of their logic concerning Jews. I will demonstrate that biblical interpretation was a particular locus of the reformers' angst concerning Jews and Judaism and explore what was at stake for them. We will return to ethical questions toward the end and, in a manner, read the Protestant reformers "against themselves" in the hope of exemplifying critical appropriation of Christian tradition on even this most difficult of topics.

2. Excavating Contexts, Unearthing Logic

There are several contexts crucial to an analysis of the Protestant reformers' views of and actions toward Jews in the sixteenth century. First, situating the reformers within a larger history, one might ask, "Did the Protestant reformers contribute anything new to the history of Jewish-Christian relations?" There is not time to recount the troubling history of forced baptisms, forced conversions, forced disputations, and forced sermon attendance of Jews by Christians. It is a history that contains accusations of Jews intending Christians harm, as well as instances of Christians killing Jews as a direct consequence of these accusations [1–3]. Yet, it is also a history that cycled through times of peaceful coexistence, intellectual collaboration, outright persecution, and allowance of basic rights of Jews while establishing public policies that restrained their flourishing. The key point of tension in this history for Christians was the fact that the vast majority of the Jews, to whom the promises of the Old Testament were made, rejected Jesus Christ as the promised Messiah, for such rejection threatened to undermine the legitimacy of the Christian faith. Hence, Christians found in Scripture explanations and prophecies of this rejection, such as depictions of the Jews as a blind, carnal, stiff-necked, and disobedient people rejected by God and replaced by the church, the "True Israel." Some Jewish scholars on this topic, such as Jeremy Cohen ([4], p. 98) and Salo Baron ([5], pp. 383–88), conclude that the Protestant reformers added nothing new to the history of Christian-Jewish relations. Indeed, Luther and Calvin furthered the depictions of Jews as blind, stubborn, and disobedient, and insisted that only those who believe in Christ are the True Israel who inherit the promises of God ([6], pp. 357, 359; [7], p. 140).

2.1. Luther and His Contexts

The Protestant reformers operated within a larger, prior tradition of Christian anti-Jewish teachings and actions—a point that should neither be lost upon us nor excuse the reformers. The need to situate the Protestant reformers within a prior historical context becomes immediately evident when one looks at the secondary literature on Luther and the Jews, which reveals opposing assertions concerning Luther's legacy. Some have presented Luther as the father of anti-Semitism, drawing a direct line from Luther to the Third Reich ([8,9]; [10], p. 8; [11], p. xi). Others assert that Luther should not be singled out any more than any other ([7], pp. 121–24, 145; [12]). To the former, from a strictly historical perspective, the charge of anti-Semitism is at least technically inaccurate and anachronistic. Most scholars agree that Luther's statements against Jews and Judaism were primarily theological in content and not racial per se ([12], p. 50; [6], pp. 367–71; [7], p. 126; [13], pp. 96–97; [14], pp. 375–76). Yet, there are undeniable parallels between the actions of the Third Reich and Luther's recommendations on how to treat Jews in his 1543 *On the Jews and Their Lies* ([15],p. 690; [7], p. 123; [16], pp. 73–74).[1] Similarly, Johannes Wallmann highlights two opposite assertions concerning the reception history of Luther's anti-Jewish writings—one group maintaining a direct tie from Luther's anti-Jewish writings to the rise of modern anti-Semitism and the other contending that Luther's prior and more positive 1523 treatise *That Jesus Christ was Born a Jew* was far more influential than his negative treatises. Wallmann convincingly demonstrates that the reality is much more of a mixed bag, with times when the positive treatise was more popular and other times when the republishing of his negative treatises indicated their popularity ([16], pp. 72–87). The conclusion here is simple and mundane, and yet secondary scholarship has too often forgotten it—namely, that history is always more complicated and messier than the dichotomies we seek to impose. Luther and Calvin were medieval men deeply shaped by prior Christian tradition, and their anti-Jewish teachings contributed to what came after them.

It is also necessary to examine the immediate contexts to which Luther's writings on Jews responded. Luther wrote five treatises dedicated to the topic of Jews and Judaism: the 1523 *That Jesus Christ was Born a Jew*, the 1538 *Against the Sabbatarians*, and three treatises in 1543—*On the Jews and Their Lies*, *On the Ineffable Name and the Genealogy of Christ*, and *Treatise on the Last Words of David*. There is a significant change in tone between Luther's 1523 treatise and later 1543 writings. In 1523, Luther expressed hope for Jewish conversion and refuted such hope in 1543; in 1523 he advocated friendly contact between Christians and Jews, but in 1543 sharply warned Christians to avoid all contact with Jews. In 1523 Luther urged Christians to treat Jews kindly and rebuffed prior medieval accusations of ritual murder and host desecration ([17], LW 45:200, 201; 47:172, 213, 241, 268, 274–75). In 1543, Luther reiterated these

---

[1] Johannes Wallmann notes that Nazis complained that Luther's anti-Jewish writings were unknown in their time ([16], pp. 73–74).

medieval accusations and recommended such things as burning their synagogues and books, forbidding Jews from any public teaching or prayer, abolishing any safe-conduct of Jews on the roads, and putting them to manual labor ([17], LW 47:217, 264, 277, 268–72, 288). Scholars debate the causes of this change. Some point to Luther's disillusionment that Jews did not convert even though Protestantism had purified the message of the Gospel, while others point to health ailments in Luther's old age that could have contributed to an increasingly bitter and hostile demeanor ([18], pp. 132–37; [19], p. 199; [20], pp. 6–19, 214). Yet, most find a deep theological consistency across Luther's lifetime concerning his teachings on Jews and Judaism ([12,14,21]; [7], pp. 124–28). Consequently, many view these changes between 1523 and 1543 not as theological changes but as responding to specific social-political events. Luther wrote his 1538 *Against the Sabbatarians* in response to the news that some Jews in Bohemia and Moravia not only were persuading Christians to be circumcised and to follow Jewish law, but also were convincing Christians that the Messiah had not yet come. Luther wrote *On the Jews and Their Lies* after learning that Jews were publicly slandering Jesus and the Virgin Mary in their writings, teachings, and prayers ([17], LW 47:65, 137). Hence, Wilhelm Maurer, Gerhard Forde, and Thomas Kaufman argue that the change in Luther was due to the immediate problem of Jewish public blasphemy, of which Luther had not been previously aware ([14], pp. 388–89, 397–400, 407, 416, 427; [18], p. 128; [13], p. 92).

Such immediate social-political contexts convincingly contributed to the specific changes in Luther's position on Jews and Judaism. Yet, naming these changes simply as contextual is misleading. It is precisely the ways in which contexts shape theology that is illuminating here. Indeed, we see a theological change in response to a particular set of events. The theological change most defensibly evident is the change from a hope in Jewish conversion to rejection of any such hope.[2] This is not simply a theological change in the view of the character of the Jew from being potentially receptive to God to being irreparably blind and disobedient; it is also a theological change in the view of the character of God and God's covenant. It points to God's rejection of the Jews for all time rather than a rejection that retained the possibility of a future Jewish conversion. It emphasizes the judging God over the God of grace and mercy. As a consequence, Luther increasingly read biblical Jews in the light of not only the Jews' rejection of Christ but also in the light of contemporary Jewish blasphemy.

2.2. Calvin and His Contexts

Specific contexts equally matter in the case of John Calvin. Unlike Luther, Calvin did not write treatises explicitly devoted to the issue of Jews and Judaism, except for a dialogue he wrote between a Christian and a Jew that he never published [22]. Scholarship on Calvin on the Jews ranges from presenting him as a firm antagonist ([5], pp. 383–88; [14], pp. 443–45; [23], p. 2) to arguing that he was no different from his contemporaries ([24,25]) to hailing him as one of the least anti-Judaic figures of his time ([26–28]; [29], pp. 102–3). Others, such as Alice Eckardt, Mary Potter Engel, and Achim Detmers, point to the complex ambiguities in Calvin's thought on Jews and Judaism. Eckardt observes that on the one hand Calvin held a high view of Mosaic Law; on the other hand, he frequently attacked Jewish exegesis. Engel demonstrates that Calvin both asserted that the Jews abrogated the divine covenant and that the one covenant remains eternal and unabrogated from the standpoint of God. Detmers and my own work point to the ambiguities of Calvin's largely positive treatment of Old Testament Jews in contrast to his mostly negative statements about New Testament and contemporary Jews, as well as Jewish exegesis ([30], pp. 120–21; [31]; [32], pp. 210–11; [33], pp. 11, 92–94, 131–32, 146, n. 23, 177, n. 66, 177–78, n. 72, 185, n. 68, 189, n. 23; [34]).

---

2   Luther clearly expressed a hope for Jewish conversion in his 1523 *That Jesus Christ was Born a Jew* ([17], LW 45:200) and his 1524 lectures on Hosea ([17], LW 18:16). By his 1528 lectures on Isaiah, Luther's portrayal of the Jews as cut off because of unbelief became more pronounced ([17], LW 16:236, 300, 17:413). By his 1543 treatises and his later lectures on Genesis, Luther more strongly stated that the Jews have ceased to be the people of God ([17], LW 47:139, 262; 2:359, 360, 361, 3:151, 4:32, 6:283).

Such ambiguities indicate the necessity of carefully attending to context. For example, Detmers contends that the polemical context of the Anabaptist devaluation of the Old Testament shaped Calvin's emphasis upon the profound unity of the Old and New Testaments ([32], p. 212). In response to the Anabaptists' elevation of the New Testament at the cost of its unity with the Old, Calvin insisted in his *Institutes* that the old and new covenants are "actually one and the same" because they share Christ as their substance ([35], 2.10.1–2). Hence, the Anabaptists were incorrect to say that the Jews of the Old Testament expected only earthly fulfilments of the covenantal promises; rather, the Jews of the Old Testament knew the fulfilment of the covenantal promises were spiritual and not earthly and ultimately dependent on God's grace, for "they had Christ as pledge of their covenant and put in him all trust of future blessedness" ([35], 2.10.17, 23). Calvin asserted Christ as the substantive unity of both testaments; they differ only in mode of delivery ([35], 2.11.1).

Calvin's theology of the unity of the testaments held direct consequences, particularly for his readings of Old Testament Jews. In contrast to Luther, who tended to read biblical Jewry in the light of Jewish rejection of Christ, Calvin emphasized Old Testament Jews as participants in God's covenant and receptors of God's providential care, even when the Old Testament prophets rebuked the Jews for their disobedience. Contrary to traditional Christian readings of several Old Testament passages (such as Ps 8, 16, 22, 59, Is 63:1–4) that depicted the Jews as the crucifiers of Christ, as a nation of depraved character, or as a people condemned by God, Calvin explicitly affirmed the Jews (albeit biblical Jews) as the people of God who exemplify God's providential care of the church ([33], pp. 77–101; [34], pp. 9–15; [36]). Yet, Calvin explicitly employed the terminology of "church" as another expression of the unity of the two Testaments centered in Christ, for when Calvin read "Israel," "Judah," or the "Jews" in the Old Testament, he equated this with the "church" of the New. Consequently, Detmers clarifies that Calvin's positive treatment of biblical Jews in no way entailed an affirmation of Jews and Judaism per se ([32], p. 212). Rather, Calvin employed Old Testament remnant theology to argue that only those Jews who believed in Christ continued in the covenant. Consequently, Detmers concludes that Calvin exhibited a form of "complete substitution of the Jewish people by the Christian Church" ([32], p. 201). Indeed, Calvin viewed the church as the faithful remnant comprising the True Israel.

Yet, I quibble with Detmer's argument that Anabaptist pressures "forced" Calvin to maintain the unity of the covenant so that only insofar as "Calvin emphasized God's fidelity to the Jewish people in the covenant could he theologically maintain the unity of the covenant" ([32], p. 212). On the contrary, Calvin grounded this unity in the conviction of a sovereign and immutable God.[3] Calvin's doctrine of God required him to maintain that God's purposes cannot be thwarted, including God's promises to the Jewish people. The unity of the covenant and his corresponding readings of Old Testament Jewry as continuing in this covenant are the necessary corollaries of his doctrine of God. Opposing Anabaptist beliefs created a context in which his arguments for the unity of the covenant needed louder voicing, but they did not "force" the concepts; his doctrine of God did that.

Even as he argued that only a remnant of the Jews (i.e., those Jews who believe in Christ as the Messiah) continue in faithful keeping of the covenant, Calvin affirmed that a full vision of God's sovereignty must always allow for the possibility that God could still at any time fulfill God's promises to the Jews. For example, in his comments on Romans 11, Calvin rejected the view that "the covenant that had formerly been made with Abraham was abrogated or that God had so forgotten it that the Jews are now completely estranged from his kingdom" ([37], p. 238). He asserted on the basis of the immutability of God and God's promises that while currently the Jews who have rejected Christ have fallen into ruin, "the nation itself, however, has not so fallen that one who is a Jew must necessarily perish or be estranged from God" ([37], p. 246). Instead, Calvin retained a clear hope of Jewish conversion, for the counsel of God "stands firm and immutable" ([37], p. 257). Moreover, Calvin noted

---

3   See Calvin's comments on Ps 102:12, Ps 102:24, Hos 2:14, Jon 3:10, Mic 2:7, Mic 7:15, Hab 2:8, Hab 3:6–9, and Hab 3:13.

Paul's appeal to Israel's history in Romans 9–11: "Paul assumes as axiomatic that God has punished the unbelief of His people, but not, however, in such a way as to have forgotten His mercy, just as [God] has often at other times restored the Jews after He had apparently banished them from His kingdom" ([37], p. 254).[4] In sum, Calvin's doctrine of God's sovereignty and immutable purposes demanded that Calvin retain the possibility of the fulfilment of God's covenant with the Jews not merely through a remnant of the Jews but a possible full restoration—yet, a restoration Calvin could only conceive of in christological terms.

I have highlighted mostly theological contexts—unity of the covenant and doctrine of God—that shaped the logic of Calvin's teachings on Jews and Judaism. This is because Calvin intentionally operated within a theological system that he meticulously expressed in a particular order and arrangement, as seen in his *Institutes*. Theological frameworks mattered a great deal to Calvin. Yet, they also emanated from and functioned within particular contexts. Prior to Calvin, the teachings of Huldrych Zwingli and Heinrich Bullinger in Zurich and Martin Bucer in Strasbourg already espoused a strong unity of the covenant and an emphasis upon the sovereignty of God that deeply shaped Calvin's theology ([32], p. 201; [39–41]; [42], pp. 81–82). Moreover, both Zurich and Strasbourg were centers of Christian Hebraism, in which Christian exegetes emphasized knowledge of Hebrew and employed Jewish exegesis to enhance knowledge of the historical contexts of the Old Testament. At the very least, Calvin's focus upon God's historical interactions with the Old Testament Jews reflected Christian Hebraists' emphases upon the original history of the Old Testament and the historical sense as a primary site of meaning [43–48].

3. What Is at Stake: Clarity of Biblical Interpretation

There are a couple of other crucial contexts to consider. First, by the time of Luther and Calvin, there were no substantial Jewish populations living in Germany and Switzerland. Jews had been expelled from Saxony in the century prior to Luther's lifetime, and a 1432 law forbid Jews to reside in Saxony. Jews conducting business and trade, however, could obtain permission for temporary residence. Yet, in 1536 the elector of Saxony passed a law forbidding Jews even to do this. Hence, Luther had to travel beyond his homeland for any direct contact with Jews. Such direct contact, as Thomas Kaufman points out, often resulted from certain Jews seeking him out ([13], pp. 73–75; [49], p. 322). For example, Luther recounted that three Jews visited him in Wittenberg (prior to the 1536 mandate) and argued with his messianic interpretation of certain Old Testament passages ([50], WATr 3:3512b, 4:5026, 4:4795; [51], WA 53:461, 50:515). After the passing of a 1536 mandate prohibiting Jews to travel for commerce, the prominent Jewish leader Josel of Rosheim wrote to Luther requesting a letter of safe conduct to travel in Saxony, which Luther denied ([17], LW 54:239).

Similarly, there were no Jewish populations in Calvin's homeland of France or in Geneva. France expelled its Jews in 1394. When Calvin converted to Protestantism and traveled to Basel, he entered a town that had expelled its Jews in 1397. According to Detmers, the first place Calvin might have had direct contact with Jews and Judaism was during his brief 1536 stay in the northern Italian city of Ferrara, where about 3000 Jews lived. Yet, Calvin never mentioned any contact with Jews at this time. Likewise, contact in Geneva was unlikely, as Geneva and its surrounding territories expelled the Jews in 1491. Yet, Detmers argues that Calvin must have been aware of the small Jewish population in Frankfurt am Main during his visit in 1539. Likewise, while Strasbourg did not allow Jews permanent residence, Jews traveled through the city for commerce. Calvin was likely privy to the debates of the Strasbourg leaders Martin Bucer and Wolfgang Capito concerning toleration of Jews and Judaism during his years in Strasbourg and his later continued contacts with the city's leaders ([32], pp. 203–6).

---

[4] For a more detailed analysis of Calvin's reading of Romans 9 to 11, see ([34], pp. 18–21; [38], pp. 189–91).

With the exception of a handful of possible encounters, the fact remains that Luther and Calvin wrote concerning Jews and Judaism within contexts in which very few actual Jews resided, let alone traveled. Hence, one might ask, "What is going on? Why do Jews appear so frequently in their writings?" Concerning Luther, one could point to the specific incidences of public Jewish blasphemy, but this does not account for the fact that Luther wrote about Jews and Judaism consistently across his lifetime. Scholars frequently observe that Luther ([14], pp. 375–76; [12], p. 50; [6], pp. 367–71; [20], pp. 140–41; [13], pp. 96–97; [7], p. 126) and Calvin's ([30], p. 121; [31], pp. 108–19; [32], pp. 215–17) engagement with Jews and Judaism overwhelming centered upon biblical interpretation. Yet surprisingly, scholars fail to connect this focus with the larger issues at stake for the Protestant reformers. In a world in which Protestant reformers such as Luther and Calvin set forth Scripture as the prime authority for Christian belief and practice, issues of biblical interpretation were of paramount importance. Specifically, Luther and Calvin insisted upon the perspicuity of Scripture—perspicuity defined by Scripture's clear revelation of Jesus Christ, justification by faith alone, and God's providential purposes for the church revealed in Christ [52–55]). Any challenge to Scripture's perspicuity, stability, and authority threatened to undermine their reforming efforts and central teachings. Hence, biblical interpretation and the perspicuity of Scripture, in particular, served as important contexts in which to understand Luther and Calvin's engagement with Jews and Judaism, for their negative statements concerning Jews and Judaism often focused upon matters pertaining to biblical interpretation. The fact that very few Jews lived among them did not deter them, for Jewish exegesis—made available by the growth of Christian Hebraism in the sixteenth century—posed a very real threat to the perspicuity, stability, and authority of Scripture. Hence, sixteenth-century Christian Hebraism is another crucial context in which to understand Protestant reformers' teachings on Jews and Judaism.

3.1. Centrality of Biblical Interpretation for Luther

Luther's negative appraisal of Jewish exegesis was prominent across his lifetime. As early as his first lectures on the Psalms (1513–15), Luther expressed his enduring concern to defend christological interpretation of the Old Testament ([12], p. 50; [7], pp. 126–28; [6], pp. 353, 363, 367–69, 371; [13], pp. 72, 96–98). In the preface, he wrote, "Every prophecy and every prophet must be understood as referring to Christ the Lord . . . For thus He Himself says: 'Search the Scriptures; it is they that bear witness to Me' (Jn 5:39). Otherwise it is most certain that the searchers will not find that for which they are searching. For that reason some explain very many psalms not prophetically but historically, following certain Hebrew rabbis who are falsifiers and inventors of Jewish vanities" ([17], LW 10:7). For Luther, prophecies of Christ's incarnation, passion, resurrection, and ascension are the primary content of Old Testament prophecy. Moreover, he insisted that all Scripture points to Christ. The fact that the Jews have rejected Christ means that they cannot by definition be right readers of Scripture, for, according to Luther, they completely miss the key subject matter ([17], LW 10:3, 7; 33:26; 34:112; 35:122, 236; [33], pp. 38–44).[5]

More specifically, Luther argued that the Jews not only fail to see Christ as the true content of Scripture, but they also lack knowledge of the chief theological loci revealed in Scripture—namely, right understandings of faith and works, law and gospel, and justification by faith alone.[6] Instead, asserted Luther, Jews trust in their lineage, glory in the law, boast in their circumcision, cling to their works, and expect a carnal fulfilment of God's promises. Hence, they read Scripture "carnally" and

---

[5] Luther wrote, "Moreover, it is certain that after the Jews had denied Christ, they lost the subject matter. For this reason they are incapable of teaching anything sound and torture themselves in vain with matters of grammar" ([17], LW 3:358).

[6] In his 1532 comments on Ps 51, Luther wrote, "The proper subject of theology is man guilty of sin and condemned, and God the Justifier and Savior of man the sinner. Whatever is asked or discussed in theology outside of this subject is error and poison. All Scripture points to this, that God commends his kindness to us and his Son restores to righteousness and life the nature that has fallen into sin and condemnation" ([17], LW 12:311).

actively promote works righteousness. Indeed, the Jews exemplify the works righteousness and trust in the wrong things that Luther's whole career stood against. He then employed Jews as an interpretive tool to unveil such wrong teachings within Roman Catholicism, for Luther frequently paralleled the Jews and the Roman Catholics. Just as the Jews trust in works, the Roman Catholics cling to their masses, sacrament of penance, and works of satisfaction. Just as the Jews trust in their physical lineage, the priests trust in their titles and vows. Just as the Jews read Scripture carnally, so do the Roman Catholics.[7] Moreover, Luther's use of the Jews as a trope to attack his opponents points to a larger antipathy toward Jews and Judaism extant in late-medieval and sixteenth-century Christian culture. In the end, Luther positioned Jews and Judaism directly contrary to Christ and the gospel and, therefore, directly contrary to his central teachings ([13], pp. 72–73). They threatened to thwart the very perspicuity of Scripture that Luther defined precisely in terms of these key teachings.

For Luther, the Jews in Scripture provided ample evidence of their blindness toward the true subject matter of God's Word. Luther's readings of medieval Jewish exegesis furthered this negative appraisal. In his condemnations of Jewish exegesis, Luther frequently pointed to the ways in which Jews corrupt or distort Scripture's meaning ([17], LW 3:115, 296, 337, 353; 4:187, 263; 6:136, 181–82, 291–92). His larger concern to preserve the clarity of Scripture quickly emerges, for he frequently lamented the ways Jews obscure the true meaning of Scripture. For example, commenting on Gen 33:18, Luther wrote, "The Jews obscure the genuine sense by their ambiguities, drawing words into varied and manifold meanings, and they do this with the set purpose of contriving questions and errors of every kind" ([17], LW 6:181–82).[8] Similarly, he commented on Gen 24:12–14, "The Jews deserve our disgust; for they obscure the proper force of words, weaken it, as it were, and make the words ambiguous" ([17], LW 4:263). Upon later awareness of public Jewish blasphemy, Luther's rhetoric expanded from viewing the Jews as blind and unable to grasp Scripture's true content to depicting the Jews increasingly as actively lying and perverting Scripture. For example, in his later lectures on Genesis (1535–45), Luther exclaimed, "[The Jews] are the most accursed people and are held captive and possessed by Satan ... I violently hate the comments of the rabbis, in which they wickedly corrupt Holy Scripture by their lies" ([17], LW 6:292).[9]

The Jews, however, were not the only target of Luther's criticisms of Jewish exegesis. Luther aimed them equally at sixteenth-century Christian Hebraists, whom he also viewed as in danger of losing Scripture's prime subject matter through their dependence on Jewish exegesis—specifically in the priority many Christian Hebraists gave to the original, historical sense of the Old Testament text ([13], p. 97; [6], p. 362). For example, the Christian Hebraist Sebastian Münster tended to follow a historical reading of the Old Testament, often neglecting traditional christological exegesis. Such concerns against Christian Hebraists acquired a sharper tone in Luther's later years, as seen in his lectures on Genesis and 1543 anti-Jewish treatises. For example, in *On the Ineffable Name*, Luther explicitly warned sixteenth-century Christian-Hebraists, "If a Christian seeks understanding in the Scriptures from Jews despite such damnation and judgment, what else does he do but that he seeks the face of a blind man, cleverness from a madman, death from life, and grace and truth from the Devil?" ([56], p. 222). For Luther, the threat to the clarity of Scripture from the Jews was very real, for he believed many of his fellow Christians had already been deceived.

In sum, Jews and Judaism were a central concern for Luther across his lifetime. Jews failed to see Christ as the true subject matter of Scripture and justification by faith alone as the key to its perspicuity. For Luther, biblical and contemporary Jews precisely exemplified wrong dependence on the Law,

---

[7] For examples, see ([33], pp. 42–44; [17], LW 3:76, 81, 89, 97, 113, 251, 343; 4:27, 32, 366; 5:104, 141; 7:36, 196; 8:168, 176;10:3, 39, 58, 61, 155, 377, 512; 11: 13, 39, 208, 512; 16:27; 17:55; 20:71, 268; 22:42, 244–45, 275, 366, 457, 510; 24:259; 26:10, 80, 246–47, 251; 29:49; 30:29, 34, 58; 34:20).

[8] Similarly he wrote on Gen 32:24, "The Jews by their ambiguous interpretations have introduced many perversions, especially darkening the passages concerning the Messiah" ([17], LW 6:136), and on Gen 35:17, "For when the Jews have doubts about a word, they resort to equivocation and multiply meanings and make it more obscure by their glosses" ([17], LW 6:266).

[9] See also ([17], LW 3:115, 296, 337, 353; 4:187, 263; 6:136, 181–82, 291–92; 22:244–45, 245, 465; 47:215, 244).

wrong trust in works for their salvation, and carnal rather than spiritual understandings of God's promises—all of which threatened to undermine clear teachings of Scripture. Moreover, the Jews' threat to the perspicuity of Scripture—particularly to christological reading of the Old Testament—was made all the more real and close to home through sixteenth-century Christian Hebraists' appropriation of Jewish exegesis and Jewish exegetical principles. For Luther, christological exegesis of the Old Testament and key reformational teachings that he genuinely believed were the perspicuous content of Scripture were at stake and demanded defense.

3.2. Centrality of Biblical Interpretation for Calvin

Biblical interpretation was equally central in Calvin's engagement with Jews and Judaism, with several similarities and some important differences. Like Luther, Calvin asserted that Christ is the content and goal of all Scripture ([57], p. 70). Hence, in rejecting Christ, Jews cannot read Scripture rightly ([58], pp. 70, 101). Like Luther, Calvin's defense of christological readings of many Old Testament passages against Jewish counter-readings exhibited the central concern for Scripture's perspicuity. A classic case is Ps 22:16, in which Christian and Jewish interpreters argue over whether a particular Hebrew word ends in a *yod* or a *vav*. Jewish interpreters opt for the *yod* with the literal reading "like a lion," while the Christian interpreters assert the *vav* with the meaning "they have pierced" to refer to the piercing of Christ's hands and feet in the crucifixion. Calvin commented, "The Jews prate much about the literal sense being purposely and deliberately overthrown by our rendering the original word as 'they have pierced' ... Very great suspicion of falsehood, however, attaches to them, seeing it is the uppermost desire of their hearts to despoil the crucified Jesus and to divest him of his character as the Messiah and Redeemer. If we receive this reading as they would have us to do, the sense would be enveloped in marvelous obscurity" ([59], vol. 1, pp. 373–74). Similarly, Calvin contended that Jews deliberately obscured Ps 109:8 in order to undermine Peter's application of this verse to Judas's betrayal of Christ (Acts 1:20). Calvin wrote, "There is good reason to believe that, in [expounding this passage] the Jewish interpreters are actuated by pure malice. What purpose can it serve to pervert the sense of a word, the meaning of which is so pointed and plain, unless that under the influence of a malignant spirit they endeavor to obscure the passage to make it appear not to be properly quoted by Peter?" ([59], vol. 4, p. 278). Calvin saw this same malicious intent in the Jews' rejection of the Gospel writers placing the words of Ps. 118:26 on the tongues of those who celebrated Jesus' entry into Jerusalem (Matt 21:9, Mk 11:9, Lk 19:38). Likewise, asserted Calvin, the Jews aimed to "mystify" the prediction of Christ in the figure of Melchizedek in Ps 110:4 ([59], vol. 4, pp. 304, 395). In sum, Calvin sought to defend against the Jews' "malevolent" attempts to obscure the clarity of the christological content of Scripture.

Calvin's concern for the "simple and plain" sense of Scripture was a second aspect that led him to criticize Jewish exegesis. For Calvin, the "simple" sense of Scripture preserved and made accessible its perspicuity. In his Old Testament exegesis, Calvin repudiated what he viewed as Jewish "fables," "fanciful foolishness," "frivolous stories," or "trifling conjectures."[10] In each case, he pointed to the "simple" meaning or "plain" sense of the text and warned the reader to avoid "Jewish subtleties." He was keenly aware of the benefits and pitfalls of the use of Jewish exegesis in his day, especially its frequent use among close Christian Hebraist colleagues—Martin Bucer foremost among them. Calvin, however, more often explicitly referred to Jewish exegesis when criticizing it. Yet, he silently employed Jewish exegesis when he believed it clarified the "simple, plain" sense of the text and buttressed the key practices of attention to historical and literary contexts, scope, and authorial intention [60]. Conversely, Calvin repudiated Jewish and Christian interpreters alike if

---

[10] See Calvin's comments on Ps 36:7, Ps 103:4, Ps 136:13, Ex 4:24, Ex 12:12, Ex 23:20, Lev 12:2, Lev 21:2, Deut 4:19, Deut 5:26, and Deut 21:10.

they strayed from these exegetical principles.[11] Yet, he accused Jews of deliberate malice, such as his comments on Ps 136:13, "We may well laugh at such fooleries, yet we hold them at the same time in detestation; for there can be no doubt that the rabbinical writers were led to this [wrong reading] by the devil, as an artful way of discrediting the Scriptures" ([59], vol. 5, p. 186). Calvin was—much like Luther—concerned to preserve the authority and perspicuity of Scripture against what he viewed as deliberate, even malicious, attempts by Jews to obscure it.

Yet, Calvin differed from Luther in a couple of crucial ways. First, Calvin was significantly less inclined in his Old Testament exegesis to deploy the Jews as an interpretive tool in which to highlight wrong trust in carnal things, dependence on the law, and works righteousness. Rather, the Jews served as a pedagogical tool to teach about God's beneficence and providential care of God's people—the church—across all ages.[12] Hence, in contrast to Luther's employment of Old Testament Jews to emphasize the distinctions between the old and new covenants, Calvin employed the stories of the Old Testament Jews as vivid depictions of the unity of the covenant across time. Preserving the unity of the covenant was distinctive to Calvin's treatment of not only biblical Jews, but also contemporary Jews. The unbelief of contemporary Jewry precisely threatened the very assertion of this unity, as seen in Calvin's closing statement in the very section of the *Institutes* where he addresses the unity of the Old and New Testaments:

> Nor would the obtuseness of the whole Jewish nation today in awaiting the Messiah's earthly kingdom be less monstrous had the Scriptures not foretold long before that they would receive this punishment for having rejected the gospel. For it so pleased God in righteous judgment to strike blind the minds of those who by refusing the offered light of heaven voluntarily brought darkness upon themselves. Therefore, they read Moses and continually ponder his writings, but they are hampered by a veil from seeing the light shining in his face. Thus, Moses's face will remain covered and hidden from them until it be turned to Christ, from whom they now strive to separate and withdraw as much as they can ([35], 2.10.23).

Here Calvin argued that Jews could not see the true goal and content of Moses' writings until they turned to Christ. The crucial problem, in other words, is that the Jews do not see the unity of the covenant who is Christ, the telos of the law. Likewise, in his unpublished dialogue between a Christian and a Jew, Calvin built the demonstration of the unity of the two Testaments into the structure of the dialogue itself by having the Jew cite New Testament passages and the Christian respond with Old Testament passages ([22]; [34], pp. 23–26).

In strong affirmation of the unity of the covenant, Calvin read Jews of the Old Testament as participants in God's eternal covenant. Thus, Calvin employed the Jews as a pedagogical tool to illustrate the experiences of Old Testament Jews as part of the one story of God's providential activity with God's people; they become the stories of the church. Hence, though Calvin offered a more positive reading of Old Testament Jews, he clearly adhered to Christ as the fulfilment of the old covenant and the church as the True Israel. Contemporary Jews threatened to undermine the unity of the covenant and endanger the very exegetical principles that Calvin maintained for the preservation of the perspicuity of Scripture.

---

[11] See, for examples, his sharp criticisms of the traditional Christian exegesis of Is 63:1, Hos 13:14, Mic 4:13, Mic 5:2, and Zech 13:7, in which Calvin appealed to these same exegetical principles of plain sense, context, and authorial intention.

[12] See Calvin's comments on Joel 2:30–31, Joel 3:9–11, Amos 5:19–20, Obadiah 18, Mic 5:7–8, Mic 5:10–15, Mic 7:9, Mic 7:16–17, preface to Nahum, Nah 1:15, Hab 3:6, Hab 3:13, Zeph 2:9–10, Hagg 2:6–9, Hagg 2:20–23, Zech 2:5, Zech 3:10, Zech 6:1–3, Zech 9:8, and Zech 12:4.

4. Drawing Lessons from Church History

We started with the question, "Did the Protestant reformers contribute anything new to the history of Christian-Jewish relations?" On a certain level, they simply continued traditional Christian teachings. Yet Luther and Calvin's prominent focus on biblical interpretation carried an exigency particular to their time and circumstances. There was an urgency in their defense of the perspicuity and authority of Scripture against Jewish corruption and obfuscation, despite the fact that very few Jews lived in Western Europe. For Luther, this took the distinct form of clarifying the differences between law and gospel and faith and works, and setting forth the clear teaching of justification by faith alone apart from (and even through) the examples of Jewish wrongful trust in their physical heritage, law, and works. For Calvin, this meant upholding the unity of the covenant found in Christ alone and advocating exegetical principles that elucidate the plain sense of Scripture. For both Luther and Calvin, Jews and Judaism posed specific threats to distinct Protestant teachings, such as justification by faith alone, the authority and perspicuity of Scripture, and, for Calvin, the unity of the covenant.

We began by saying that we cannot deal with this difficult topic responsibly without revisiting ethical issues, but a responsible engagement also entails first excavating the contexts and unearthing the logic—some of which this paper has aimed to provide. Just as the reformers accentuated biblical interpretation, I begin with a focus on exegesis. In a provocative article, Andrew Gow argues that Luther's exegesis of Scripture is a form of Christian colonialism. He contends that "in Luther's case, Christ-centered readings had a directly polemical function that colonized and appropriated Hebrew Bible texts" ([61], p. 243). Employing an example of Luther's reading of Isaiah, Gow concludes, "Luther insists on knowing the meaning of the Isaiah passage in a way that excludes Jewish readings, thus appropriating it for Christian truth and denying any other meaning it might have" ([61], p. 245). Indeed, Luther often interpreted Old Testament passages in this manner. The question Gow's article raises for me is, "What makes exegesis colonizing?" With Gow's definition, Calvin's exegesis was equally colonizing, for he interpreted all the stories of Old Testament Jewry as the stories of the church and insisted that they culminate in Christ. If one defines a colonizing exegesis by its appropriation and reconfiguration of the Hebrew Scriptures in order to make Christian truth claims, then Luther and Calvin are not the only ones guilty of a colonizing exegesis; pretty much all of Christianity is guilty of this at one point or another. I contend that such appropriation and reconfiguration for specific truth claims are not in themselves what makes something colonizing—or more precisely, they are not what is ethically questionable. Ethical problems arise when such actions are combined with the denigration of the other and the denial of the other's claim to these texts to define their own identity. Luther and Calvin not only interpreted Scripture to make distinct Christian claims and to buttress Christian identity, but they also vilified Jews, Judaism, and Jewish exegesis. I contend that the former is a necessary aspect of distinct religious identities, and I contend that the latter is where Christians have sinned and acted in ways contrary to the very principles of the Christian faith. History repeatedly shows that denigrating another too often leads to oppressive and violent acts that I, at least, cannot accept as consistent with the principles of the Christian faith. This is not intended to promote a form of relativism; rather, it advocates for real and competing truth claims with the plea for Christians to learn much better how to make such truth claims in a more ethical and faithful fashion.

Hence, such issues around exegesis translate out to broader issues of Christian identity and the ways in which it negotiates that identity, especially when Christianity's truth claims impinge upon the identity of another—whether Jews or multiple "others." Luther and Calvin's examples demonstrate what can happen when Christians care more about the content of their defense than whether their method is ethical and faithful. This does not mean that one has to hold a belief with any less conviction. It does mean that one should be able to do so without disparaging the other. When I teach about the history of Christian-Jewish relations, I often identify it as the "fall" of Christianity, for it serves as a lens for the temptations Christianity faces in many subsequent interactions with the "other" in history. It serves as a mirror for what happens when self-protection, security, or the necessity to be right at any cost becomes Christianity's primary focus rather than the call to humility, goodness, godliness, peace, and putting others before ourselves. This history asks Christians penetrating questions about how one holds truth claims faithfully—how one holds them with conviction while also holding them in a manner consistent with the belief in a God who would die on a cross and take the sin and violence of the world onto God's very own Self, precisely to end all violence and oppression.

Thus, taking a close and painful look at the history of Christian-Jewish relations also calls Christians to read Christianity "against itself." I end with a few examples specific to reading Luther and Calvin "against themselves." Luther and Calvin's profound doctrine of sin and human depravity at the very least should warn Christians that sinful inclinations toward self-protection still powerfully tempt us toward trust in the wrong things (such as articulations of the truth) rather than in the God in whom there is always mystery that finite human constructions could never fully apprehend. Moreover, Luther and Calvin's powerful teachings of the agency of God's Word, in which the Word is the true actor in any human transformation, exhorts Christians to the humble recognition of themselves as the mere vessels of this Word. It clarifies the crucial distinction between the verbs "to convert" and "to witness." No Christian can convert another; only God can do that. Hence, coercive actions on the part of Christians are an abuse of God's Word. Rather, Christians are called to bear witness of the truth they know in Jesus Christ and let God do what God may with that witness. Furthermore, Luther and Calvin viewed all humanity as having the image of God and repeatedly warned that no one person can possess the whole truth; likewise, no one person possesses full knowledge of a right reading of Scripture ([37], p. 4; [17], LW 34:285–86). This calls for profound humility and calls for the necessity of negotiating truth communally with an openness to the image of God in even the "other." Lastly, the practice of reading of Scripture "against ourselves" calls for the reading of Christian history "against ourselves" to illuminate the circumstances under which one becomes a "persecuting society" [62] in contrast to the circumstances under which one becomes a cruciform people shaped by the crucified Christ who laid down his life that others might see the love of God.

Conflicts of Interest: The author declares no conflict of interest.

References

1. Ora Limor, and Guy G. Strousma. *Contra Iudaeos: Ancient and Medieval Polemics between Christians and Jews*. Tübingen: J.C.B. Mohr, 1996.
2. Robert Bonfil. "Aliens within: The Jews and Antijudaism." In *Handbook of European History 1400–1600: Late Middle Ages, Renaissance and Reformation*. Edited by Thomas A. Brady Jr., Heiko A. Oberman and James D. Tracy. Leiden: Brill, 1994, pp. 263–302.
3. David Nirenberg. *Anti-Judaism: The Western Tradition*. New York: W. W. Norton & Company, 2013.
4. Jeremy Cohen. "Traditional Prejudice and Religious Reform: The Theological and Historical Foundations of Luther's Anti-Judaism." In *Anti-Semitism in Times of Crisis*. Edited by Sander L. Gilman and Steven T. Katz. New York: New York University Press, 1991, pp. 81–102.
5. Salo W. Baron. "John Calvin and the Jews." In *Essential Papers on Judaism and Christianity in Conflict from Late Antiquity to the Reformation*. Edited by Jeremy Cohen. New York: New York University Press, 1991, pp. 380–400.
6. Mark U. Edwards. "Against the Jews." In *Essential Papers on Judaism and Christianity in Conflict: From Late Antiquity to the Reformation*. Edited by Jeremy Cohen. New York: New York University Press, 1991, pp. 345–79.
7. Mark Thompson. "Luther and the Jews." *Reformed Theological Review* 67 (2008): 121–45.
8. Peter F. Wiener. *Martin Luther: Hitler's Spiritual Ancestor*. London: Hutchinson, 1945.
9. William L. Shirer. *The Rise and Fall of the Third Reich*. New York: Simon & Schuster, 1960.
10. Michael Berenbaum. *The World Must Know: The History of the Holocaust as Told in the United States Holocaust Memorial Museum*, 2nd ed. Baltimore: John Hopkins University Press, 2006.
11. Eric W. Gritsch. *Martin Luther's Anti-Semitism: Against His Better Judgment*. Grand Rapids: Eerdmans, 2012.
12. Heiko A. Oberman. *The Roots of Anti-Semitism: In the Age of Renaissance and Reformation*. Translated by James I. Porter. Philadephia: Fortress, 1981.

13. Thomas Kaufmann. "Luther and the Jews." In *Jews, Judaism, and the Reformation in Sixteenth-Century Germany*. Edited by Dean Phillip Bell and Stephen G. Burnett. Leiden: Brill, 2006, pp. 69–104.
14. Wilhelm Maurer. "Die Zeit der Reformation." In *Kirche und Synagoge: Handbuch der Geschichte von Christen und Juden. Darstellung mit Quellen*. Edited by Karl-Heinrich Rengstorf and Siegfried von Kortz-fleisch. Stuttgart: Klett, 1968, vol. 1, pp. 363–452.
15. Diarmaid MacCulloch. *Reformation: Europe's House Divided*. London: Penguin, 2003.
16. Johannes Wallmann. "The Reception of Luther's Writings on the Jews from the Reformation to the End of the 19th Century." *Lutheran Quarterly* 1 (1987): 72–97.
17. Martin Luther. *Luther's Works*. Edited by J. Pelikan and H. Lehman. 55 vols. Philadelphia: Fortress. pp. 1957–86, Hereafter cited as "LW".
18. Gerhard O. Forde. "Luther and the Jews." *Lutheran Quarterly* 27 (2013): 125–42.
19. Eric Gritsch. "The Jews in Reformation Theology." In *Jewish-Christian Encounters over the Centuries: Symbiosis, Prejudice, Holocaust, Dialogue*. Edited by Marvin Perry and Frederick M. Schweitzer. New York: Peter Lang, 1994, pp. 197–213.
20. Mark U. Edwards Jr. *Luther's Last Battles: Politics and Polemics, 1531–46*. Ithaca: Cornell University Press, 1983.
21. Erich Vogelsang. *Luthers Kampf gegen die Juden*. Tubingen: J.C. B. Mohr, 1933.
22. John Calvin. "Calvin, Jews, and Intra-Christian Polemics." Ph.D. dissertation, Temple University, Philadelphia, PA, USA, 1987; pp. 229–61.
23. Shimon Markish. *Erasmus and the Jews*. Edited by Anthony Olcott. Chicago: University of Chicago Press, 1986.
24. Anne Jippe Visser. *Calvijn en de Joden*. 's-Gravehage: Boekencentrum, 1963.
25. Jacques Courvoisier. "Calvin und die Juden: Zu einem Streitgespräch." In *Christen und Juden: Ihr Gegenüber vom Apostelkonzil bis Heut*. Edited by Wolf Dieter and Karl Thieme. Mainz: Matthias Grünewald, 1961, pp. 141–46.
26. Hans Joachim Kraus. "Israel in the Theology of Calvin: Towards a New Approach to the Old Testament and Judaism." *Studies in Christian-Jewish Relations* 22 (1989): 75–86.
27. Calvin Augustus Pater. "Calvin, the Jews, and the Judaic Legacy." In *In Honor of John Calvin: Papers from the 1986 International Calvin Symposium*. Edited by Edward Furcha. Montreal: McGill University Press, 1987, pp. 256–96.
28. Jack Hughes Robinson. *John Calvin and the Jews*. New York: Peter Lang, 1992.
29. Clark W. Williamson. *Has God Rejected His People? Anti-Judaism in the Christian Church*. Nashville: Abingdon, 1982.
30. Alice L. Eckardt. "The Reformation and the Jews." In *Interwoven Destinies: Jews and Christians through the Ages*. Edited by Eugene J. Fisher. New York: Paulist, 1993, pp. 111–33.
31. Mary Potter Engel. "Calvin and the Jews: A Textual Puzzle." *The Princeton Seminary Bulletin* 1 (1990): 106–23.
32. Achim Detmers. "Calvin, the Jews and Judaism." In *Jews, Judaism, and the Reformation in Sixteenth-Century Germany*. Leiden: Brill, 2006, pp. 197–217.
33. G. Sujin Pak. *The Judaizing Calvin: Sixteenth-Century Debates over the Messianic Psalms*. New York: Oxford University Press, 2010.
34. G. Sujin Pak. "A Break with Anti-Judaic Exegesis: John Calvin and the Unity of the Testaments." *Calvin Theological Journal* 46 (2011): 7–28.
35. John Calvin. *Institutes of the Christian Religion*. Edited by John T. McNeill. Translated by Ford Lewis Battles. Library of Christian Classics (LCC); Philadelphia: Westminster, 1960, vol. 20, All references to this text above cite book, chapter, and section numbers.
36. Barbara Pitkin. "Imitation of David: David as a Paradigm for Faith in Calvin's Exegesis of the Psalms." *Sixteenth Century Journal* 24 (1993): 843–63. [CrossRef]
37. John Calvin. *The Epistles of Paul the Apostle to the Romans and to the Thessalonians*. Edited by Ross Mackenzie. Grand Rapids: William B. Eerdmans, 1995.
38. Peter Barnes. "Calvin and the Jews." *The Reformed Theological Review* 68 (2009): 175–93.
39. Emil G. Kraeling. "Zwingli and Calvin and the Old Testament." In *The Old Testament since the Reformation*. London: Lutterworth, 1955, pp. 21–32.

40. Heinrich Bullinger. *A Brief Exposition of the One and Eternal Testament or Covenant of God.* In *Fountainhead of Federalism: Heinrich Bullinger and the Covenantal Tradition.* Translated by Charles S. McCoy, and J. Wayne Baker. Louisville: Westminster/John Knox, 1991, pp. 99–138.

41. J. Wayne Baker. *Heinrich Bullinger and the Covenant: The Other Reformed Tradition.* Athens: Ohio University Press, 1980.

42. Wulfert de Greef. "Calvin's Understanding and Interpretation of the Bible." In *John Calvin's Impact on Church and Society, 1509–2009.* Edited by Martin Ernst Hirzel and Martin Sallmann. Grand Rapids: William B. Eerdmans, 2009, pp. 67–89.

43. Frank Rosenthal. "The Rise of Christian Hebraism in the Sixteenth Century." *Historia Judaica* 7 (1945): 167–91.

44. Jerome Friedman. *The Most Ancient Testimony: Sixteenth-Century Christian-Hebraica in the Age of Renaissance Nostalgia.* Athens: Ohio University Press, 1983.

45. Jerome Friedman. "Protestants, Jews, and Jewish Sources." In *Piety, Politics, and Ethics: Reformation Studies in Honor of George Wolfgang Forell.* Edited by Carter Lindberg. Kirksville: Sixteenth Century Journal Publisher, 1984, pp. 139–56.

46. Eric Zimmer. "Jewish and Christian Hebraist Collaboration in Sixteenth Century Germany." *Jewish Quarterly Review* 71 (1980): 69–88. [CrossRef]

47. Stephen G. Burnett. "Reassessing the 'Basel-Wittenberg Conflict': Dimensions of the Reformation-Era Discussion of Hebrew Scholarship." In *Hebraica Veritas? Christian Hebraists and the Study of Judaism in Early Modern Europe.* Edited by Allison P. Coudert and Jeffrey S. Shoulson. Philadephia: University of Pennsylvania Press, 2004, pp. 181–201.

48. Stephen G. Burnett. *Christian Hebraism in the Reformation Era (1500–1660: Authors, Books, and the Transmission of Jewish Learning.* Leiden: Brill, 2012.

49. Kirsi Stjerna. "Luther and his Jewish Conversation Partners: Insights for Thinking about Conversion, Baptism, and Saving Faith." *Currents in Theology and Mission* 40 (2013): 319–35.

50. Martin Luther. *D. Martin Luthers Werke. Kritische Gesamtausgabe.* 72 vols. Weimar: H. Böhlau. pp. 1883–2007, Hereafter cited as "WA".

51. Martin Luther. *D. Martin Luthers Werke. Kritische Gesamtausgabe. Tischreden.* 6 vols. Weimar: H. Böhlau. pp. 1912–21, Hereafter cited as "WATr".

52. Mark Thompson. "Biblical Interpretation in the Works of Martin Luther." In *A History of Biblical Interpretation, Volume 2: The Medieval through the Reformation Periods.* Edited by Alan J. Hauser and Duane F. Watson. Grand Rapids: William B. Eerdmans, 2009, pp. 299–318.

53. David J. Lose. "Luther and the Evangelical Clarity of Scripture and Sermon." *Lutheran Forum* 31 (1997): 32–35.

54. James Patrick Callahan. "*Claritas Scripturae*: The Role of Perspicuity in Protestant Hermeneutics." *Journal of the Evangelical Theological Society* 39 (1996): 353–72.

55. Klaas Runia. "The Hermeneutics of the Reformers." *Calvin Theological Journal* 19 (1984): 121–52.

56. Martin Luther. "On the Ineffable Name." In *The Jews in Christian Theology: Martin Luther's Anti-Jewish Von Schem Hamphoras, Previously Unpublished in English, and Other Milestones in Church Doctrine Concerning Judaism.* Edited by Gerhard Falk. Jefferson: McFarland & Co., 1992.

57. John Calvin. "Preface to Olivétan's New Testament." In *Calvin: Commentaries (Library of Christian Classics).* Translated by Joseph Haroutunian. Philadelphia: Westminster, 1958, vol. 23, pp. 58–73.

58. John Calvin. *Commentary on a Harmony of the Evangelists, Matthew, Mark and Luke.* Translated by Rev. William Pringle. Grand Rapids: Baker, 1984, vol. 1.

59. John Calvin. *Commentary on the Book of Psalms.* Translated by Rev. James Anderson. Grand Rapids: Baker, 1999, vol. 1–5.

60. G. Sujin Pak. "Luther, Bucer, and Calvin on Psalms 8 and 16: Confessional Formation and the Question of Jewish Exegesis." *Dutch Review of Church History* 85 (2005): 169–86. [CrossRef]

61. Andrew Gow. "Christian Colonialism: Luther's Exegesis of Hebrew Scripture." In *Continuity and Change: The Harvest of Late Medieval and Reformation History: Essays presented to Heiko A. Oberman on his 70th Birthday.* Edited by Robert Bast and Andrew C. Gow. Leiden: Brill, 2000, pp. 229–52.

62. Robert Ian Moore. *The Formation of a Persecuting Society: Power and Deviance in Western Europe, 950–1250.* Oxford: Blackwell, 1987.

Article

Martin Luther and Lucas Cranach Teaching the Lord's Prayer

Bruce McNair

Department of History, Campbell University, 143 Main Street, Buies Creek, NC 27506, USA;
mcnair@campbell.edu

Academic Editor: Christopher Metress
Received: 10 February 2017; Accepted: 31 March 2017; Published: 11 April 2017

Abstract: Martin Luther wrote and preached on the Lord's Prayer many times over a 20-year period. When we consider his work on the Prayer we see significant developments as the historical context changes, so that he finds new ways to express his most fundamental theological principles, such as justification by faith alone, the alien and proper work of God, the corruption of the will and the hiddenness of God. Luther's works on the Prayer were intended to teach complex ideas in easily accessible ways, and still do that for today's undergraduates. In particular, Luther included in the Large Catechism of 1529 a series of Lucas Cranach woodcuts that provide unique illustrations of his developing theological principles.

Keywords: Martin Luther; Lord's Prayer; prayer; Cranach; Catechism; Erasmus; Bible; justification; Reformation

---

1. Introduction

In courses that cover the Reformation, it is always important to tie Martin Luther's reforms to the historical context in which they occurred. For example, the 95 theses need to be understood in the context of late medieval Church practices of penance and indulgences. Modern students may not have first-hand experience of indulgences, but most do know the Lord's Prayer. Luther used the Lord's Prayer both in his own prayers, and as a vehicle for communicating his most fundamental theological concepts, such as justification by faith alone, the alien and proper work of God, the corruption of the will and the hiddenness of God. While each of these concepts involves complex theological doctrines, Luther's writings on the Lord's Prayer can make these concepts easily accessible to students and show the historical context in which they developed. Particularly helpful for teaching these concepts is the *Large Catechism* of 1529, for which Lucas Cranach provided illustrations of Luther's teachings, something not commonly found in Luther's writings. These illustrations were intended to reinforce Luther's points, but they also reflect the ways in which his interpretations of the Prayer changed as the historical context changed.

In this study, I will examine how Luther presents some of his fundamental theological concepts to laypeople in his teachings on the Lord's Prayer and how, in the case of the *Large Catechism*, Lucas Cranach illustrated these concepts. It is important for students to understand that Luther's reforms were not static, but developed over time and were influenced by historical events. Luther's writings on the Prayer are easily accessible and show both his main teachings and the historical context in which they occurred[1].

---

[1] For the history of the interpretation of the Lord's Prayer, see (Stevenson 2004). On Luther specifically, see (McNair 2005); *Recherches sur le Notre Pere* (Carmignac 1969) which also has an outstanding bibliography; "Luther et Calvin, commentateurs

2. Luther's Works on and Use of the Lord's Prayer

Over the course of his career, Luther preached and wrote upon the Lord's Prayer twenty-one times[2] (Carmignac 1969, pp. 166–70). His seven most extensive studies of the Prayer were all intended for the laity. *An Exposition of the Lord's Prayer for Simple Laymen* (Luther 1969, 42.19–81; Luther 1883, 2.80–130), based on a series of sermons he gave in 1517, was published in 1519. The *Personal Prayer Book* of 1522 (Luther 1969, 43.11–45; Luther 1883, 10(II).375–406) was intended as a replacement for the popular medieval prayer books, and the format follows the traditional Roman Catholic prayer book structure but with new interpretations. His *Ten Sermons on the Catechism* (Luther 1969, 51.169–82; Luther 1883, 30(I).94–109) were delivered in 1528, and the *Large* and *Small Catechisms* (Luther 1959) appeared in 1529. These three works cover the traditional sections of Christian catechisms, that is, the Ten Commandments, the Apostles' Creed, the Lord's Prayer and the sacraments. His *Commentary on the Sermon on the Mount* is a series of sermons he gave in the early 1530s and, lastly, *A Simple Way to Pray* (Luther 1969, 43.193–211; Luther 1883, 38.58–75), written in 1535, is a published letter to his barber and gives instruction on daily prayer.

These writings on the Lord's Prayer were central to Luther's efforts to change the practices of his congregation regarding prayer, including their use of medieval prayer books. These prayer books, such as Books of Hours or Breviaries, emphasized reciting prescribed prayers and following the canonical hours. Luther describes his own prayer methods in his writings, namely, how first thing in the morning and again in the evening, preferably kneeling or standing before an open window, he would recite the Ten Commandments, then the Apostles' Creed and some Scripture, followed by the Lord's Prayer, saying each phrase of the Prayer and elaborating upon it before going on to the next phrase[3]. After the Lord's Prayer, he prayed the same way through the Ten Commandments and the Apostles' Creed as time permitted or, as he says, unless he fell asleep. In his two *Catechisms*, Luther's order of Commandments, Creed and then Lord's Prayer actually rearranges the traditional form of catechisms, which used the order of Creed, Lord's Prayer and then Commandments. The traditional order corresponded to the virtues of faith, hope and love, whereas Luther revised the order because he instead understood the Commandments, Creed and Prayer to represent a medical diagnosis of the human condition, respectively the description of the sickness, the announcement of the cure and the medicine needed (Wengert 2009).

Luther's purpose in using the Commandments, the Creed and the Lord's Prayer also differed significantly from medieval prayer books in that his goal was to teach laypeople to develop their own prayers, rather than to repeat the Lord's Prayer or other prayers a prescribed number of times a day using repetitive methods such as the rosary. These changes to the medieval method of prayer led to rumors that Luther rejected prayer of any kind, for in the *Large Catechism* of 1529 he says opponents were "alleging that since we reject false and hypocritical prayers we teach there is no duty or need to pray (Luther 1959, p. 421)"[4]. He denied this, saying that he rejected only the abuse of prayer. For Luther, prayer is abused when it is not based on what is found in Scripture. This error results from the fact that, though we know there is a God, God is hidden and we need him to reveal by his Word how and what to pray. For Luther, God has revealed in the Lord's Prayer what we are to pray

---

du Notre Pere" (Leinhard 1992) compares Luther's *Catechisms* with Calvin's *Institutes*; *Das Vaterunser: Umrisse zu einer Geschichte des Gebets in der Alten und Mittleren Kirche* (Dibelius 1903) also examines Luther's place in the interpretive tradition. For a general study of Luther's understanding of prayer, see (Lehmann 1985) and (Hebart 1984). For Lucas Cranach, see (Moser 2005). For the *Catechisms*, see (Wengert 2009).

[2] Accounting for those works which are republished, there are fourteen separate occasions.

[3] He describes this in his *Prayer Book* of 1522, *Catechisms* of 1529 and *A Simple Way to Pray* of 1535. In his 1522 *Deutsche Bibel*, (Luther 1883, 6.32) Luther translates Matthew 6:9–13, "Unser vater inn dem himel. Dein name sei heilig. Dein reich kome. Dein wille geschehe auff erden wie inn himele. Unser teglich brott gib unns heutt, und vergib uns unsere schulde wie wir unsernn schuldigern vergeben, unnd fure unns nitt inn versuchung, sondern erlose uns von dem ubel, denn dein ist das reich, und die krafft, unnd die herlickeit in ewickeit. Amen."

[4] Also *Ten Sermons on the Catechism* (Luther 1969, 51.170). There is an extensive literature on the Catechisms, see (Wengert 2009) with bibliography.

and therefore we know he will hear it. Luther ties prayer to the second commandment, "Thou shalt not take the name of the Lord thy God in vain," which he interprets as a command to call upon God. Likewise, the command "Ask, and it will be given you" (Mt 6:7) shows for Luther that God has promised to hear and answer prayer. It is the revealed nature of the Lord's Prayer and the promises attached to it that make it unique among prayers.

Luther's method of praying by expanding upon the different petitions of the Lord's Prayer one at a time was the same method he used in explicating the Prayer[5]. In the remainder of this essay, I will examine Luther's interpretations of six of the seven petitions and consider the Cranach woodcuts from the *Large Catechism* that were used to illustrate Luther's theological concepts. Since, over the 20 years he writes on the prayer, Luther continually found new ways to explain his theological principles, I will also discuss how his interpretations changed over time and were influenced by historical events.

3. The First Petition of the Prayer—Preaching True Faith

In his 1519 *Exposition on the Lord's Prayer*, Luther's focus in the first petition, "Hallowed be Thy name," (Figure 1) is on what this petition says about us. As he says, "when we pray that God's name be hallowed in us, this implies that it is not yet holy in us; if it were, we should not have to pray for it" (Luther 1969, 42.33). He thinks that when we pray this petition we confess that we have robbed God of what rightly belongs to him, namely, that his name be holy in us and we should be terrified of the judgment that we deserve. However, God has told us to pray this way because he intends to be merciful and, in confessing that God's judgment about us is true, we justify God and so are justified by God.

In the 1520s, as Catholic opposition and discord among reformers grew, Luther came to interpret this petition differently, with a greater concern for the threat posed by false teachings that were leading people astray. Thus, in the 1522 *Prayer Book*, he sees the petition as asking for help to honor God, to serve others, to pray for proper things and not to be deceived by false doctrine. He states in the *Prayer Book* that in this petition we ask God to "help us root out all false belief and superstition. Help us bring to naught all heresies and false doctrines which are spread under the guise of your name" (Luther 1969, 43.30–31). God's help comes through his Word, so this petition is asking God for his Word through preaching, which reflects how Luther saw preaching just as important as the traditional focus on the Eucharist.

Hallowed Be Thy
Name
LC 1529

Figure 1. First petition.

---

5   Luther's division of the Lord's Prayer into seven petitions follows a tradition which dates back to Augustine. Another tradition which dates to Tertullian divides it into six petitions, and was followed in the Eastern church and by other reformers such as Calvin. Luther does not, however, follow Augustine in assigning a gift of the Spirit to each of the petitions (Stevenson 2004).

In the *Large Catechism* of 1529, both Luther's explication of the first petition and Lucas Cranach's woodcut (Figure 1) reflect this concern for preaching. The image is of a pastor preaching to his congregation, associating this petition with the need for true preaching to counter false doctrine[6]. This image reinforces Luther's increasing emphasis on both the need for pastors to preach properly and for the congregation to listen to the Word of God. As Luther writes in the *Large Catechism*, "we ought constantly to cry out against all who preach and believe falsely and against those who attack and persecute our Gospel and pure doctrine and try to suppress it, as the bishops, tyrants, fanatics and others do" (Luther 1959, p. 426). For students, then, Cranach's woodcut can be understood as part of a larger shift in Luther's teaching toward an increased emphasis on the need to combat through preaching the false doctrines that threatened Christians.

After Protestants failed to achieve either unity at the Marburg Colloquy in 1529 or reconciliation with the Catholics at the Diet of Augsburg in 1530, Luther's concern over false teaching became more strident. In his 1530 *Commentary on the Sermon on the Mount*, he says that the first petition opposes "every kind of false belief and worship, all of hell, and all sin and blasphemy" (Luther 1969, 21.146). In *A Simple Way to Pray* of 1535 he says the petition asks God to "destroy and root out the abominations, idolatry and heresy of the Turk, the Pope and all false teachers and fanatics" (Luther 1969, 43.195).

4. The Second Petition—Kingdoms

As with the first petition, Luther's interpretation of the second petition of the Lord's Prayer, "Thy kingdom come," (Figure 2) shows a change in emphasis over time, namely, in his thought concerning different types of kingdoms. In the 1519 *Exposition*, he contrasts God's kingdom with the kingdom of the devil. He says the kingdom of the devil is in this world, while the kingdom of God is in the godly person. He writes, "all of us dwell in the devil's kingdom until the coming of the kingdom of God." (Luther 1969, 42.38). He says that in praying for God's kingdom to come, we confess that it has not yet come to us and that we are still outside of his kingdom. Although deserving judgment for this, when we justify God's judgment by confessing his Word as true, God heals and pardons us. Also, because God's kingdom is hidden from us, we do not enter it, rather here we pray that it will come to us. He writes, "if you want to know the kingdom of God, do not go far afield in search of it ... it is not only close to you, it is in you." (Luther 1969, 42.41).

In his work on the two *Catechisms* of 1529, he alters his interpretation of the second petition, emphasizing that God's kingdom comes whether we pray for it or not. As he says in the *Small Catechism*, "To be sure, the kingdom of God comes of itself, without our prayer; but we pray in this petition that it may also come to us." (Luther 1959, p. 346). We cannot hasten or delay God's kingdom; rather, we pray that it may come to us so we can enjoy something that is already underway. For Luther, God's kingdom comes to us through the faith that is brought by the Holy Spirit.

---

[6] All images used here from Lucas Cranach are in the public domain and available at many sites, see for example (Wikimedia Commons n.d.).

Thy Kingdom
Come. Acts 2
LC 1529

Figure 2. Second petition.

This principle that God's kingdom comes to us by the Holy Spirit is illustrated by Cranach's *Large Catechism* woodcut (Figure 2). The woodcut is accompanied by a reference to Acts 2, showing the moment when the Holy Spirit comes upon the disciples. Each disciple is shown with a tongue of fire, and the Holy Spirit, as a dove, is above them. In the *Large Catechism*, Luther writes, "So we pray that [God's] kingdom may prevail among us through the Word and the power of the Holy Spirit, that the devil's kingdom may be overthrown and he may have no right or power over us" (Luther 1959, p. 427).

In the same year as the *Catechisms*, the second Diet of Speyer of 1529 rescinded the ability of political leaders to decide the religion of their territories, an ability that had proven to be very favorable to Protestant leaders. This was followed by the failure of Protestant and Catholic unity at the Diet of Augsburg of 1530 and the formation of the Protestant Schmalkaldic League of 1531 to oppose the Holy Roman Emperor and Catholic princes in the Empire militarily. Amid these political developments and increasing tensions, by the 1530s the focus of Luther's interpretation of the second petition changed from the coming of God's kingdom to protecting believers from kingdoms opposed to God. In the 1530 *Commentary on the Sermon on the Mount*, for instance, he says that in the second petition we ask that God would "shatter all the kingdoms that rage against His kingdom, so that it alone may remain" (Luther 1969, 21.146). Moreover, according to the 1535 *A Simple Way to Pray*, these raging kingdoms are in this world and are people in authority, both clerical and political, who take their power, wealth and position and use them for evil. He says, "they are many and mighty; they plague and hinder the tiny flock of God's kingdom who are weak, despised and few." (Luther 1969, 43.195). In this 1535 work, Luther stresses that only by God's constant protection do the faithful of God's kingdom survive the attacks of the kingdoms of this world. Luther's writing on the Prayer after the time of the *Catechisms*, then, shows that the changing political context influenced his explication of the second petition to focus less on the spiritual battle between God's kingdom and the kingdom of the devil, and more on the dangers posed by political authorities and their earthly kingdoms.

5. The Third Petition—The Alien and Proper Work of God

Luther's interpretations of the third petition, "Thy will be done on earth as in heaven", (Figure 3) generally concern the corruption of human will and one of his favorite theological principles, the alien and proper work of God. For Luther, God's alien work is to break the sinful nature of believers by convicting them of sin before the Law and making them aware of the punishment sin deserves. Central to this alien work is the crucifixion of Jesus. The proper work of God is to justify believers by faith alone and to enable believers to will what God wills. Central to this proper work is the resurrection of Jesus.

In his 1519 *Exposition* he distinguishes between what he terms the "old Adam" and the justified believer and he rejects the idea that we have some ability to do good by our own will. For Luther, because a believer is both fully just and unjust, the "old Adam" is a desire for evil, which corrupts the will and renders the individual unable, apart from by grace, to obey God's revealed will, which is the Law. As a result, God must break down and rebuild the will; he must destroy in order to renew. Luther writes, we "must despair utterly of ever having or attaining a good will … A good will is found only where there is no will. Where there is no will, God's will, which is the very best, will be present." (Luther 1969, 42.48). For Luther in 1519, the third petition shows we do not have a free will that can choose the good and so be rewarded by God for its virtue. Instead, our will must be overcome by God, which is a process begun when we accept God's judgment of us as true and so here we are praying that God do his alien work of breaking our will and his proper work of rebuilding it, so by grace it can choose the good and love God.

Thy Will Be
Done on Earth as
it is in Heaven
Matthew 27
LC 1529

Figure 3. Third petition.

In the *Large* Catechism, Cranach's woodcut (Figure 3) for this petition references Matthew 27 and is an image of Jesus carrying the cross, surrounded by persecutors. This image reflects two things. First, Jesus' crucifixion is central to Luther's idea of the alien and proper work of God, in that believers cannot do God's will unless they have first been broken before the Law and its punishments. Second, the image shows how, by the time of the *Catechisms* of 1529, Luther's understanding of the third petition of the Prayer has become increasingly concerned with the attacks of the devil and persecutors. As he says in the *Large Catechism*, the devil and the world will bring suffering to believers, "For where God's Word is preached, accepted, or believed and bears fruit, there the blessed holy cross will not be far away" (Luther 1959, p. 429).

This shift toward an emphasis on persecution is maintained in later explications of the third petition. In *A Simple Way to Pray* of 1535, for instance, Luther says this third petition shows that no Christian may have peace in this life since God is constantly stripping the will of evil and defending the Gospel from the devil, his minions and ourselves. He says that though the world fights against God's kingdom and children, nevertheless in this petition we take confidence that God's will shall prevail both in the world and in ourselves. He writes that the world tries "with every evil intention to destroy [God's] name, word, kingdom and children. Therefore, dear Lord, God and Father, convert them and defend us" (Luther 1969, 43.196). As with the two previous petitions, his interpretation here shows a growing concern with opposition to his reforms from both Catholics and other Protestants. However, despite these shifting concerns, it is important for students to understand that for each of the first three petitions Luther's primary purpose remains one of pastoral guidance, with the goal of teaching people fundamental theological principles such as the alien and proper work of God, the corruption of the will and the hiddenness of God, in an uncomplicated way.

6. The Fourth Petition—Bread

Developments regarding the fourth petition, "Give us this day our daily bread," (Figure 4) reveal the impact of Luther's work on translating the Bible into German. According to the *Exposition* of 1519, the "bread" of this petition is the Word of God. However, because God is hidden we cannot summon God's Word and so unless God decides to reveal his Word to us, this bread remains hidden also. Nevertheless, God has bound himself by a promise to be present to the faithful in preaching and in the sacraments, and therefore part of the fourth petition is prayer for the clergy so that faithful preaching is available and the sacraments are properly administered. Prayer for the clergy is essential for access to God's Word, and the lack of good clergy and the sacraments are punishments for not praying this petition sincerely. He writes, "the bread, the Word and the food are none other than Jesus Christ our Lord himself . . . Christ our bread is given in a twofold manner. In the first place, outwardly, by persons, for instance, by priests and teachers. And this is done in two different ways: first, through words; second, through the sacrament of the altar" (Luther 1969, 42.56–7).

This connection between the bread of the fourth petition and the Eucharist follows two significant traditions. First, in Christian history the version of the Lord's Prayer found in Matthew has traditionally taken precedence over the one found in Luke, and Luther adopts this same method. Second, in the Vulgate Bible Jerome translated the Greek word *epiousion* of Matthew (6:11) with the Latin *supersubstantialem*, a word meaning the bread 'necessary for existence.' *Supersubstantialem* was a word invented by Jerome and used nowhere else in the Vulgate. For the version in Luke (11:3), Jerome used *quotidianum* or 'daily' bread. Luther in 1519 accepts the patristic tradition found in Jerome and other Fathers and which was common in both the Eastern Church and the medieval Catholic church, namely, understanding 'the bread necessary for existence' in the Lord's Prayer in terms of the Eucharist (Stevenson 2004, pp. 117–50)[7].

When Erasmus published his Greek New Testament with a new Latin translation in 1516, in both Matthew and Luke he used *quotidianum* (Erasmus 1986b, p. 11)[8]. In his *Annotations* which accompanied his New Testament, Erasmus defended Jerome's use of *supersubstantialem* as a valid rendering of the Greek but thought *quotidianum* was better. When Luther translated the Bible into German in 1522 he used Erasmus' edition of the New Testament, and in translating both Matthew and Luke used *täglich*, 'daily.' This then influenced his studies of the Prayer. In 1519 he had understood the bread as the Word of God in the sacrament. By his 1528 *Sermons on the Catechism*, however, he entirely set aside this interpretation of bread in terms of the sacrament and adopted a more material understanding[9].

---

[7] For example, Thomas Aquinas interprets the "bread" as Christ, and in terms of John 6 (Aquinas 1861, 1.71).
[8] In his *Annotations* (Erasmus 1986a, p. 34), Erasmus defends Jerome's use of *supersubstantialem* as a valid rendering of the Greek in support of the idea of God providing us spiritual bread.
[9] Calvin in his 1558 commentary on the Gospels clearly agrees with Luther when he says Christ is here speaking of bodily food, not spiritual, and criticizes Erasmus' defense of *supersubstantialem* (Calvin 1993, 1.321–25).

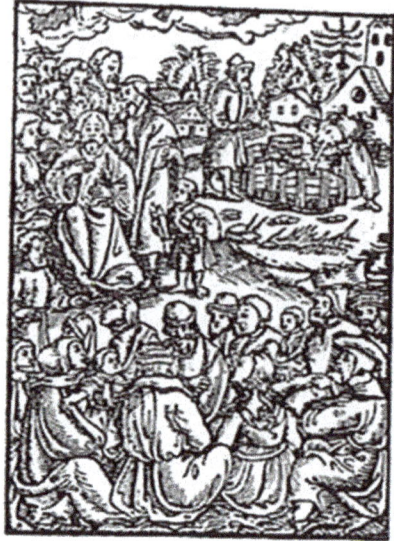

Give Us This Day
Our Daily Bread
John 6
LC 1529

Figure 4. Fourth petition.

The *Large Catechism* woodcut (Figure 4) for the fourth petition refers to John 6 and shows Jesus feeding the multitude. In the image there is a boy with a few loaves and fishes beside Jesus. In the background there are casks of water, or perhaps beer, which is not in the Bible verse, but no doubt familiar to Luther's readers. Noticeably, the picture is not about Jesus and the disciples at the Last Supper in the upper room, which would connect the bread in the petition to the sacrament. Rather it illustrates the more physical interpretation of bread to which Luther adheres from the 1520s on.

In both the *Large* and *Small Catechisms* of 1529 he says that in the fourth petition we are praying for our crops, peace and good government, and acknowledging that bad rulers, war, hunger, a poor economy and other such calamities are all in God's hand. We are here praying for governmental authorities, justice and loyal subjects and against the devil and his followers who constantly try to disrupt society. This material interpretation of bread shows a clear break with the medieval and patristic tradition, as well as his own 1519 *Exposition* on the fourth petition, and dates to his translation of the Bible in 1522. No doubt this interpretation was reinforced by the crop failures of the mid 1520s and the Peasants War of 1525, and is one he retains throughout his later writings. For instance, in *A Simple Way to Pray* of 1535, Luther notes that in this petition we pray that God "grant us thy blessing also in this temporal and physical life. Graciously grant us blessed peace. Protect us against war and disorder" (Luther 1969, 43.196). He says this petition is a prayer for emperors, princes, townsmen and farmers, good harvests and our family.

7. The Fifth Petition—The Problem of the If

Luther's interpretations of the fifth petition, "forgive us our debts as we forgive our debtors," (Figure 5) reveal a struggle to solve a significant theological problem, namely, does God only forgive our sins when we first forgive our neighbor[10]? In his 1519 *Exposition*, Luther states that praying this

---

[10]   In his German Bible and writings, Luther renders Matthew 6:12a as "vergib uns unsere schulde", which in the American edition of his works (Luther 1969) is always "forgive us our debts." In using "debts" Luther follows standard late medieval practice. Regarding the use of "debts" or "trespasses", the most influential English translations are the Tyndale Bible (1525),

fifth petition is a sin of disobedience for those who refuse to forgive their neighbor, are spiritually offended by their neighbor's lifestyle, or consider themselves better than others. He notes that a person's sins will "not be imputed if they denounce their sins, ask for mercy and forgive their debtors" (Luther 1969, 42.70). It is the "if" that caused Luther concern, since if God's forgiveness is based upon our prior action of forgiving our neighbor, then this would appear to be contrary to the principle of justification by faith alone. An early solution to the problem is found in his 1528 *Sermons on the Catechism*, where he states that in asking God to forgive our sins, it is "not that He does not give it [forgiveness] without our prayer . . . But [this petition] is to be done in order that we may acknowledge it. He adds that God, "enjoins it upon you as a sign, that you may be assured that, if you forgive, you too will be forgiven" (Luther 1969, 51.178–9).

Forgive Us Our
Debts as We Forgive
Our Debtors.
Matthew 18
LC 1529

Figure 5. Fifth petition.

As Luther develops his thought on this fifth petition, he finds the answer to the problem lies in the hiddenness of God, meaning that God cannot be known unless he reveals himself and even then he does so in such a way that he appears contrary to what is expected. Just as God is hidden, so too is his forgiveness. In Cranach's woodcut for the *Large Catechism* (Figure 5), the verse reference is to Matthew 18, and the image tells the story of the unmerciful servant. At the top of the woodcut the servant is forgiven by his king of an immense debt and then, at the bottom of the image, that servant refuses to forgive another servant of a minuscule debt. In the parable, the servant is forgiven, but upon refusing to forgive another, is thrown by the king into prison and tortured.

The woodcut depicts the man who hopes for forgiveness while being unforgiving himself, but confronting him is God's command to forgive and the punishment for not forgiving. For Luther, God's Word contains both Law and Gospel. God's forgiveness and mercy (Gospel) are here hidden under the command (Law) that one forgive one's neighbor. We naturally focus on the command, not realizing that God's forgiveness here is hidden. He writes, "Not that [God] does not forgive sin even without and before our prayer; and he gave us the Gospel, in which there is nothing but forgiveness,

the First Book of Common Prayer (1549) and the Rhiems Bible (1582), all of which use "trespasses", and the King James Version (1611) which uses "debts."

before we prayed or even thought of it. But the point here is for us to recognize and accept this forgiveness." (Luther 1959, p. 432). What the fifth petition reveals is that, "if you forgive, you have the comfort and assurance that you are forgiven in heaven." (Luther 1959, p. 433). Thus, for Luther, forgiving our neighbor is not a prerequisite for our own forgiveness, but a sign of the promise that we are forgiven, and in this promise there is assurance. God's Word here enables believers to recognize the hidden forgiveness that is already present.

In *A Simple Way to Pray* of 1535, Luther's primary concern is with the first part of this petition, "Forgive us our debts." He says this asks God, "Do not look upon how good or how wicked we have been but only upon the infinite compassion which thou hast bestowed upon us in Christ." Luther is not as concerned with the second half of the petition, adding, "Anyone who feels unable to forgive, let him ask for grace so that he can forgive; but that belongs in a sermon." (Luther 1969, 43.197).

8. The Seventh Petition—Sickness and Death

It might be expected that in his exposition of the seventh petition, "deliver us from evil," (Figure 6) Luther's interpretations would, over time, follow the same pattern as with previous petitions and focus increasingly on his theological opponents and the threats they posed to the faith. Surprisingly, however, he instead shows a growing concern with sickness and death. In his *Exposition* of 1519, for example, he says that although we often take the seventh petition as a prayer for deliverance from pain and distress, we should instead pray for what is emphasized in the first three petitions, namely, God's honor. He writes, "we should pray for deliverance from evil so that trials and sin may cease and that God's will may be done and his kingdom come, all to the glory and honor of his holy name" (Luther 1969, 42.76).

But Deliver Us From
Evil. Matthew 15
LC 1529

Figure 6. Seventh petition.

In the *Large Catechism*, Luther moves away from emphasizing God's honor in the seventh petition and introduces instead ideas about human sickness and affliction. Luther says that since all evil comes from the devil, we pray in this petition to be protected and delivered from him, since he seeks our life, afflicts our bodies and brings "all the tragic misery and heartache of which there is so incalculably much on the earth." (Luther 1959, p. 435). Once again, Cranach's woodcut (Figure 6) complements this new emphasis, referencing Matthew 15. In the biblical passage and the image, a Canaanite woman begs Jesus to heal her daughter, but Jesus at first refuses to do so, saying that he does not throw the children's food to dogs. She responds that even dogs get the crumbs on the floor, whereupon Jesus praises her faith and heals her daughter. Cranach places a dog in the foreground by the kneeling woman, illustrating Jesus' initial answer and her response. For Luther, just as the woman accepts Jesus' likening her to a dog and uses his own words in her request, so too in the Lord's Prayer we use Jesus' own words to find the medicine for the sickness and misery in the world.

In *A Simple Way to Pray* of 1535, Luther shifts the emphasis away from sickness and towards a new theme, death, and says that though we long for death we ask that God aid us amidst such great evil and grant us a firm faith when we die. He writes that in this petition we pray for God to "help us to pass in safety through so much wickedness and villainy; and, when our last hour comes, in thy mercy grant us a blessed departure from this vale of sorrows so that in the face of death we do not become fearful or despondent but in firm faith commit our souls into thy hands" (Luther 1969, 43.197–8).

9. Concluding Remarks

Luther's writings on the Lord's Prayer are still a good introduction to his main ideas and they provide a window into the historical context in which those ideas developed. He clearly has fresh insights into the Prayer each time he returns to it over a period of two decades. In his earliest writing on the Prayer, he seeks to dispel any notions of our possible goodness, whereas his writings of the 1520s reflect how, as opposition increased from Catholics and other Protestants, he saw the Prayer as teaching and enabling believers to live a godly life while under attack from false teachers. His interpretations in the 1520s also show a growing concern about good government and pressing economic issues. Finally, his writings of the 1530s become more vehement against opponents and more focused on sickness and death. These interpretive changes coincide with such events as his work on translating the Bible into German in 1522, the economic and social problems of the mid 1520s and the failure both of Protestant unity and reconciliation with the Catholics by the 1530s. Nonetheless, even as the historical context changes, the Prayer continues to be a way for Luther to teach significant theological principles to his parishioners, such as the hiddenness of God, the corruption of the will, the alien and proper work of God and justification by faith alone. He intended each of the writings on the Lord's Prayer to make complex theological concepts easily accessible to an audience of laypeople and in the case of the *Large Catechism*, these concepts are illustrated well by Lucas Cranach.

Conflicts of Interest: The author declares no conflict of interest.

References

Aquinas, Thomas. 1861. *Commentum in Matthaeum et Joannem Evangelistas*. Parma: Fiaccadori.

Calvin, John. 1993. *Commentary on a Harmony of the Evangelists*. Translated by William Pringle. Grand Rapids: Baker Books.

Carmignac, Jean. 1969. *Recherches sur le Notre Pere*. Paris: Letouzey.

Dibelius, Otto. 1903. *Das Vaterunser: Umrisse zu einer Geschichte des Gebets in der Alten und Mittleren Kirche*. Topelmann: Giessen.

Erasmus, Desiderius. 1986. *Erasmus' Annotations on the New Testament: The Gospels. Facsimile of the Final Latin Text (1535) with all Earlier Variants (1516, 1519, 1522 and 1527)*. Edited by Anne Reeve. London: Duckworth.

Erasmus, Desiderius. 1986. *Novum Instrumentum, Basel 1516*. Stuttgart: Frommann-holzboog.

Hebart, Friedemann. 1984. The Role of the Lord's Prayer in Luther's Theology of Prayer. *Lutheran Theological Journal* 18: 6–17.

Lehmann, Martin. 1985. *Luther and Prayer*. Milwaukee: Northwestern Publishing House.

Leinhard, Marc. 1992. Luther et Calvin, commentateurs du Notre Pere. *Revue d'Histoire et de Philosophes Religieuses* 72: 73–88.

Luther, Martin. 1883. *D. Martin Luthers Werke: Kritische Gesamtausgabe*. Thuringia: Weimar.

Luther, Martin. 1959. *The Book of Concord*. Translated and edited by Theodore Tappert. Philadelphia: Fortress Press.

Luther, Martin. 1969. *Luther's Works*. Philadelphia: Fortress Press.

McNair, Bruce. 2005. Luther and the Pastoral Theology of the Lord's Prayer. *Logia: A Journal of Lutheran Theology* 14: 41–46.

Moser, Peter. 2005. *Lucas Cranach: His Life, His World and His Art*. Bamberg: Babenberg.

Stevenson, Kenneth. 2004. *The Lord's Prayer: A Text in Tradition*. Minneapolis: Fortress Press.

Wengert, Timothy. 2009. *Martin Luther's Catechisms: Forming the Faith*. Minneapolis: Fortress Press.

Category: Woodcuts by Lucas Cranach (I). *Wikimedia Commons*. Available online: https://commons.wikimedia.org/wiki/Category:Woodcuts_by_Lucas_Cranach_(I) (accessed on 6 April 2017).

Article

Luther, Bach, and the Jews: The Place of Objectionable Texts in the Classroom

Beth McGinnis [1] and Scott McGinnis [2,*]

[1] Division of Music, School of the Arts, Samford University, 800 Lakeshore Dr., Birmingham, AL 35229, USA; ermcginn@samford.edu

[2] Department of Religion, Samford University, 800 Lakeshore Dr., Birmingham, AL 35229, USA

*   Correspondence: tsmcginn@samford.edu; Tel.: +1-205-726-4260

Academic Editors: Peter Iver Kaufman and Christopher Metress
Received: 16 February 2017; Accepted: 26 March 2017; Published: 1 April 2017

Abstract: This article examines the pedagogical challenges and value of using objectionable texts in the classroom by way of two case studies: Martin Luther's writings on Jews and two works by J.S. Bach. The use of morally or otherwise offensive materials in the classroom has the potential to degrade the learning environment or even produce harm if not carefully managed. On the other hand, historically informed instructors can use difficult works to model good scholarly methodology and offer useful contexts for investigating of contemporary issues. Moral judgments about historical actors and events are inevitable, the authors argue, so the instructor's responsibility is to seize the opportunity for constructive dialogue.

Keywords: Martin Luther; Johann Sebastian Bach; anti-Judaism; anti-Semitism; pedagogy

1. Introduction

Although the Castle Church in Wittenberg famously appears in Martin Luther's biography as the site of the (possibly mythical but nevertheless) dramatic posting of the *Ninety-Five Theses*, the "mother church of the Reformation" actually lies a short walk to the east: the *Stadtkirche*, or City Church, dedicated to St. Mary. It was here that Luther as university professor and city preacher regularly proclaimed those early doctrines that would become foundational for the reformation breaking out all over Germany, here where the first mass was celebrated in German rather than Latin, and here where the laity received communion in both kinds. Visitors to the church today marvel not only at Lucas Cranach's magnificent altarpiece painting, but may also be found outside staring up at a stone relief on the southeast corner of the building. There they see a particularly grotesque image that dates to the medieval period: the *Judensau*, or Jewish pig (See Figure 1). In the carving a rabbi lifts the tail of a sow and stares intently as if in deep contemplation while other Jews are depicted as suckling underneath.

The *Judensau* was by no means unique to Wittenberg but could be found all over Germany and beyond.[1] The image not only epitomizes the coarseness and ugliness of medieval anti-Semitism but also continues to provoke controversy among moderns, who debate whether to relegate it to a museum or contextualize it in some way in its place, especially in the light of the many visitors expected in Wittenberg for the 500th anniversary of the Reformation (Harvey n.d.).[2] In a way, this modern debate over the fate of the Wittenberg *Judensau* helps to cast a number of questions that illustrate the

---

[1] See (Shachar 1974).

[2] E.g., see the petition at https://www.change.org/p/remove-the-wittenberg-judensau. A similar debate arose around the fiftieth anniversary of Kristallnacht, after which a sculpture was placed on the ground immediately beneath the *Judensau* to commemorate the Jews murdered during the Holocaust.

pedagogical issue at hand: how should professors handle offensive texts and other artifacts of the past in the context of the classroom? What are the professor's responsibilities in introducing students to offensive materials? To put the question more sharply, what obligations—moral or otherwise—do educators have in investigating and teaching about the past? To consider these questions, in what follows we examine two case studies that illustrate the challenges that arise regularly in the context of our teaching: first, Luther's writings on Jews, and second, two vocal works by Johann Sebastian Bach, the composer working in the Lutheran tradition two centuries later. We argue teachers should embrace the opportunity such controversial works present in order to (1) model historically informed readings and (2) investigate the ethical issues raised by historical study. To do one without the other, however, limits the effectiveness of introducing controversial works in the classroom and carries the potential for harm.

Figure 1. The Wittenberg *Judensau*.

2. Luther and the Jews

Although the Wittenberg *Judensau* predated Luther by two centuries, it nevertheless received favorable mention in his 1543 writing *Von Schem Hamphoras* (*Of the Unknowable Name*):

> Here at Wittenberg, in our parish church, there is a sow carved into the stone under which lie young pigs and Jews who are sucking; behind the sow stands a rabbi who is lifting up the right leg of the sow, raises the behind of the sow, bows down and looks with great effort into the Talmud under the sow, as if he wanted to read and see something most difficult and exceptional; no doubt they gained the Shem Hamphoras from that place (Falk 1992).

Later followers of Luther took inspiration from his writing and placed an inscription over the relief: "Rabini Shem hamphoras," a nonsensical name meant to ridicule the medieval Jewish mystical reference to the unspeakable divine name.

Martin Luther's attitudes toward Jews and Judaism have been the subject of intense scrutiny by historians and others, in terms of both the role those attitudes play in Luther's broader theology and their place in the history of Western anti-Semitism (Kaufmann 2006; Hillerbrand 1990; Oberman 1984; Edwards 1983).[3] This scrutiny predated the Second World War and indeed was underway among Luther's contemporaries and in the period immediately following his death. However, favorable

---

[3] The literature is vast, and it is beyond the scope of this article to provide a comprehensive review. Works particularly useful for those preparing to teach Luther's writings on Jews include: (Kaufmann 2006, pp. 69–104; Hillerbrand 1990; Oberman 1984; Edwards 1983).

mentions by Nazi propagandists and the move by some to draw a direct line from Luther to Hitler and the Holocaust show the truth of Thomas Kaufmann's observation that it "would be naïve or careless to think that a German Protestant church historian could approach the extraordinarily complex topic of 'Martin Luther and the Jews' without considering the fatal historical effects" of Luther's writings. At the same time, Kaufmann finds equally problematic the idea that there is a necessary or inevitable connection between the two (Kaufmann 2006, p. 69).

Complex and problematic: the two terms could also be said to describe the task of instructors assigned to introduce the sixteenth-century reformer to undergraduate students. One of the first questions to arise is that of texts: out of the vast corpus of Luther's writings, which should claim a spot in the limited real estate of course syllabi? Luther's attitudes concerning Jews are frequently summarized by dividing them into two periods, earlier and later, that span the majority of his writing career. The earlier period may be represented by the 1523 treatise *That Jesus Christ Was Born a Jew*. Writing not long after his excommunication by Leo X, Luther used the unbelief of the Jews as a cudgel against the Catholic Church: "If I had been a Jew and had seen such dolts and blockheads govern and teach the Christian faith, I would sooner have become a hog than a Christian" (Luther 1962, p. 200). He goes on to encourage a welcoming attitude toward Jews in order to facilitate their conversion. But two decades hence, Luther had seemingly performed a complete about-face. In the more frequently cited and taught[4] *On the Jews and Their Lies* (1543), he advocated burning Jewish synagogues and homes, confiscating Jewish property, forbidding rabbis to preach, and removing travel protections. The reasons for his change continue to be debated, while the work stands as one of the most explicit anti-Semitic statements of the Reformation era, a period that had no lack of vitriol. How might these two works be put to work in the classroom, and what might be made of their apparent contrast? The historical circumstances and contents of each warrant closer attention.

The occasion of Luther's first major writing about Jews, *That Jesus Christ Was Born a Jew*, was the quashing of rumors being circulated by his enemies, namely that Luther taught that Jesus was the natural son of Joseph and that Mary was not a virgin. From a pedagogical standpoint, it is useful to note that here Luther was not so much speaking *to* Jews as *about* them; his primary audience was a Christian one and the occasion of the writing was a dispute among Christians. As was often the case, Luther turned the tables on his opponents by taking what could have been a purely defensive moment and adapting it to his own purposes. In the first part of the treatise he succinctly refuted the charges against him and argued that Jesus was a descendent of Abraham through his mother Mary, a virgin. He did so to refute his detractors but, more important, he also claimed that his argument "might perhaps win some Jews to the Christian faith." In Luther's estimation, Jews had every reason to reject Christianity: they had been treated as "dogs rather than human beings" and suffered loss of property. Even those who had been baptized had been exposed to a false Christianity that was "mere babble without reliance on Scripture." In sum, Luther understood the experience of Jews up until his day as one of maltreatment and sometimes coerced inclusion in a soulless faith (Luther 1962, p. 200).

After thus indicting his critics, Luther ostensibly switched audiences and attempted in the second part of the treatise to persuade Jews that Jesus is the true messiah. It is worth pausing here with students to note the role of text and subtext, that is, to consider whether Luther was primarily making a positive argument to convert Jews, or simply continuing to use the example of the Jews to berate his Catholic opponents. For Luther the case hinged on the proper interpretation of Scripture. For instance, in Genesis 49 when the patriarch Jacob says "the scepter shall not depart from Judah, nor a teacher from those at his feet, until the Shiloh comes," historical circumstances necessitated, he averred, that this could only be a reference to Jesus; or, in Daniel 9 Luther argued the text can only refer to the destruction of the temple by the Romans, which led to the conclusion that Jesus is the true messiah, and so on.

---

[4] For instance, Samford University's Core Texts Reader, a collection of primary texts used in the freshman core curriculum, includes selections from two works by Luther: *On the Freedom a Christian* (1520) and *On the Jews and Their Lies* (1543).

Here we see Luther the controversialist has given way to Luther the professor of biblical exegesis, although the roles are certainly intermeshed and never truly separable. The assumption that appears to power the argument throughout is that good, historically grounded exegesis should win the day and persuade Jews who have suffered abuse by Catholics. In this spirit, Luther concluded with an uplifting admonition:

> Therefore, I would request and advise that one deal gently with them and instruct them from Scripture; then some of them may come along. Instead of this we are trying only to drive them by force, slandering them, accusing them of having Christian blood if they don't stink, and I know not what other foolishness. So long as we thus treat them like dogs, how can we expect to work any good among them? Again, when we forbid them to labor and do business and have human fellowship with us, thereby forcing them into usury, how is that supposed to do them any good? If we really want to help them we must be guided in our dealings with them not by papal law but by the law of Christian love. We must receive them cordially, and permit them to trade and work with us, that they may have occasion and opportunity to associate with us, hear our Christian teaching, and witness our Christian life. If some of them should prove stiff-necked, what of it? After all we are not all good Christians either (Luther 1962, p. 229).

Several points are worth noting here: (1) Luther rooted his positive stance toward the Jews and the basis of his criticism of Catholics in his evangelical intent; (2) the means of that evangelism should be the proper discernment of the true meaning of Scripture; (3) particularly notable given his later writings, Luther drew a connection between socio-economic oppression, the Christian ethic of love, and Jews' receptiveness to the gospel; and (4) he tempered his optimism and acknowledged many will resist.

For many historians the latter point is the key to finding continuity among Luther's various writings about the Jews despite their apparent contradictory perspectives. Indeed, two decades later, Luther's optimism about the conversion of Jews exposed to the true gospel had evaporated, to be replaced with a thoroughgoing hostility. *On the Jews and Their Lies* (1543) shocked not only his opponents but many of his colleagues as well with the vehemence of its rhetoric and the extent of the recommended strictures to be leveled against Jews. He repeated the well-worn and fantastical medieval charges that Jews poison wells, kidnap children, drink their blood, and desecrate the host. Based on the guilt of the Jews, Christians were "not at fault in slaying them." Rather than decrying the ill treatment of Jews as he had two decades earlier, Luther now understood it as the "terrible wrath of God these people have incurred and still incur without ceasing" (Luther 1971, p. 267). Given that anti-Semitic violence was now thought to have the divine imprimatur, Luther proceeded to instruct the magistrates on a number of punitive measures which may be roughly divided between the religious and the economic. First, the burning of synagogues and schools, as well as seizure of books and other materials, was to be done in the name of suppressing blasphemy. These measures appear to have stemmed from Luther's frustration with the lack of Jewish converts to Lutheran Christianity as well as rumors that Jews were attempting to convert Christians to Judaism. Alongside these religious strictures, a variety of other measures were directed at constricting Jewish economic and social activity and influence. Homes were to be burnt so that Jews would remember "they are not masters in our country, as they boast." Safe conduct was to be abolished, given they had no business in the countryside "since they are not lords, officials, tradesmen, or the like." Additionally, confiscated wealth would be used to reward Jews who did convert, and Jews would be put to work in the fields since it was not fitting they idle away their time by "boasting blasphemously of their lordship over the Christians by means of our sweat" (Luther 1971, pp. 269, 270, 272). Taken together, the economic focus of these recommendations indicate a profound unease with the very presence of Jews in the midst of Christians and resentment at what economic space was allowed to them.

Historians have suggested a variety of reasons for Luther's apparent shift—ill health, negative encounters with Jews, rumors of Jews converting Christians—but if we place the latter work in context the contrast begins to diminish. Luther, believing he was living in the last days, saw the enemies of Christ coalescing around him: the Jews joined papists, Turks, Anabaptists, and others as those who impeded the spread of the gospel and thus exposed themselves to the final, wrathful judgment of God. In Luther's mind, the Jews' evangelical moment seemed to have passed, and he channeled what he believed was the divine disgust, using the most vituperative language he had at hand. Thus, in this context one might conclude that Luther's shift is one of style, not substance (Oberman 1984, pp. 113–17).

While historical contextualization may go a way toward the first goal of introducing students to the world in which Luther wrote, we still must consider the weight of these texts as they come into our own age and classrooms. One useful approach is to locate the anti-Semitism of the early modern era against the larger backdrop of processes by which societies established boundaries and maintained social control through the identification of the "Other," any group that existed on the margins and had little social and economic power to resist societal persecution (Moore 2007).[5] Toward this end, Hans Hillerbrand juxtaposed the Jews alongside Anabaptists, witches, beggars, and prostitutes as a way of considering the fate of the "Other" in the Reformation (Hillerbrand 1998). Hillerbrand argued that what was at work was the ability of society—defined here as "those exercising political power...to control, or intellectual power...to create consciousness"—to prescribe value judgments about difference, and crucially, to make those differences visible (Hillerbrand 1998).[6] If difference per se is not the defining characteristic of the "Other" in society but instead it is when difference is defined as deviance that the "Other" comes into focus, then the question that naturally follows is "toward what end?" In his landmark study *Orientalism*, Edward Said examined the essential role that the construction of the Orient played for the formation of Western identity. The East provided an alternative "self" that in comparison to the West was judged to be inferior (Said 1978). Returning to Luther, we can see how, for example, this meant that Jewish exegesis of the Scriptures could not simply be an alternative reading; it must be wrong, or more precisely, diabolically wrong, for Luther's Christian reading of the Old Testament to be correct. Also, in this context Luther's recommendation of economic restrictions for Jews becomes more closely aligned with his claim of exegetical superiority: Jews were to remember that "they are not masters in our country" (Luther 1971, p. 269), a territory one might define theologically as much as geographically.

It perhaps should not go without saying that using this interpretative lens need not equate to ascribing motive or intent to Luther or any other actor in the sixteenth century. That is to say, it is possible, indeed advisable, first to locate Luther's writings in the context of sixteenth-century debates over biblical and theological interpretation. Luther did not know the "Other"; he knew only the diabolically inspired forces aligned against the gospel, forces to be resisted through the correct reading of the Scriptures (Oberman 1989). Yet the pedagogical task necessarily extends beyond the past into the present in the context of the classroom, where students encounter texts and ideas and understand them through their own interpretative contexts, and crucially, they do so in the presence of other students who may or may not share their contexts. Establishing a productive intersection of these multiple interpretative frameworks is the crucial work of reading texts in the community of the classroom. We will have more to say about this key challenge faced by teachers after we consider a second case study.

3. Bach and the Jews

Two centuries after Luther, in his first year in Leipzig (1724), J. S. Bach composed the *St. John Passion* on a libretto from the Luther Bible's translation of John's gospel. Fast-forwarding to April 1995, a performance of the *St. John Passion* was scheduled for Parents' Weekend at Swarthmore College in

---

[5] For a useful application of this concept in a medieval context, see (Moore 2007).
[6] (Hillerbrand 1998, pp. 247–48). He raises in passing a pedagogically useful question: Does the recognition of difference invariably lead to value judgments?

Philadelphia. Several students who were members of the choir refused to perform because they viewed the work as anti-Semitic. Swarthmore, a Quaker institution, did go through with the performance, and on Palm Sunday, but contextualized it with discussions, program notes, and symbolic empty chairs in the chorus. In the summer of the same year, the Oregon Bach Festival planned a performance of the *St. John Passion* as part of an observance of the fiftieth anniversary of World War II, again eliciting negative reactions. In response, the Festival added discussions, an ecumenical religious service, and Jewish works to the schedule. These incidents set off a national musicological controversy and evolved into a ripe teachable moment for Bach scholar Michael Marissen, who had been a Swarthmore professor since 1989. Shortly afterward, Marissen published the thorough and thoughtful study *Lutheranism, Anti-Judaism, and Bach's St. John Passion,* which interprets the historical context of Bach's passion for today's listeners and performers (Marissen 1998; Marissen 2016; Belfer 2016).[7]

The text Bach used for the *St. John Passion* consists of passages taken directly from Luther's translation of John 18 and 19, along with eighteenth-century poetic commentaries. The compiler of this libretto is unknown. This text specifically identifies the people who taunt Jesus and cry out for his crucifixion not as the "crowd" or "mob" but as the "Jews," and Bach's musical setting is equally as vivid and dramatic as the text. This is the aspect of the passion that has most distressed modern listeners. Jewish composer and conductor Lukas Foss, who escaped to the United States from Nazi Germany in 1937, began substituting the word "Leute," or "people," for "Jüden" in his performances of the passion, and other twentieth-century conductors followed suit (Lydon 2015).[8] In 2000 when the Oregon Bach Festival reprised their performance of the passion and again held discussions about its anti-Semitism, Marissen and other panelists reached the consensus that open dialogue was better than censoring or changing the work. Everyone does not share this opinion, however. A controversial 2012 Berlin cathedral performance of the passion replaced some of the original text with lines from Jewish and Muslim poetry and liturgy translated into German (Da Fonseca-Wollheim 2012).

To understand what sparked the controversies, it is helpful to hear an example. Listen to the Vienna choirboys sing *"Kreuzige, kreuzige!"* at about 58:00 in this 1985 performance of the *St. John Passion* conducted by Nikolaus Harnoncourt (Harnoncourt 2015)[9]

https://www.youtube.com/watch?v=QbVTxRicMGM

This example illustrates the reason musical passion settings exist in the first place: it is one thing to read in John's gospel that the crowd yelled, "Crucify him," but it is quite another to hear the episode in Bach's striking rendition. In Leipzig Bach was considered a musical preacher, and part of his job was to exhort the faithful to greater devotion. Both he and the Lutheran Church understood the power music has to stir the heart, and the central impetus behind Bach's church music was to wield that power toward specific ministerial purposes. For Michael Marissen, these pastoral purposes are the key to understanding the *St. John Passion*. While Bach's music does nothing to soften the negative portrayal of the Jews that is already present in the gospel of John, the passion's greater concern is to convict Bach's Lutheran contemporaries of their sin and draw them to repentance. Marissen also pointed out that compared with the passion settings of other Baroque composers such as Handel and Telemann, Bach's *St. John Passion* is relatively restrained in its depiction of the Jews (Marissen 1998, pp. 29–30, 47).

This is not to say, however, that there is no anti-Judaism in Bach. In another study, Marissen considered Cantata 46, which Bach composed for the tenth Sunday after Trinity, also in his first year in Leipzig (1723) (Marissen 2003; Marissen 2016).[10] The liturgical focus for this particular Sunday was the

---

[7] (Marissen 1998). Recently Marissen also published his collected writings on the religious contexts of Bach's music (Marissen 2016). Simultaneously, his wife Lauren Belfer published a historical novel (Belfer 2016) about the discovery of a (fictive) previously unknown Bach cantata with a violently anti-Jewish text.

[8] For an overview of this controversy with a timeline and reading list, see (Lydon 2015).

[9] Harnoncourt's groundbreaking work in historically informed performance is well known. In addition to his extensive discography, see (Harnoncourt and Pauly 1988; Harnoncourt and Pauly 1997).

[10] (Marissen 2003). Marissen also published a lightly revised version of this article in (Marissen 2016, pp. 63–121).

historical and spiritual "Israel." Sermons and prayers for that day drew a clear connecting line, starting with the destruction of Jerusalem by the Babylonians in the sixth century B.C.E., continuing through the Jews' rejection of Jesus as the Messiah, and ending with the destruction of Jerusalem by the Romans in 70 C.E. The gospel reading was Luke 19:41–48, in which Jesus weeps over Jerusalem and then drives the money-changers out of the Temple. In the vespers service on the tenth Sunday after Trinity, the epistle reading was replaced by the story of the Roman destruction of Jerusalem, as told by first-century historian Josephus. Liturgical music for the day followed suit: a typical motet would be a setting of Psalm 137, "Super flumina Babylonis" (Terry 1926; Marissen 2016).[11]

Bach's Cantata 46 sits squarely within this established liturgical tradition. The opening chorus is a dissonant, minor, chromatic fugue on the text from Lamentations 1:12: "Behold, yet, and see if any sorrow be like my sorrow, which has struck me. For the Lord has made me full of distress on the day of his fierce wrath" (Marissen 2016, p. 97). Two pairs of solo movements follow: a tenor recitative and bass aria, and an alto recitative and aria. The tenor compares Jerusalem's downfall to the Old-Testament destruction of Gomorrah, but claims it would have been better if Jerusalem had been destroyed utterly. Bach used the same melodic interval, a tritone, for "Gomorrah," "Christ's enemy," and the image of God breaking a staff—a symbolic act of final judgment. From Medieval times, the tritone has been considered the harshest interval, and known as the *diabolus en musica*. This prominent interval, along with chromatic harmonies, a disjunct vocal line, and key relationships that are incongruous for Bach's time, creates a harshly accusing tone. The slide trumpet and agitated strings of the bass aria conjure a military scene as the text paints God's wrath against Israel as a storm, long threatened and finally broken forth. The trumpet constitutes an ancient musical shorthand for battle, and this style of string writing, known as *stile concitato*, was in Bach's time a convention for militant effects. The much gentler alto recitative and aria shift the focus from the Jews, on whom God was believed to have passed final judgment, to Bach's Lutheran congregants, who could presumably still repent and receive grace. Listen to the musical contrast in this recording conducted by Helmuth Rilling (Rilling 2011).

> https://www.youtube.com/watch?v=dGSJ1_2imA0

The overarching structure of the cantata, then, employs the fate of Israel as an object lesson to convict Lutheran Christians and turn them to repentance. Both the text and Bach's musical setting serve to elicit a specific spiritual response. To modern ears, however, the harsh portrayal of the Jews and of God's judgment against them is jarring. Acknowledging such anti-Jewish polemic in Bach's vocal music has been difficult for the musicological community to reconcile with his foremost status among composers, and among composers of Christian music to boot. However, the controversy has fruitful teaching applications.

For music students, it can be a case study for examining how music takes on extra-musical significance. Consider the various and complex ways music and text interrelate in Cantata 46. The liturgical context, biblical context, and musical context all carry associations. Leipzig churchgoers would have heard Bach's cantata alongside other liturgical elements connecting God's judgment against the Jews with their rejection of Jesus and with biblical passages expressing God's wrath. They would have heard the trumpet and *stile concitato* strings as militaristic but interweaving recorders as a gentle lament. They would have heard the dissonance of the tritone, which also held symbolic significance at a deeper analytical level for contemporary musicians. Somewhat more abstract is Bach's use of canonic imitation in the opening chorus—a device he frequently employed as a musical pun when setting texts having to do with law, since "canon" literally means "rule" or "law."

Even more arcane, yet still salient, are the cantata's harmonic relationships. Bach scholar Eric Chafe has detailed how Bach and his predecessors and contemporaries used anabasis, or modulation to keys with more sharps, and catabasis, or modulation to keys with more flats, to set texts with

---

[11] Information on the liturgy from (Terry 1926), reproduced in (Marissen 2016, p. 76).

positive and negative themes, respectively (Chafe 1991; Chafe 2000). Marissen has pointed out a "bizarre tonal fracture" and "striking harmonic catabasis" in the opening chorus of Cantata 46, a "harmonic breach" Marissen interpreted as an image of destruction, "aptly reflecting the chorus's biblical lines concerning the Lord's fierce wrath against the city of Jerusalem" (Marissen 2016, p. 97). These key relationships may be inaudible to all but the most musically sophisticated listeners, and the extra-musical associations they carry are made even more complex by the fact that thinking of harmonic modulation as either "upward" or "downward," as Chafe does, is in itself a metaphor (Lakoff and Johnson [1980] 2003; Schulenberg 1995). Nevertheless, harmonic modulation was certainly significant for Bach, the most sophisticated of musicians, composing in conversation with others who spoke a similar musical language.

This is why it makes sense to resist the temptation to view Bach's music as pure music without inherent extra-musical meaning. Such a view is attractive, especially to musicians for whom musical meaning is paramount. However, the concept of music as an entity unto itself developed in music aesthetics only at the beginning of the nineteenth century, and even then only applied to instrumental music (Bonds 1997). While the nineteenth and twentieth centuries saw no shortage of scholars who read even Bach's vocal music from this absolute point of view, the approach is anachronistic and unhistorical (Taruskin 1995; Marissen 2016).[12]

Or, to be more accurate, this approach is rooted in its own historical and cultural context (McGinnis 2006).[13] Early Bach studies grew out of debates over the status of instrumental music. Turn-of-the-nineteenth-century critics such as E. T. A. Hoffmann proposed that instrumental music could, through its sheer form and structure, reflect and even manifest the forms of a neo-Platonic ideal realm, and Bach's nineteenth-century biographer Philipp Spitta extended this claim to Bach's vocal church music (Spitta 1951). Spitta established a chronology of Bach's works using watermark and handwriting evidence, then drew conclusions about Bach's development as a composer based on this chronology. In Spitta's view, Bach became increasingly careful over the course of his career to preserve the integrity of the Lutheran chorale tune, so that his "later" cantatas only surround and adorn the chorales without changing them substantially. For Spitta, this meant Bach's church cantatas adhered increasingly more closely to the chorale tunes and therefore increasingly more closely to the "objective" truth the chorales carried. As such, Bach's late church cantatas reflected a realm of philosophical truth otherwise accessible through strictly instrumental music but not vocal.

Spitta's chronology and the conclusions he drew from it remained unshaken until the mid-1950s, when Alfred Dürr and Georg von Dadelsen proposed a new chronology that combined liturgical information with watermark and handwriting evidence (Herz 1985; Kerman 1985).[14] By then, both music and musicology were playing on the field of mid-century modernism and using the languages of math and science in the service of rational inquiry (McGinnis 2003).[15] The atmosphere was much more skeptical and secular, and biographers less prone to hagiography than in Spitta's time. Dürr's and Dadelsen's (now classic) revised chronology called into question Spitta's teleological interpretation of Bach's career, and consequently his characterization of Bach as devout Lutheran.

Furthermore, as the rise of the historical performance movement in the late twentieth century saw an accompanying uptick in the number of studies focusing on the historical, liturgical, and theological contexts of Bach's music, (Kerman 1985)[16] other scholars countered with the aesthetic point of view that Bach's texts and religious contexts are tangential to a true understanding of his music as great

---

[12] For an uncompromising examination of formalist approaches to Bach, see (Taruskin 1995). Also see (Marissen 2016, pp. 1–5).
[13] For a brief overview of nineteenth- and twentieth-century approaches to connecting Bach's music with the extra-musical, see (McGinnis 2006). Marissen's preface to (Marissen 2016) surveys the state of the field in the past twenty years.
[14] For outlines of major developments in post-World-War-II Bach scholarship, see (Herz 1985; Kerman 1985).
[15] With the phrase "playing on the field," we refer to sociologist Pierre Bourdieu's theories of social and political positioning. For an application of these theories to musical modernism, see (McGinnis 2003).
[16] For an overview see (Kerman 1985).

art (Schulenberg 1995).[17] It is certainly tempting to take this aesthetic approach when confronted with offensive material such as anti-Jewish polemic in Bach's music, to ignore text and context and concentrate rather on the sheer magnificence of the music itself. Could not Bach's music be even more relevant if we interpret it in light of our own worldview, giving him a pass when the values of his society conflict with those of our own?

To do so, however, is to miss the benefit of learning from history, and to miss out on the power art has not only to entertain but to edify. If Bach, who was not only intellectually brilliant but also deeply devout, composed anti-Jewish music, we understand both the composer and his works better if we investigate the circumstances. More important, we hone our own moral sense when we put ourselves in Bach's place: a pastoral musician employing the most effective rhetoric he can to lead his flock to the salvation of their souls. When we face up to history's low points as well as the high ones, we can become better and more ethical as individuals and societies. What blind spots do we ourselves have, we might ask, that might become evident three centuries from now?

4. Conclusions

Earlier we suggested that the educator's task with regard to objectionable material is twofold: (1) provide a proper historical context in which to understand the work and (2) provide space for students to consider and address the ethical questions that arise from the study of such works. Furthermore, we suggested that to do one without the other is to fail. If we merely stand in judgment against the ethical failings of past actors without seeking to understand the context that gave rise to them, we risk missing the lessons of history—seeing the habits of thought, speech, and action that culminate in unethical conduct. That is, we fail to learn from history. At the opposite extreme, to become trapped in the past, as it were, in our consideration of works such as *On the Jews and Their Lies* and Cantata 46 without bringing the question forward risks ignoring how past thought might link to present attitude and action.

As an example of this, consider a distinction that emerges regularly in the secondary historical literature, that is, the distinction drawn between anti-Judaism and anti-Semitism. Different scholars attach various nuances to the terms, some quite strictly, but the former is usually taken to refer to opposition to Jewish theological positions and especially exegetical strategies regarding the Hebrew Bible/Old Testament. In contrast, the latter term denotes opposition to, or worse, hatred of Jews as a people. This hatred plays on vile racial stereotypes and conspiracy theories, frequently justifies violence and persecution, and is understood by many to have its origins in racial theories of the nineteenth century. This distinction, while valid in historical analysis and useful in certain contexts, nevertheless carries risks as well, inasmuch as it may downplay or ignore potential connections between theology and violent action. Put succinctly, religious ideas have social consequences (Geertz 1973; Oberman 1984).[18] In the context of the classroom, a risk teachers face is the inclination of students and perhaps teachers themselves to contain objectionable ideas of Luther, Bach, and others within the bounds of theological discourse or music aesthetics—the world of ideas. Instead, teachers of history can help students make the connections between ideas and actions in the past, identify

---

17 See, for example, (Schulenberg 1995).
18 The claim here is a large one, the full defense of which is beyond the scope of this essay, but it should be noted that it relies upon an essentially social understanding of religion, as well as one that includes both idea and practice. A useful starting point is that of anthropologist Clifford Geertz, who defined religion as "a system of symbols which acts to establish power, pervasive, and long-lasting moods and motivations in men by formulating conceptions of a general order of existence and clothing those conceptions with such an aura of factuality that the moods and motivations seem uniquely realistic." See (Geertz 1973). One should also consider the possibility that religious ideas follow, rather than produce, social practice, an approach implied by Hillerbrand when he observes that "the definition of the Other in the sixteenth century was impossible unless theology served as handmaiden" (Hillerbrand 1998, p. 265). On the utility of the distinction between anti-Judaism and anti-Semitism, see also (Oberman 1984, p. xi).

patterns that recur in history, and make judgments based on their interpretations of the evidence at hand. But should the work end there? Indeed, can it?

In a recent class at our university we explored how music can help construct identities—of self and "Other"—that either reinforce or challenge societal norms. Our topic was the racist portrayals of African Americans in nineteenth-century black minstrel shows, and before confronting these portrayals the class laid down ground rules for discussion. Through these rules or guiding principles the students recognized that racism is not only part of our common history but also a thread running through our present discourse. As we prepared for our class discussion, they predicted that studying this issue in a historical context would help us think more clearly in our own. In the case of the minstrel shows, we found that the shows' portrayal of black slaves served particular functions in nineteenth-century American society: primarily, to reinforce social norms by characterizing slaves as dimwitted, happy-go-lucky, and content with life. This characterization of an "Other" by society's powerful served in part to uphold the institution of slavery, and it met subtle and creative challenges in the slaves' own minstrel shows and in parodic genres such as the cakewalk. These layers of portrayal constituted acts of social positioning in much the same way that Luther positioned himself against Catholicism via his portrayal of the Jews, or Bach set the Jews up as an object lesson for his Lutheran congregants. As our class came to understand each portrayal as either supportive or subversive to the dominant systems of society, we also began to turn the lens to our own society, and to question the function of the identities we construct.

William Faulkner famously wrote "The past is never dead. It's not even past" (Faulkner 1975). There is no better lens for understanding the present than careful reading of the past. When we introduce difficult texts and ideas into the classroom, students inevitably make moral judgments. Recognizing that fact and bringing those judgments into the discourse of the classroom is the hard work of education, not without risk, but rich with potential benefits for all.

Acknowledgments: The authors acknowledge with appreciation the organizers and attendees of the *Teaching the Reformations* conference held at Samford University, October 2016, for their useful queries and comments, as well as those of the anonymous reviewers.

Author Contributions: Each author contributed equally to the writing of this article.

Conflicts of Interest: The authors declare no conflict of interest.

References

Belfer, Lauren. 2016. *And After the Fire*. New York: Harper.

Bonds, Evan. 1997. Idealism and the Aesthetics of Instrumental Music at the Turn of the Nineteenth Century. *Journal of the American Musicological Society* 50: 387–420. [CrossRef]

Chafe, Eric. 1991. *Tonal Allegory in the Vocal Music of J. S. Bach*. Berkeley and Los Angeles: University of California Press.

Chafe, Eric. 2000. *Analyzing Bach Cantatas*. New York: Oxford University Press.

Da Fonseca-Wollheim, Corinna. 2012. Unleashing Musical Passions: Updating Bach, or Defacing Him? *The Times of Israel*, March 23. Available online: http://www.timesofisrael.com/updating-bach-or-defacing-him/ (accessed on 5 October 2016).

Edwards, Mark U., Jr. 1983. *Luther's Last Battles*. Ithaca: Cornell University Press, pp. 115–42, et passim.

Falk, Gerhard. 1992. *The Jew in Christian Theology: Martin Luther's Anti-Jewish Vom Schem Hamphoras, Previously Unpublished in English, and Other Milestones in Church Doctrine Concerning Judaism*. Jefferson: McFarland & Company, pp. 182–83.

Faulkner, William. 1975. *Requiem for a Nun*. New York: Vintage, Act 1, Scene 3.

Geertz, Clifford. 1973. Religion as a Cultural System. In *The Interpretation of Cultures*. New York: Basic Books, p. 90.

Harnoncourt, Nikolaus. 2015. Johannes Passion BWV 245—Harnoncourt. Available online: https://www.youtube.com/watch?v=QbVTxRicMGM (accessed on 1 October 2016).

Harnoncourt, Nikolaus, and Reinhard G. Pauly. 1988. *Baroque Music Today: Music as Speech*. Portland: Amadeus Press.

Harnoncourt, Nikolaus, and Reinhard G. Pauly. 1997. *The Musical Dialogue: Thoughts on Monteverdi, Bach, and Mozart*. Portland: Amadeus Press.

Harvey, Richard. n.d. Entfernen Sie die Wittenberger Judensau! (Main) Remove the Wittenberg Judensau! Available online: https://www.change.org/p/remove-the-wittenberg-judensau (accessed on 1 October 2016).

Herz, Gerhard. 1985. Toward a New Image of Bach. In *Essays on J. S. Bach*. Studies in Musicology No. 73. Ann Arbor: UMI Research Press, pp. 149–84.

Hillerbrand, Hans. 1990. Martin Luther and the Jews. In *Jews and Christians*. Edited by James H. Charlesworth. New York: Crossroad Publishing, pp. 127–50.

Hillerbrand, Hans. 1998. The 'Other' in the Age of the Reformation: Reflections on Social Control and Deviance in the Sixteenth Century. In *Infinite Boundaries: Order, Disorder, and Reorder in Early Modern German Culture*. Edited by Max Reinhart. Kirksville: Truman State University Press.

Kaufmann, Thomas. 2006. Luther and the Jews. In *Jews, Judaism, and the Reformation in Sixteenth-Century Germany*. Edited by Dean Phillip Bell and Stephen G. Burnett. Leiden: Brill.

Kerman, Joseph. 1985. *Contemplating Music: Challenges to Musicology*. Cambridge: Harvard University Press, pp. 49–59.

Lakoff, George, and Mark Johnson. 2003. *Metaphors We Live by*. Chicago: University of Chicago Press. First published 1980.

Luther, Martin. 1962. *Luther's Works*. Edited by Jaroslav Pelikan and Helmut T. Lehmann. Philadelphia: Fortress Press, vol. 45.

Luther, Martin. 1971. *Luther's Works*. Edited by Jaroslav Pelikan and Helmut T. Lehmann. Philadelphia: Fortress Press, vol. 47.

Lydon, Christopher. 2015. J. S. Bach's Bitter-Sweet Passion. *Radio Open Source: Art, Ideas, and Politics with Christopher Lydon*, March 29. Available online: http://radioopensource.org/st-john/ (accessed on 5 October 2016).

Marissen, Michael. 1998. *Lutheranism, Anti-Judaism, and Bach's St. John Passion*. New York: Oxford University Press.

Marissen, Michael. 2003. The Character and Sources of the Anti-Judaism in Bach's Cantata 46. *Harvard Theological Review* 96: 63–99. [CrossRef]

Marissen, Michael. 2016. *Bach & God*. New York: Oxford University Press.

McGinnis, Beth Rowell. 2006. The Wind Blows where It Will: Hymnannies, Passion Chorales, and Sacred Jazz. In *Bound on Earth: A Festschrift for Edmon Lewin Rowell, Jr.* Edited by Marc A. Jolley, Graydon F. Snyder and Don Haymes. Macon: Mercer University Press, pp. 28–31.

McGinnis, Margaret Elizabeth. 2003. Playing the Fields: Messiaen, Music, and the Extramusical. Ph.D. dissertation, University of North Carolina at Chapel Hill, Chapel Hill, NC, USA; pp. 4–11, 79–125.

Moore, Robert I. 2007. *The Formation of a Persecuting Society: Authority and Deviance in Western Europe 950–1250*, 2nd ed. Malden: Blackwell Publishing.

Oberman, Heiko A. 1984. *The Roots of Anti-Semitism in the Age of Renaissance and Reformation*. Philadelphia: Fortress Press.

Oberman, Heiko. 1989. *Luther: Man between God and the Devil*. New Haven: Yale University Press.

Rilling, Helmuth. 2011. JS Bach Cantata BWV 46 Rilling. Available online: https://www.youtube.com/watch?v=dGSJ1_2imA0 (accessed on 1 October 2016).

Said, Edward. 1978. *Orientalism*. New York: Random House.

Schulenberg, David. 1995. 'Musical allegory' Reconsidered: Representation and Imagination in the Baroque. *The Journal of Musicology* 13: 203–39. [CrossRef]

Shachar, Isaiah. 1974. *The "Judensau": A Medieval Anti-Jewish Motif and Its History*. London: The Warburg Institute.

Spitta, Philipp. 1951. *Johann Sebastian Bach: His Work and Influence on the Music of Germany, 1685–1750*. Translated by Clara Bell and J. A. Fuller-Maitland. London: Novello.

Taruskin, Richard. 1995. Facing Up, Finally, to Bach's Dark Vision. In *Text and Act: Essays on Music and Performance*. New York: Oxford University Press, pp. 307–20.

Terry, Charles Sanford. 1926. *Joh. Seb. Bach: Cantata Texts, Sacred and Secular; with a Reconstruction of the Leipzig Liturgy of his Period*. London: Constable.

Article

John Calvin and John Locke on the *Sensus Divinitatis* and Innatism

J. Caleb Clanton

Department of History, Politics, & Philosophy, Lipscomb University, One University Park Drive, Nashville, TN 37204, USA; caleb.clanton@lipscomb.edu; Tel.: +1-615-966-5727

Academic Editor: Christopher Metress
Received: 4 December 2016; Accepted: 13 February 2017; Published: 20 February 2017

Abstract: Inheritors of the Calvinist Reformed tradition have long disagreed about whether knowledge of God's nature and existence can be or need be acquired inferentially by means of the standard arguments of natural theology. Nonetheless, they have traditionally coalesced around the thought that some sense or awareness of God is naturally implanted or innate in human beings. A root of this orientation can be found in John Calvin's discussion of the *sensus divinitatis* in the first book of *The Institutes of the Christian Religion*. This paper outlines a pedagogical strategy for organizing and evaluating Calvin's treatment of the *sensus divinitatis*, chiefly by putting it in tension with John Locke's polemic against innatism in Book I of *An Essay concerning Human Understanding*. I begin by reconstructing Calvin's depiction of the *sensus divinitatis*, as well as his case for thinking that it is innate. I then explain how Locke's critique of innatism offers a fairly direct response to Calvin and, hence, a useful framework for exploring the limits of Calvin's treatment of the *sensus divinitatis*.

Keywords: Calvin; *sensus divinitatis*; natural theology; Locke; innatism; innate ideas

1. Introduction

Suppose there is such a person as God. Should we assume that we could come to know about this God without recourse to something like scriptural revelation or direct revelatory experiences? Would the kinds of philosophical arguments that, say, St. Thomas Aquinas offers be adequate to the task? More generally, would supernaturally unaided human reasoning ever be capable of leading us to knowledge of God's nature and existence?

The unease that many inheritors of the Calvinist Reformed tradition have expressed in attending to these sorts of questions is epitomized in some ways in the bitter punch-up between Karl Barth and Emil Brunner in the 1930s. In light of Brunner's call for his generation of theologians to "find the way back to a true *theologia naturalis*," even the one-word title of the essay Barth wrote in response to Brunner echoes the anxiety that some Reformed thinkers continue to feel: *"Nien!"* ([1], p. 59). And while a continuous thread of Reformed thinkers has endorsed some form of natural theology since as far back as the early sixteenth century ([2], pp. 9–40), Nicholas Wolterstorff has claimed recently that a *revulsion against* theistic arguments has been "characteristic of the Continental Calvinist tradition" ([3], p. 7). Along similar lines, Alvin Plantinga has said that, "for the most part," the Reformed attitude toward proving God's existence "looks a little like the attitude some Christians adopt towards faith healing: it can't be done, but even if it could, it shouldn't be" ([4], p. 49).

Though Reformed thinkers have long disagreed about whether knowledge of God's nature and existence can be or need be acquired inferentially, they have nonetheless traditionally coalesced around the thought that some sense or awareness of God is naturally implanted or innate in human beings—that we have some sort of *cognitio Dei insita*, even if we do not or cannot have *cognitio Dei acquisita* ([2], p. 57; [5], pp. 42–43; [6], pp. 95–104). A root of this orientation can be found in John Calvin's discussion of the *sensus divinitatis* in the opening book of *The Institutes of the Christian Religion*. Because that discussion comprises one the most influential contributions to the development of Protestant theology—and hence to the last five centuries of Western history—it is certainly fitting for college professors to cover it in their general education courses, as well as in other undergraduate theology, philosophy, history, and humanities courses.

The purpose of this paper is to outline a way of organizing and evaluating Calvin's treatment of the naturally implanted awareness of God, chiefly by putting it in tension with John Locke's famous polemic against innatism in Book I of *An Essay concerning Human Understanding*. My intention is not so much to proffer specific techniques of classroom delivery as it is to sketch a way of approaching the ideas to which the texts in question give rise. Suffice it to say that I trust that my approach to reading Calvin and Locke in tandem will have meaningful applications in a variety of undergraduate courses. For example, philosophy professors might find it worthwhile to use Calvin as an alternative way of motivating one of the central debates of the modern period between rationalists and empiricists. Of course, the standard way of discussing Locke's empiricism these days is by positioning Descartes as the rationalist foil. But undergraduates often fail to see what is at stake when the matter is presented in this way; hence they often find much of Locke's *Essay* unmotivated and, frankly, boring. Happily, Calvin's innatism, when read in combination with Locke, can help students—especially religious students—see what hangs in the balance. Or, to take another example, religion professors might use this side-by-side reading of Calvin and Locke as a historically informed way of wrestling with questions related to the proper grounding of religious faith—Do we need to rely on arguments, or is it something else at play? And, more generally, humanities and core texts professors can use this approach as an entry point into some of the great canonical texts of the Reformation and modern period.

The paper proceeds as follows. I begin by reconstructing Calvin's depiction of the *sensus divinitatis* (§2), as well as his case for thinking that it is innate (§3). I then explain how Locke's critique of innatism offers a fairly direct way of engaging with Calvin's ideas and, hence, a helpful way of motivating students' interest in either thinker's views (§4). Of course, this way of setting things up should not be taken to imply that Locke took himself to be responding directly to Calvin. But my contention is that reading Calvin in tension with Locke helps shed light on both thinkers, as it provides a useful framework for undergraduates to explore the limits of Calvin's treatment of the *sensus divinitatis*, as well as the limits of Locke's rejection of innatism (§5). And not only does this approach have the historical pay-off of introducing students to two of the most towering Protestant figures of the Christian intellectual tradition, but it also sets the stage for a philosophical and theological inquiry of ongoing significance. Are we born blank slates, for example, and are all the contents of our minds derived of some sort of prior experience? Can we have knowledge of God's existence, and if so, *by what means*? Can belief in God be properly basic? How should we interpret key passages in Romans 1 and 2? And so on.

Before moving on, let me say what I think is a reasonably manageable reading assignment for undergraduates related to the issues discussed herein. I would recommend that students read chapters 1–6 of Book I of Calvin's *Institutes*, as well as chapters 2 and 4 of Book I of Locke's *Essay*, distributed over two class periods. For greater theological context, one might also find it helpful to assign Romans 1 and 2, as well as the relevant sections in Calvin's and Locke's respective commentaries on Romans ([7], pp. 46–52, 72–75; [8], pp. 280–98).

I turn now to Calvin.

2. Calvin on the Sensus Divinitatis

Chapter 3 of Book I of Calvin's *Institutes* opens with these words: "That there exists in the human minds and indeed by natural instinct, some sense of Deity, we hold to be beyond dispute" ([9], I.iii.1). Now, it is worth stressing to students that there are two distinct claims on offer here. The first is that human minds possess a sense of Deity (or, what one translator renders as an "awareness of divinity" ([10], I.iii.1). The second claim is that we possess this sense or awareness innately. We should pause here to consider each of these assertions separately.

First off, what exactly is this thing that Calvin thinks we possess—suppose we call it the "sensus" for short? To be sure, he depicts it in various ways. On one pass, for example, he characterizes it as a divinely instilled "*idea* of the Godhead, the memory of which he [God] constantly renews and occasionally enlarges" ([9], I.iii.1; emphasis added). On another pass, he describes the sensus as an *awareness* that "that there is a God, and that he is their Maker" ([9], I.iii.1). Along similar lines, he depicts it as a "common *conviction* possessed by the mind" (specifically the "conviction that there is a God"), as a "sense of religion," and as an "*impression* of a Deity" ([9], I.iii.1; emphases added). Still further, he characterizes the sensus as "that uniform *belief* in God" with which we are imbued as though with a "seed" from which the "religious propensity springs" ([9], I.iii.2; emphasis added). He additionally describes the sensus as the "*remembrance* of God" that is "spontaneously suggested" to the human mind "from within, by a natural sense" ([9], I.iv.2; emphasis added).

That the sensus is *innate* to the human mind—and that it is innate precisely because God put it there—is the second claim Calvin regards as indisputable. He writes, for example, that the sensus is "thoroughly fixed...in our very bones" ([9], I.iii.3)—that it is "stamped on the breast of all men," and "inscribed on every heart" ([9], I.iii.1)—and he depicts it as an idea of God that "always exists in every human mind" ([9], I.iii.2). The sensus is, he says, "indelibly engraven on the human heart" and "naturally engendered in all ([9], I.iii.3). And even more to the point at hand, he contends that the sensus is "not a doctrine which is first learned at school, but one as to which every man is, from the womb, his own master" ([9], I.iii.3). In other words, the sensus is not something we acquire by, say, inferring it from something even more basic and naturally knowable to human minds. Rather, the sensus is, as it were, always already nonderivatively in the mind as a "seed of divine knowledge so wondrously deposited" by God *ab initio* ([9], I.v.15).

In connection to that last point, it can be helpful for students to know that a number of scholars contend that Calvin's depiction of an innate sensus resembles, and was plausibly derived of, the Epicurean and Stoic notion of a *prolepsis* (or, preconception) of God, particularly as it appears in Cicero's *De Natura Deorum* ([11], pp. 284–85; [12], p. 96; [13]). What, exactly, is a prolepsis? Edward Adams explains that, for Stoics and Epicureans, a prolepsis was thought to be an innate, commonly possessed "basic notion which arises naturally without mental effort or instruction," the truth of which can be "taken for granted" without the need for argument and which can function as the measure against which other propositions are judged ([11], p. 285). Accordingly, in Adams's view, "For Calvin, the sensus divinitatis is a 'preconception' [=prolepsis] of God in line with the Stoic theory" ([11], p. 285). This plausibly Ciceronian dimension of Calvin's sensus will be significant for reasons that will become apparent below.

For now, though, we might wonder why, in Calvin's view, the sensus would need to be innate in the first place, as opposed to being acquired inferentially. He offers at least three reasons. First, the innateness of the sensus is sufficient "to prevent any man from pretending ignorance" of God's existence and, hence, of one's obligation to worship God ([9], I.iii.1). Obviously enough, if one were non-culpably unaware of God's existence, then one would have a legitimate excuse for not believing in or worshipping God. However, an innate possession of the sensus would indeed foreclose even the possibility of such an excuse, an excuse which we lack according to Romans 1:20. A second and related purpose for which the sensus is innate is so that "all to a man...may be condemned by their own conscience when they neither worship him [God] nor consecrate their lives to his service" ([9], I.iii.1). The thought here is that, if everyone had an innate sense of God, then they would be convicted *as though from within* of their own shortcomings with respect to God. This is presumably a nod to the Apostle Paul's mention in Romans 2:14–15 of an accusatory law written on the human heart.

There is, I think, yet a third reason for the innateness of the sensus in Calvin's view. Despite the fact that he never makes this point explicit in the *Institutes,* it is nonetheless clear from his *Commentary on Romans* that Calvin thinks the innateness of the sensus is also consistent with, if not simply an elaboration of, Paul's words in Romans 1:19. To see the point in high relief, it is helpful to keep in mind that English translations of this passage typically vary between saying that what is knowable about God is either "plain *to* humans" (e.g., NRSV) or "manifest *in* humans" (e.g., KJV). The preposition here—*to* or *in*—appears to be significant for Calvin, since he seems to think that it speaks to the means by which God would be knowable—whether inferentially or non-inferentially, for example—and, hence, whether there would be a need for something like an innate sensus in the first place. He writes, for example:

> Insane then are all they who seek to know of themselves what God is: for the Spirit, the teacher of perfect wisdom, does not in vain invite our attention to what may be known…and by what means this is known, he immediately explains. And he said, *in* them rather than *to* them, for the sake of greater emphasis…he seems here to have intended to indicate *a manifestation, by which they might be so closely pressed, that they could not evade; for every one of us undoubtedly finds it to be engraven on his own heart* ([7], p. 48; emphases added).

The take-away point here is that, as Calvin reads Paul, what is knowable about God is manifest *in* us, as opposed to being shown *to* us. And Calvin apparently takes this to mean that something like the sensus is implanted in humans—engraven on our hearts as the unmerited gift of God—as opposed to being something that is acquired through the efforts of the human endeavor—say, by reasoning about the evidence shown *to* us.

3. Calvin's Argument for the Innateness of the Sensus

Students are right to wonder why we should think that humans possess such a sensus, and—more to the point at hand—why we should think that we possess it *innately*. So the natural question is to ask at this juncture is: What reasons does Calvin marshal in support of those claims?

His reasoning on the matter can be organized into a two-step argument. First, he argues that the sensus is, in fact, *universally* possessed by everyone—a claim for which he offers several supporting considerations and defenses. And, second, he contends that the universality of the sensus implies its innateness. Accordingly, his argument—what we might dub Calvin's *argument from universal possession*—can be rationally reconstructed as follows:

(C1)   Every human possesses [a] an idea of God and [b] some sort of sense/awareness/conviction/belief that there is a God. [=universality thesis]

(C2)   If [a] and [b] are universally possessed, then [a] and [b] are innate. [=implication thesis]

(C3)   Thus, [a] and [b] are innate. [from C1 and C2]

(C4)   Thus, every human possesses [a] and [b] innately. [from C1 and C3]

Calvin's case for premise C1 is not to claim that it is known through reason *a priori*, or even through scriptural revelation ([12], p. 95). Rather, his case appears to be a combination of empirical observation and inductive generalization. He claims, for example, that "*experience* testifies that a seed of religion is divinely *sown in all*" ([9], I.iv.1; emphases added). The thought here, presumably, could be fleshed out as follows: All observed humans exhibit, in some form or fashion, the possession of the sensus in question. Moreover, there are no genuine exceptions to this observation, even among those whom we might most expect to find exceptions—viz., those among "the dullest tribes farthest removed from civilization" and those who "seem to differ least from the lower animals" ([9], I.iii.1). Nor would idol-worship and other superstitious practices count as legitimate counterexamples. In fact, Calvin regards those practices as even further evidence *in support* of the universality thesis, the thought being that they simply represent a perversion of the sensus, and, as one commentator says, "it is impossible to pervert what does not exist" ([12], p. 95). So, in an apparent nod to Cicero ([14], I.xvi), Calvin asserts that "there is no nation so barbarous, no race so brutish, as not to be imbued with the conviction that there is a God" ([9], I.iii.1). Accordingly, the bottom line for Calvin seems to be that, in the absence of counterexamples, we can simply generalize from our everyday observations to premise C1.

Now, we should note that, in addition to the universality thesis, something like the implication thesis would be needed to get from C1 to C3 and C4. Without it, for example, Calvin would have nothing to offset the worry that a uniform sense of God could emerge as, say, a product of human convention or chance or, at any rate, something other than God's design (such that the uniform sense in question would ultimately be unreliable). And, indeed, Calvin appears to assume something like premise C2 as a given. He asserts, for example: "Since, then, there has never been, from the very first, any quarter of the globe, any city, any household even, without religion, *this amounts to a tacit confession, that a sense of Deity is inscribed on every heart*" ([9], I.iii.1; emphasis added). Additionally, he goes on to say toward the close of the same chapter that, in light of the fact that "some idea of God always exists in every human mind.... All men of sound judgment will therefore hold, that a sense of Deity is indelibly engraven on the human heart" ([9], I.iii.2–3). The gist here appears to be that the universal possession of the sensus implies, or is at least best explained by, its innateness; hence, premise C2.

Unfortunately, though, Calvin is less than fully transparent about what he regards as warrant for the implication thesis of premise C2, despite the fact that he assumes it—and needs to assume it—all the same. In light of the context of the passages cited above, one conjecture is that Calvin may have simply borrowed the thought from Cicero. Cicero held, for example, that

> since their [the gods'] existence is pretty universally admitted not only among philosophers but also among those who are not philosophers, let us own that the following fact is also generally allowed, namely, that we possess a 'preconception,' ...or 'previous notion' of the gods ([14], I.xvii).

Apparently, Cicero regarded the universal acceptance of a proposition as some sort of indication that we also possess an innate prolepsis of the concepts that comprise the proposition in question. And if Calvin is as indebted to Cicero's work on these matters as some scholars have suggested, then we have at least a plausible account of what may have inspired Calvin to hold premise C2, even if we are still in the dark as to what is supposed to warrant that assumption.

Leave that particular concern to the side for now. Calvin tries to defend his overall case for the universal possession and innateness of the sensus against two different objections. The first objection is the charge that "religion was devised by the cunning of a few individuals" as a means of manipulating society ([9], I.iii.2). We might think of this as something of a proto-Marxist objection: religion is a kind of manufactured opium for the masses, peddled by a pushy pusher. The critic's thought here would be that, since religion is nothing more than a manipulative fiction, the universality thesis is clearly false (the pushers themselves would obviously be exceptions to premise C1), and the implication thesis is false as well (universality would be achieved through widespread deception, not innateness).

Calvin's concedes that perhaps "designing men" have indeed introduced falsehoods into religion, but he thinks that the efficacy of religious fictions in manipulating the masses actually neutralizes the objection at hand ([9], I.iii.2). Why is this? In short, Calvin thinks that the masses would not be so easily manipulated by religion if something like the sensus were not already operating in the background. Presumably, one cannot use for manipulation what is not present to manipulate, and given that the masses are so easily wrought by religion, Calvin thinks we have even further evidence in support of the universal possession of the sensus. Hence he claims, for example, that the designing men in question "could never have succeeded in this [manipulation] had the minds of men not been previously imbued with that uniform belief in God, from which, as from its seed, religious propensity springs" ([9], I.iii.2).

The second objection Calvin considers is the charge that, contra premise C1, there are those who simply lack an awareness of God ([9], I.iii.2). Opponents of premise C1 will of course point to various nonbelievers throughout history. Still, while Calvin concedes that there are individuals who "deny the being of a God," he contends that even those folks will, from time to time, encounter an awareness of God, whether they want to or not ([9], I.iii.2). "Though the conviction may occasionally seem to vanish for a moment," Calvin writes, "it immediately returns and rushes in with new impetuosity" under certain circumstances ([9], I.iii.2). There are, in other words, no thoroughgoing atheists in the foxholes of life. What evidence does he offer in support of this kind of view? In effect, he tells us to take a look at what happens to the tough when the tough really gets going. He writes: "When at their ease, they [the reprobate] can jest about God, and talk pertly and loquaciously in disparagement of his power; but should despair, from any cause, overtake them, it will stimulate them to seek him, and *dictate ejaculatory prayers*, proving that they were not entirely ignorant of God but had perversely suppressed feelings which ought to have been earlier manifested" ([9], I.iv.4; emphasis added). Apparently, in other words, those ejaculatory prayers, amount to telltale evidence that the folks in question were not, in fact, unaware of God all along.

4. Locke's Polemic against Innatism

Students will naturally wonder about how successful Calvin's argument from universal possession is? Is it plausible to think that humans possess a sense of God *innately*? It is here, I think, where it helps to have undergraduates consider Locke's critique of innatism as a way of critically engaging with Calvin. So I turn now to Locke.

According to Nicholas Jolley, the impetus behind Locke's attack on innatism was not only the desire to correct philosophical error, but also "the desire to expose a threat to the open society" ([15], p. 32). Locke's worry, Jolley claims, was that the doctrine of innatism "serves as an excuse for removing classes of propositions from the sphere of rational scrutiny" and, hence, that innatism "plays into the hands of those of an authoritarian cast of mind" ([15], p. 32). Assuming Jolley is correct, then, we might say that Locke challenged innatism in part because he regarded it as the tool of tyrants, dogmatic moralists, and demagogic pulpiteers. And although Locke rejected all forms of innatism, it is easy enough to imagine that, given just how frequently innatism was invoked vis-à-vis religion in his day, Locke probably had *religious* iterations of innatism in his sights ([16], p. 199[1]).

Now, admittedly, it might at first seem strange—if not simply anachronistic—to turn to Locke when thinking specifically about Calvin, especially in light of the fact that scholars virtually never discuss them in tandem with respect to the sensus, for example[2]. But I think this is nonetheless a sensible thing to do, for at least three reasons. First off, the link between Locke and Calvin on these matters is far less surprising than one might suspect on first glance. While Locke does not make explicit in the *Essay* which advocates of innatism he means to be attacking, scholars typically see him as taking aim at such seventeenth century thinkers as Descartes and the Cambridge Platonists, as well the Anglican Bishop of Worcester, Edward Stillingfleet ([16], pp. 200–2; [18], p. 46; [19], pp. 35–43). The Stillingfleet connection in particular is worth highlighting here. In a work with which Locke was clearly very familiar (viz. Stillingfleet's *Origines Sacrae* [1662]), Stillingfleet pulls explicitly from Cicero's discussion of the prolepsis of God, as well as Cicero's so-called argument from universal consent, in formulating his own case for the existence of God ([19], pp. 37–38). And, as noted above, there are solid reasons for thinking that Calvin was also influenced by Cicero's discussion of the prolepsis of God as well. Thus, to the extent that the residue of Cicero can be found in *both* Stillingfleet *and* Calvin, and given that Locke was almost certainly taking aim at the Stillingfleet's Ciceronian variety of innatism, it is actually not that surprising on final analysis that Locke's polemic against innatism would connect up as neatly in response to Calvin as I believe it does. Second, and more important, even if Calvin's *Institutes* was the furthest thing from Locke's mind when he penned the *Essay*, his polemic against innatism is certainly no less *logically* relevant to an evaluation of Calvin's views on the sensus. Plainly enough, if Locke is right to reject innatism, then Calvin's account of the sensus—together with those elements of his theology that are parasitic on it—is clearly problematized to the extent that it

---

[1] For more on the relevant theological context surrounding Locke's discussion of innatism, see [17].
[2] For the only notable exception that I am aware of, see [12], which I discuss below.

presupposes a refuted brand of innatism. And, third, as I have already indicated, there is certainly pedagogical value to reading Locke and Calvin together, in part because doing so helps put important epistemological and theological issues in plain view—and in a way that introduces undergraduates to two of the most important figures in Western history.

Locke's critique of innatism can be organized into two broad stages[3]. He first offers a series of objections aimed at undercutting the standard case *for* innatism. And, second, he presents a series of reasons for thinking that innatism is not only rationally unsupported, but false. I turn now to representative examples of each stage of his polemic against innatism.

4.1. Undercutting the Case for Innatism.

Locke defines innatism as the view according to which "there are in the understanding certain innate principles; some primary notions, κοιναι εννοιαι [=common notions], characters, as it were, stamped upon the mind of man, which the soul receives in its very first being; and brings into the world with it" ([21], I.ii.1). As he sees it, the typical case *for* innatism goes roughly as follow:

> There is nothing more commonly taken for granted, than that there are certain principles, both speculative and practical...universally agreed upon by all mankind: which therefore, they argue, must needs be constant impressions, which the souls of men receive in their first beings, and which they bring into the world with them, as necessarily and really as they do any of their inherent faculties ([21], I.ii.2).

We can formalize this argument—what we can call the *argument from universal agreement for innatism*—in the following way:

(U1) There are certain principles, $P_1...P_n$, universally agreed to by all mankind. [=universality thesis]

(U2) If P is the focus of universal agreement, then P is innate. [=implication thesis]

(U3) Thus, $P_1...P_n$ are innate. [from U1 and U2]

The similarities between the argument Locke recites here and Calvin's argument from universal possession are easy enough for students to spot. Both are comprised of an empirical claim about universality, together with a claim about what that universality supposedly implies. We could nitpick a bit more, to be sure: for Calvin, the relevant universality is the *possession* of an idea/awareness/conviction/belief, whereas for Locke the relevant universality pertains to *assent* to a proposition. Additionally, the arguments differ with respect to the scope of the implication thesis: while Calvin's is focused restrictedly on the universality (and hence innateness) of the sensus in particular, the argument Locke recites captures a more generalized case for innatism. At any rate, given the structural parallels between the two arguments, strikes against U1–U3 will on most occasions double as strikes against C1–C4.

Locke rejects both premises of the argument from universal agreement. Starting with premise U2, he reasons as follows: Even if one were to grant that there are propositions to which everyone assents (like, say, the principle of non-contradiction or the proposition "there is a God"), that universal agreement alone would not be enough to entail the innateness of the propositions in question, precisely because we would have other (and, Locke thinks, *tidier*) explanations for such universality. For example, those propositions could have been taught to children by their earliest caretakers or, more generally, by the customs of society, which Locke depicts as "a greater power than nature, seldom failing to make them worship for divine what she hath inured them to bow their minds [to]" ([21], I.iii.25). Alternatively, the universal agreement in question could stem from the fact that the truth-value of the proposition in question is simply self-evident in the sense that the mind is able to

---

[3] In general, my approach to Locke's response to innatism follows [19]. My discussion is also informed by [20].

directly perceive the agreement (or, disagreement) between the constituent ideas without the aid of any intermediate ideas—and not in the least because the principle is innate ([21], IV.ii.1; [19], p. 46). Accordingly, insofar as universal agreement would be explainable by appeal to things other than innateness, premise U2 is certainly problematic, in which case the argument from universal consent is, at least as worded above, unsound.

Locke also rejects premise U1: "there are none [principles] to which all mankind give an universal assent" ([21], I.ii.4). His reasoning is that if *any* principle has a shot at soliciting universal assent, it would have to be something as elementary as, say, the principle of identity (viz., "whatsoever is, is") or the principle of non-contradiction. But, alas, children and idiots do not even *perceive* those principles in their minds ([21], I.ii.5). And, in Locke's view, if children and idiots do not perceive those principles in their minds, then they surely cannot *understand* them or, in turn, *assent* to them. Accordingly, even the most plausible candidates for universal agreement fail to garner universal assent.

Such a critique of the argument from universal agreement might strike undergraduates as utterly fatal, were we to ignore Locke's contentious assumption that an idea or proposition could not possibly be imprinted *in* a mind if it is not (or, at least, *was* not) consciously perceived *by* that mind (at some point). But of course the savvier proponent of innatism will inevitably want to punch back here: the point is not that every human mind (occurrently) perceives actual ideas and principles *ab initio*, but rather that every human mind has an innate potential or capacity or disposition to perceive (and, hence, assent to) those ideas and propositions under this or that condition. Accordingly, once we trade in *occurrent* innatism for its more sophisticated *dispositional* cousin—and once we properly qualify the universality and implication theses to specify the relevant conditions under which these ideas and principles would indeed be perceived and agreed to by the mind—the argument from universal agreement can stand firm against Locke's attack on premise U1. Or so Locke's savvy innatist opponent might argue.

Now, it is worth noting that many of Calvin's interpreters read him as endorsing precisely this sort of *dispositional* variety of innatism, as opposed to an occurrent variety, which is a point to which I return below. For now, though, consider how a dispositional account of innatism might run. As William Uzgalis observes, the dispositional innatist could insist that

> innate propositions are capable of being perceived under certain circumstances. Until these circumstances come about the propositions remain unperceived in the mind. With the advent of these conditions, the propositions are then perceived ([22], sect. 2.1).

To his credit, Locke considers a range of the disposition-actualization conditions to which his dispositional innatist opponent might turn. Dispositional innatists might claim, for example, that the mind perceives, and hence assents to, the relevant principles . . .

[a] . . . "as soon as men come to the use of reason" ([21], I.ii.7); or
[b] . . . when the use of reason "assists them in the discovery of the ideas and principles" ([21], I.ii.7); or
[c] . . . as soon as the proposition is proposed and all the terms involved are understood ([21], I.ii.17).

As Locke sees it, though, none of those qualifications to the universality thesis and the implication thesis will work to vindicate innatism. For example, with respect to condition-[a], Locke claims that it is simply "false and frivolous" to say that everyone assents to certain propositions (e.g., the principle of non-contradiction) *at the very moment* of being endowed with reason ([21], I.ii.12). Observation simply begs to differ.

Suppose, then, we try to qualify the universality thesis and the implication thesis with condition-[b]. Locke's response: if a proposition were to count as innate insofar as it is discovered by reason, then *every* proposition that is discoverable by reason—including complicated mathematical theorems, for example—would get to count as innate, which Locke thinks is simply ludicrous (though, of course, *dispositional* innatists might very well want to disagree on this point!).

Or, lastly, suppose we say, with proponents of condition-[c], that an idea is innate just as long as it is assented to upon being heard and properly understood. Locke contends that this particular criterion of innateness gives rise to counterexamples. Samuel Rickless explains one such counterexample as follows:

> ...it is plain that the proposition that yellow is not red is assented to as soon as it is proposed and its constituent terms are understood. Hence, [according to the criterion in question], this proposition is innate. Yet the ideas of yellow and red are acquired through sense perception, and so are not innate ([19], p. 51).

The problem here, of course, is that the innateness criterion in question seems to give rise to an unacceptable absurdity: given this innateness criterion, the proposition in question ("yellow is not red") would be at once innate and not innate. So, for Locke, condition-[c] is out.

Ultimately, then, Locke finds both premises of the argument from universal agreement problematic. And if Locke is right to reject the argument from universal agreement as unsound, the proponent of innatism—as well as the proponent of Calvin's sensus—lacks a clear case in support of her views. Admittedly, even if one cannot articulate the putative case *for* innatism, that alone would not entail that innatism—or Calvin's account of the innate sensus—is false, just rationally unsupported. But Locke is not done yet; enter his rebutting case against innatism.

4.2. Rebutting Innatism

In addition to critiquing the standard case *for* innatism, Locke offers several reasons to think that innatism is simply false[4]. For starters, Locke thinks that the simple fact that there are no propositions that actually enjoy universal assent not only does the work of undercutting the argument from universal consent, but it also effectively doubles as a falsification of innatism. This is because, as he says, "I agree with these defenders of innate principles, that *if they are innate, they must needs have universal assent*" ([21], I.ii.24). And since there are no principles to which all agree, by modus tollens, there are no innate ones, either.

Of course, we should bear in mind that this sort of rebuttal loses its teeth if we substitute a dispositional analysis of innatism for an occurrent version of it. But suppose we leave that issue to the side for the moment, though. Locke offers a separate rebutting defeater to innatism. With respect to *practical* principles (e.g., "it is wrong to murder"), there are several reasons for thinking that they are not innate, according to Locke. First, if they were truly stamped on the human heart innately, those principles would have to be self-evident; and they certainly are *not* self-evident—all practical principles stand in need of argument, he says. Second, if practical principles were actually innate, then there would be no way humans could so easily transgress them with such "confidence and serenity" ([21], I.iii.9). But, sadly, "Robberies, murders, rapes, are the sports of men," Locke says, which is the opposite of what we would expect if moral principles were stamped on the human heart at birth ([21], I.iii.9). Additionally, he argues that, if there were truly innate practical principles on the human mind, we should expect that someone would have already catalogued what those principles are supposed to be ([21], I.iii.14). But, unfortunately, no such catalogue exists.

Locke's ultimate swipe at innatism can be reconstructed in terms of the following argument:

(L1) If the ideas that make up putatively innate principles are themselves not innate, then the principles in question could not be innate.

(L2) The ideas that make up putatively innate principles (including the idea of God) are not innate.

---

4 For an excellent and extensive survey of Locke's rebutting arguments against innatism, see ([19], pp. 52–59). My discussion takes several cues from [19], but for the sake of brevity, I focus solely on those considerations that I think are most relevant to the matter at hand.

(L3)   Thus, the principles in question (including those involving the idea of God) could not be innate. [from L1 and L2]

Locke focuses his energy on defending premise L2. His approach is to identify those speculative and practical principles that are most frequently cited as being innate and then demonstrate how the ideas that constitute those principles are, in fact, *not* innate.

It is at this juncture where students can extract from Locke what may be most relevant as a possible rebutting defeater to Calvin's account of the sensus. Locke concedes that "if any idea can be imagined innate, the idea of God may, of all others, for many reasons be thought so" ([21], I.iv.8). But, unlike Calvin, he thinks there are multiple reasons for thinking that the idea of God in particular is simply not innate.

First, Locke contends that, in observing newborns, we simply gather no evidence that they have any ideas (including the idea of God) that would make up the putatively universally assented to principles (including the proposition 'there is a God') ([21], I.iv.2). He writes, for example:

> How late is it before any such notion [of God] is discoverable in children? And when we find it there, how much more does it resemble the opinion and notion of the teacher, than represent the true God ([21], I.iv.13).

Second, if the idea of God were innate, it would have to be an idea everyone possessed. But, *pace* Calvin's appeal to Ciceronian anthropology, Locke thinks there is plenty of evidence that the idea of God is not—and never has been—*universally* possessed. He notes atheists from antiquity and cites a litany of navigational reports in his own day of whole nations—both civilized and "uncultivated"—that "want the idea and knowledge of God altogether" ([21], I.iv.8). Note that we again see on display Locke's assumption that a mind does not possess an idea of something if it does not occurently perceive the idea in question. Again, though, leave that problem to the side for now.

Third, even among those who have some idea of God, there is little to no consistency in their conception of it, except in name only ([21], I.iv.14–15). What is more, even if the idea of God were universally possessed and consistently conceived, it does not follow from that alone that the idea is innate any more than it would that the idea of fire is innate: the idea of God, like the idea of fire, could be easily acquired *a posteriori*, spread far and wide, and passed down through the generations ([21], I.iv.9–11).

Fourth, for Locke, the innateness of the idea of God is simply unnecessary for God's goodness in light of what he regards, for example, as perfectly successful inferential approaches for doing natural theology. He says, for example:

> Nor do I see how it derogates more from the goodness of God, that he has given us minds unfurnished with these ideas of himself, than that he hath sent us into the world with bodies unclothed, and that there is no art or skill born with us: for, being fitted with faculties to attain these, it is want of industry and consideration in us, and not of bounty in him, if we have them not. It is as certain that there is a God, as that the opposite angles, made by the intersection of two straight lines, are equal ([21], I.iv.16).

And, lastly, Locke contends that if God were to have implanted some idea of God in the human mind, then "it is most reasonable to expect it should have been some clear and uniform idea of himself" ([21], I.iv.17). What we see instead are unclear and non-uniform (or, simply unperceived or nonpossessed) ideas of God, which Locke thinks amounts to evidence against the idea's innateness.

The bottom line here is that, given the many reasons in support of premise L2, and in combination with premise L1, it appears that we have a *positive* case for thinking innatism is not only rationally unwarranted, but false.

5. Is Locke's Case against Calvin Decisive?

Students will inevitably wonder where this side-by-side reading of Calvin and Locke takes us. What damage, if any, does Locke do to Calvin? Has Locke undermined Calvin's argument from universal awareness, for example? And, beyond that, has Locke given us reasons for rejecting the thought humans have an innate sensus?

How we answer those questions will inevitably depend, at least in part, on whether we read Calvin as an *occurrent* innatist or a *dispositional* innatist. For example, if Calvin means to be saying that the sensus is occurrently innate, then by nearly any measure Locke's critique of innatism has indeed laid waste to Calvin's sensus.

That said, as noted above, many of Calvin's interpreters read him as endorsing a dispositional variety of innatism. Michael Sudduth notes, for example, that

> Reformed theologians have typically denied that this knowledge [of God] is conscious or occurrent knowledge impressed on the mind from the time of birth. It is best construed as an innate disposition, present from birth, to form a belief in God in a spontaneous manner upon mental maturation and experience of the world ([2], p. 57).

Plantinga, to take one very notable example of this Reformed approach, reads Calvin as asserting merely that "God has implanted in us all an innate tendency, or nisus, or disposition to believe in him," which Plantinga further depicts as a "strong propensity or inclination towards belief" that gets "triggered or actuated by widely realized conditions" ([4], pp. 51–52). Even more recently, Plantinga has interpreted Calvin as saying that, from birth, we have the *capacity* for knowledge of God—not *actual* knowledge ([23], p. 173). Along similar lines, Paul Helm construes Calvin's sensus as a "human *faculty* or disposition to interpret certain data in certain ways," in combination with "what the *sensus* [qua faculty] senses" ([12], p. 91)

What difference does this sort of interpretative difference make? Helm goes as far to say that Calvin's treatment of the sensus (when understood as a faculty or disposition) is ultimately able to withstand, and even *embrace*, Locke's attack on innatism. Helm writes, for example:

> [I]t is not accurate to say that Calvin's account of the [sensus divinitatis] is of an innate idea of God. He is not committed to the position that all men and women are born with a fully-formed concept of God. *Had he known of John Locke's critique of innate ideas, including the innate idea of God, Calvin could or would have concurred* ([12], p. 94; emphasis added).

Presumably, the thought here is that, to the extent that Calvin was talking only about innate *dispositions* or *inclinations*—as opposed to innate occurrent *ideas* or *knowledge*—nothing in Locke's polemic against innatism deals a deathblow against the innateness of the sensus. For example, if Helm is right, Locke presents us with no decisive reason for rejecting premise U1 as false—nor has he succeeded in rebutting innatism. Or so one might say.

But there are at least two general points worth considering in response to Helm on this matter. The first is this: *even if* we interpret Calvin as a dispositional innatist, it is not as though Locke's critique of innatism somehow leaves Calvin's account utterly untouched. Suppose we grant, for instance, that Calvin claims only that the sensus is a universally possessed innate *disposition* to form beliefs about God in such-and-such conditions. But even if Calvin's brand of innatism is strictly dispositional in nature, Locke has still, at a minimum, shifted the burden of proof back on the proponent of Calvin's argument from universal possession. A full defense of that argument against Locke's critique would require its proponents to: [a] offer an account of the specific conditions under which the sensus is actuated such that its output can be perceived by the mind; [b] offer a reason for thinking that such a disposition is universally possessed in the first place; [c] offer a reason for thinking that the universality of such a disposition is best explained by innateness; and [d] explain why the innateness of this disposition is needed as an alternative to inferential approaches to natural theology. Admittedly, another option available to proponents of Calvin's sensus would be to present a completely different case for the innateness of the disposition in question than the argument from universal possession. But that would push us well beyond Calvin, so it seems.

In any case, the burden of proof would not end there. In addition to needing a positive case *for* the innateness of the sensus (*qua* disposition), proponents of Calvin's sensus would need to defend against the rebutting considerations Locke offers. And as Rickless rightly observes, dispositional innatism might be resilient to some aspects of Locke's rebuttal, but it is not somehow immune to them *all* ([19], p. 64)—e.g., Locke's point that the innateness of the idea of God is unnecessary for God's goodness in view of successful inferential approaches to natural theology or Locke's worry that, if the idea of God were innate, it should be an idea that is *clear to every mind*. So even if we insist on viewing Calvin's innatism through dispositional lenses, so to speak, more work would be needed to defend that account against the sort of worries Locke raises. To be sure, developing and defending such a dispositional innatism may very well pay dividends in the long run for religious epistemology, for instance: perhaps dispositional innatism is the right way to think about the grounding of religious faith, especially in light of some of the hurdles facing the standard arguments of natural theology. So, at the least, one of the possible benefits of dispositional innatism is that it potentially leaves more arrows in the quiver of religious apologetics.

That said, still another difficulty remains for Calvin's interpreters, and this brings me to the second general point in response to Helm: it is far from obvious that *Calvin* actually endorses a dispositional variety of innatism in the first place such that his account of the sensus can simply skirt (much of) Locke's critique of (occurrent) innatism. Readers can surely be forgiven if they find it strange that Calvin's sensus is described by some of his interpreters in terms of an innate capacity or a faculty or a disposition, especially when Calvin himself seems to depicts it fairly straightforwardly as an *idea*, an *awareness*, a *conviction*, a *belief*. Are each of those terms somehow analyzable as dispositions or capacities or inclinations? Perhaps so, but *that* is far from obvious.

Part of the problem here may be that Calvin was himself simply unclear on the matter. Wolterstorff admits, for example, that Calvin "was not entirely consistent in his view as to the structure of that indigenous seed of religion: sometimes he thought of it as the innate belief in the existence of a creating and obligating God; rather more often he thought of it as the innate disposition" ([24], p. 165). And even Plantinga, who reads Calvin as a dispositional innatist, acknowledges in a footnote to his discussion of the sensus that "Calvin interpretation is not my project here" and, further, that he concedes that it can sometimes "sound as if Calvin thinks *knowledge* of God is innate, such that one has it from birth" ([23], p. 172, n 7; [23], p. 173). All the same, Plantinga surmises, "My guess is Calvin thinks…what one has from one's mother's womb is not this knowledge of God; but a *capacity* for it. Whatever Calvin thinks, however, it's *our* model" ([23], p. 173; emphasis added).

Other interpreters are neither as quick nor as confident in attributing—or imparting—a dispositional variety of innatism to Calvin. Commenting on Plantinga's interpretation of Calvin in particular, Sudduth writes: "I would argue in response to this increasingly prevalent interpretation of Calvin that, despite its philosophical plausibility, it is—*as an interpretation of Calvin*—somewhat misleading" ([25], pp. 59–60; emphasis added). Sudduth points out, for example, that

> Calvin is quite emphatic about the 'sense of divinity…engraved upon men's minds' as constituting knowledge of God. The sensus divinitatis is *not* a mere disposition or belief-forming mechanism that is innate, *but the knowledge itself is innate* ([25], p. 60; emphases added).

Similarly, Adams argues that the sensus for Calvin "is not simply a gut-feeling, intuition or vague impression, but a cognition, an intellectual consciousness of God the creator" ([11], p. 284).

At a minimum, then, it is fair to say that serious debate remains as to how we should interpret Calvin on the matter: despite whether construing the sensus as an innate disposition is a charitable interpretation *of the sensus*, it is not obvious whether this amounts to an interpretation *of Calvin* that is allowable by the text. That means there is much to discuss regarding whether Locke's polemic against innatism, in the end, poses a fatal threat to *Calvin's* treatment of the sensus. And in view of those disputes, several significant philosophical and theological questions remain. Are we born blank slates—and blank in what respect? Could knowledge of God's existence be the natural output of a properly functioning human mind when confronted with the conditions that activate an innate disposition to believe? Or is knowledge of God's existence acquired only by means of an inference from more basic beliefs? What is the nature of that inference, and what are we to say if no such inference seems convincing in light of the objections?

It remains, as it always does, for students to wrestle with these issues for themselves. My hope is that the foregoing helps to move that inquiry along in fruitful ways.

Acknowledgments: For helpful comments on a previous draft of this paper, the author thanks the attendees of his paper session at the "Teaching the Christian Intellectual Tradition" Conference on the Reformations (Samford University, Birmingham, AL, USA, 6–8 October 2016).

Conflicts of Interest: The author declares no conflict of interest.

References

1. Emil Brunner, and Karl Barth. *Natural Theology: Comprising "Nature and Grace" by Professor Dr. Emil Brunner and the Reply "No!" by Dr. Karl Barth.* Eugene: Wipf and Stock, 2002.
2. Michael Sudduth. *The Reformed Objection to Natural Theology.* Burlington: Ashgate, 2009.
3. Nicholas Wolterstoff. "Introduction." In *Faith and Rationality: Reason and Belief in God.* Edited by Alvin Plantinga and Nicholas Wolterstorff. Notre Dame: University of Notre Dame Press, 1983.
4. Alvin Plantinga. "The Reformed Objection to Natural Theology." *Proceedings of the American Catholic Philosophical Association* 15 (1980): 49–63. [CrossRef]
5. Michael Sudduth. "Revisiting the 'Reformed Objection' to Natural Theology." *European Journal for Philosophy of Religion* 2 (2009): 37–62.
6. Thomas A. Woolford. "Natural Theology and Natural Philosophy in the Late Renaissance." Ph.D. Thesis, Trinity College, University of Cambridge, Cambridgeshire, UK, November 2011.
7. John Calvin. *Commentaries on the Epistle of Paul the Apostle to the Romans.* Edited and translated by John Owen. Grand Rapids: Christian Classics Ethereal Library, n.d. Available online: http://www.ccel.org/ccel/calvin/calcom38.pdf (accessed on 16 September 2016).
8. John Locke. "A Paraphrase and Notes on the Epistle of St. Paul to the Romans." In *The Works of John Locke in Nine Volumes*, 12th ed. London: Rivington, 1824, vol. 7, Sects. II and III; Available online: http://oll.libertyfund.org/titles/locke-the-works-vol-7-essays-and-notes-on-st-pauls-epistles (accessed on 16 September 2016).
9. John Calvin. *The Institutes of the Christian Religion.* Translated by Henry Beveridge. Grand Rapids: Christian Classics Ethereal Library, n.d. Available online: http://www.ccel.org/ccel/calvin/institutes/ (accessed on 16 September 2016). All references to this text above cite book, chapter, and section numbers.
10. John Calvin. *The Institutes of the Christian Religion.* Edited by John T. McNeil. Translated and indexed by Ford Lewis Battles. Philadelphia: The Westminster Press, 1960. All references to this text above cite book, chapter, and section numbers.
11. Edward Adams. "Calvin's View of Natural Knowledge of God." *International Journal of Systematic Theology* 3 (2001): 280–92. [CrossRef]
12. Paul Helm. "John Calvin, the Sensus Divinitatis, and the Noetic Effects of Sin." *International Journal for Philosophy of Religion* 43 (1998): 87–107. [CrossRef]
13. Egil Grilis. "Calvin's Use of Cicero in the Institutes I:1-5: A Case Study in Theological Method." *Archiv fur Reformationsgeschichte* 62 (1971): 5–37. [CrossRef]
14. Marcus Tullius Cicero. *De Natura Deorum (On the Nature of the Gods).* Translated by Francis Brooks. London: Methuen, 1896. Available online: http:oll.libertyfund.org/titles/539 (accessed on 16 September 2016).
15. Nicholas Jolley. *Locke: His Philosophical Thought.* New York: Oxford University Press, 1999.
16. Richard Ashcraft. "Faith and Knowledge in Locke's Philosophy." In *John Locke: Problems and Perspective.* Edited by John W. Yolton. New York: Cambridge University Press, 1969, pp. 194–223.
17. Victor Nuovo. "Locke's Christology as a Key to Understanding his Philosophy." In *The Philosophy of John Locke: New Perspectives.* Edited by Peter R. Antsey. New York: Routledge, 2003, pp. 129–53, (esp. at p. 141).
18. John W. Yolton. *Locke: An Introduction.* New York: Basil Blackwell, 1985.
19. Samuel Rickless. "Locke's Polemic against Nativism." In *The Cambridge Companion to Locke's "Essay Concerning Human Understanding."* Edited by Lex Newman. New York: Cambridge University Press. pp. 33–66.

20. Jeffrey Tlumak. *Classical Modern Philosophy: A Contemporary Introduction*. New York: Routledge, 2007.
21. John Locke. "An Essay concerning Human Understanding, Part 1." In *The Works of John Locke, in Nine Volumes*, 12th ed. London: Rivington, 1824, vol. 1. Available online: http://oll.libertyfund.org/titles/761 (accessed 16 September 2016). All references to this text above cite book, chapter, and section numbers.
22. William Uzgalis. "John Locke." In *The Stanford Encyclopedia of Philosophy*, 2016. Available online: http://plato.stanford.edu/archives/spr2016/entries/locke/ (accessed on 6 June 2016).
23. Alvin Plantinga. *Warranted Christian Belief*. New York: Oxford University Press, 2000.
24. Nicholas Wolterstorff. "The Reformed Tradition." In *A Companion to Philosophy of Religion*. Edited by Philip L. Quinn and Charles Taliaferro. Malden: Blackwell, 1999, pp. 165–70.
25. Michael L. Czapkay Sudduth. "The Prospects for 'Mediate' Natural Theology in John Calvin." *Religious Studies* 31 (1995): 43–68. [CrossRef]

Article

Teaching Music in the Reformed/Calvinist Tradition: Sphere Sovereignty and the Arts

John MacInnis

Music Department, Dordt College, 498 4th Ave NE, Sioux Center, IA 51250, USA; john.macinnis@dordt.edu; Tel.: +1-712-722-6202

Academic Editor: Christopher Metress
Received: 8 February 2017; Accepted: 28 March 2017; Published: 31 March 2017

Abstract: This article shares objectives, teaching methods, and sources of inspiration as I lead 21st-century students in engaging a Reformed/Calvinistic vision for the arts generally, and music specifically. Special explanation is made of Calvinistic concepts such as sphere sovereignty and *sensus divinitatis*. To conclude, I discuss aspects of a recent composition titled *The God of Material Things* by Jonathan Posthuma, a graduate of our college music program, whose work exemplifies many of the elements that my colleagues and I hope distinguish the accomplishments of music students beyond their education at Dordt College.

Keywords: music; Calvinism; sphere sovereignty, reformed theology, *Sensus Divinitatis*; arts education

1. Introduction

In 1898, Abraham Kuyper delivered a series of lectures at Princeton Seminary with the aim of articulating a Calvinist vision for all of life, not just theology. Kuyper addressed topics such as politics and science, and he dedicated a lecture to describing a Calvinist vision for the arts. As a music professor who also teaches in the core curriculum at a confessional Calvinist college, I often use Kuyper's lecture on the arts, among other things, to engage my students as they wrestle with the Calvinist tradition in relation to music. My goal is not indoctrination; rather, we engage Kuyper's ideas as an opportunity for students to form their own opinions and to develop insight for living productively and faithfully as musicians and people invested in musical culture, wherever God may call them. This article explains a number of my objectives, teaching methods, and sources of inspiration (e.g., the Calvinistic concept of sphere sovereignty) as I lead 21st-century students in engaging a Calvinist vision for the arts generally, and music specifically.[1] To conclude, I discuss aspects of a recent composition titled *The God of Material Things* by Jonathan Posthuma, a graduate of our college music program, whose work exemplifies many of the elements that my colleagues and I hope distinguish the accomplishments of music students beyond their education at Dordt College.

To begin, I would note that many of the ideas emphasized by the Reformed tradition should be considered broadly Christian.[2] For example, Reformed thinkers were not the first to challenge dualistic assumptions about the "sacred" and the "secular" or whether a life dedicated to the arts is a lesser calling than, say, ministry or missions. Moreover, the Reformed faith is thoroughly mainstream,

---

1   In this essay, I have endeavored to present my teaching goals and practices clearly, succinctly, and, I hope, winsomely. In truth, though, my lesson plan sometimes goes left, and wrestling with the Reformed tradition in a given class is messier than I anticipated. On those days, as always, student engagement helps me to challenge my assumptions and clarify my own thinking, which results in the sorts of insight that I share here—in hope that it is beneficial to others.

2   By "Reformed tradition" I intend the branch of Protestantism that traces its beliefs and practices to the teachings developed by John Calvin in the 16th century. Today, churches calling themselves Reformed or Calvinist can be found all over the world and collectively display a remarkable and beautiful diversity.

and, on our best day, Reformed scholars may sound very similar to the best human thinkers of today and long ago, Christian or not. Lastly, the following is not intended as doctrinaire. That is, these are my own ideas about teaching music as a Reformed believer and the various ways that tradition inspires me personally.

2. Music Itself Speaks

My largest contribution to our core curriculum is "Introduction to the Arts," a class in which I am presented with a sizable cross section of our campus student body. The class is populated with students studying nursing, business, and engineering, as well as an assortment of humanities and arts majors. Leading the class is a team of professors specializing in music, film, theatre, and visual art, who all work together to present a comprehensive vision for living aesthetically sensitive lives in this world. In the course of a semester, students enroll in two consecutive subsections to study specific art forms, and, additionally, everyone gathers for several topically driven conversations on how the arts speak to each other as well as their significance within our culture.[3] My music subsection usually consists of eighteen class periods, so I must be focused and selective concerning what I talk about and how I engage my students, so that my time with them provides a lasting and life-giving influence on the course and quality of their lives.

For several years, I have structured my subsections around musical topics that students confirm are most relevant and interesting to them: music for films, television, and interactive media, popular music, and church music. Within each topic, I address topics such as musical meaning and intertextual relationships, the craft of making music, musical form, and music's functions in various settings. To keep clear for students the intent of the class and its purpose within the college's core curriculum, I repeatedly ask: "Are we able to discern and articulate what God intends art and music to be in this good world, here and now?" Our discussions move in two separate directions: (1) What does God intend for art and music in my life personally?; (2) What should be the place of the specialized artist in my community?

I usually begin this class with film music because it is familiar to students, visually stimulating, and often well crafted. I show clips from the classic 1933 film *King Kong* and highlight composer Max Steiner's use of leitmotif to amplify actor emotions, indicate shifting perspectives, and add a compelling layer of meaning to the film overall. Then, I show a torture scene from Quentin Tarantino's 1992 film *Reservoir Dogs* to highlight the power of diegetic music to shape the viewer. In his choice of music for this scene, Tarantino aims to place the film viewer in a specific psychological state and to implicate her in the horrifying on-screen action (Kalinak 2010). At this point, many of my students are surprised that music can be so powerful.

When we take up a study of music in interactive media, I introduce my class to the craft and artistry of video game composer James Hannigan,[4] and, in the context of that presentation, I describe Marshall McLuhan's famous idea that "the medium is the message".[5] Once I've convinced them that a video-game medium, however it may be structured, is itself a message, I find the students are receptive to accepting that music, by virtue of its construction and production, also constitutes a message that speaks powerfully and, indeed, shapes its audience.

Students take away two leading ideas from these classes on music and associated media: Music itself speaks, even apart from attendant subject matter, just as much as it adds rich strata of meaning. And, without effort, these layers of meaning are often lost to us. For contrast, I ask students how they have experienced music lately, and if they think they have received all that music

---

[3] For a discussion of one topic engaged collaboratively in CORE 160, "Introduction to the Arts," cf. (MacInnis 2014).

[4] Many of James Hannigan's compositions along with composer commentary can be heard on his website (www.jameshannigan.com)

[5] McLuhan's remarkable thesis was that, in the end, the characteristics of any given medium shapes a person or a society as much as, if not more than, the message content delivered by that medium (McLuhan 1964).

offered them on any given day and in any given situation. Normally, my students readily acknowledge that they desire more from their music. They want the joy of hearing music, understanding its language, and being challenged and changed by what it says, rather than confining their experience of music to a speechless and wearisome hum, whose meanings are stereotypical and superficial.

3. The Reformed Call for Attentiveness

In a word, I show my students the importance of attentiveness, of watchfulness in their musical activities and music listening, so that their lives may be full and rich. But the matter cannot be left here. My practice, then, is to press them to give a fuller account for why attentiveness is important. The easy answer is that God does not want us to limit ourselves; God wants us to use God's gifts, such as music, and not to misuse or neglect them.[6] This principle is fine, but the Reformed tradition teaches a deeper truth: God reveals God's self to us through creation and the creative activities of humans. That is, we are awake and watchful because music, as with all other things in our lived experience, is an opportunity to know and engage with God.

In his *Institutes of the Christian Religion*, John Calvin opens with a discussion of the knowledge of God. Calvin argues that we are wise to know both God and ourselves, that both species of knowledge are mutually referential,[7] and that, in some sense, every person already possesses knowledge of God:

> That there exists in the human mind, and indeed by natural instinct, some sense of Deity [*divinitatis sensum*], we hold to be beyond dispute, since God himself, to prevent any man from pretending ignorance, has endued all men with some idea of his Godhead, the memory of which he *constantly renews and occasionally enlarges*, that all to a man, being aware that there is a God, and that he is their Maker, may be condemned by their own conscience when they neither worship him nor consecrate their lives to his service. (Calvin 1949, p. 43)

In his book *Warranted Christian Belief*, philosopher Alvin Plantinga extensively develops Calvin's assertion about this ubiquitous *sensus divinitatis*. Plantinga proposes that the *sensus divinitatis* is a cognitive mechanism that, given stimulus and the proper functioning of that mechanism, produces beliefs about God within us.[8] (Plantinga 2000, p. 173ff) For the purposes of the present discussion, it is striking that the sense of Divinity, as the concept is proposed by Calvin and developed by Plantinga, is prompted and characterized by our lived experience as humans in this universe. Calvin, in his *Institutes*, goes on to explain that the universe can be considered a sort of mirror in which one may view God:

> And, first, wherever you turn your eyes, there is no portion of the world, however minute, that does not exhibit at least some sparks of beauty; while it is impossible to contemplate the vast and beautiful fabric as it extends around, without being overwhelmed by the immense weight of glory. Hence, the author of the Epistle to the Hebrews elegantly describes the visible worlds as images of the invisible (Hebrews 11:3), the elegant structure of the world serving us as a kind of mirror, in which we may behold God, though otherwise invisible. (Calvin 1949, p. 51)

Furthermore, for Calvin, diligent and academic study of the universe, in all its complexity, serves to augment and elaborate what may be known about God. That is, anyone active in the world knows there is a God, that God is powerful and wise, and that there must be an appropriate response

---

[6] Cf. Jesus's parable of the talents, (Matthew 25:14–30).

[7] For Calvin, to know oneself is inducement and opportunity to know God. Cf. Calvin's *Institutes* (Calvin 1949, p. 38): "Every person, therefore, on coming to the knowledge of himself, is not only urged to seek God, but is also led as by the hand to find him."

[8] For Plantinga, this sense of Divinity requires maturity and functions independently of logical argument. Furthermore, Plantinga distinguishes between the *sensus divinitatis* and the work of the Holy Spirit producing faith within the believer.

to such greatness, but the student of a given discipline has access to further testimony that enhances the quality and shapes the character of that knowledge. Calvin writes:

> In attestation of his wondrous wisdom, both the heavens and the earth present us with innumerable proofs, not only those more recondite proofs which astronomy, medicine, and all the natural sciences, are designed to illustrate, but proofs which force themselves on the notice of the most illiterate peasant, who cannot open his eyes without beholding them. It is true, indeed, that those who are more or less intimately acquainted with those liberal studies are thereby assisted and enabled to obtain a deeper insight into the secret workings of divine wisdom. (Calvin 1949, p. 51)

And, to be sure, Calvin includes the accomplishments of human creativity as opportunities to know of God's activity in the universe:

> The swift and versatile movements of the soul in glancing from heaven to earth, connecting the future with the past, retaining the remembrance of former years, nay, forming creations of its own—its skill, moreover, in making astounding discoveries, and inventing so many wonderful arts, are sure indications of the agency of God in man...Shall we be deemed the inventors of so many arts and useful properties that God may be defrauded of his praise, though experience tells us plainly enough, that whatever we possess is dispensed to us in unequal measures by another hand? (Calvin 1949, p. 54)

So, within the Reformed tradition, it is proposed that basic beliefs about God are formed and deepened in response to our engagement with the world, in all its diversity and complexity, what Calvin often termed the *theatrum gloriae Dei*, i.e., the theatre of God's glory (Calvin 1949, p. 156). To apply this discussion to the arts, and music specifically, we find that the study of music and the experiences of performing and hearing music constitute so many opportunities to know God, to engage with God, and to have one's insights about God deepened and extended.

For example, while recently practicing the sixth trio sonata for organ by J. S. Bach (BWV 530), I found myself marveling that such beauty is possible in the world, that the capacity to create intricate and stirring sounds is so freely given to humans, that men and women can be blessed with time and training to study and understand this music. Most importantly, in the study and practice of Bach's art, my main impulse was to praise and give thanks, ascribing the glory of what I was experiencing to God. (And perhaps that is what Bach himself intended when he penned S.D.G. (*Soli Deo Gloria*, "Glory to God Alone") after the last fugue in his famous *Well Tempered Clavier*, Book I). Knowing firsthand the character and wisdom expressed in Bach's music, after many hours of study, I thought that I had learned something about the wisdom and character of God.[9]

The same holds true for people attending to art as audience members. For example, it is expected that individuals will respond emotionally to music, even though they are not actively participating in the music making. Depending on the nature of the emotional states evoked within a person by music, which may be subtle, complex, and powerful, they open a person's mind to a richer experience of the world and compel his conclusions about God. It is a situation similar to *feeling* wonder when surveying the complex and vast workings of creation (cf. Psalm 8:3–4: "What is man that thou art mindful of him?"); the quality of this emotional state accompanies and drives our judgment that the Creator is great. Likewise, our experience feeling love for others and being loved ourselves characterizes our

---

[9] Indeed, David Bently Hart is not spare in his praise of Bach's music as a vehicle for Christian truth: "Bach is the greatest of Christian theologians, the most inspired witness to the *ordo amoris* in the fabric of being; not only is no other composer capable of more freely developing lines or of more elaborate structures of tonal mediation (wherever the line goes, Bach is there also), but no one as compellingly demonstrates that the infinite is beautiful and that beauty is infinite. It is in Bach's music, as nowhere else, that the potential boundlessness of thematic development becomes manifest: how a theme can unfold inexorably through difference, while remaining continuous in each moment of repetition, upon a potentially infinite surface of varied repetition." (Hart 2003)

conclusions about God's love and the affirmation that God is love. Music is an art uniquely suited to exploring and cultivating one's emotional life, for performer and audience member, and it is perfectly normal to conclude in response to music, "God must be something like that." Calvin himself said that God "constantly renews and occasionally enlarges" our sense of divinity; the discipline of music constitutes just such an occasion.

But what about the varying levels of musical quality experienced in any given day? In a situation that is similar to Calvin's astronomer viewing the night sky, I suppose it is safe to say that our sense of the Divine is justifiably at work when we are presented with music generally, as it is when we are presented with stars generally. But, the *sensus divinitatis* has more to work with when we are engaged with greater musical complexity, subtle and evocative interpretations, and more refined artistic skill. I do not intend a complexity for its own sake; rather, I mean a musical complexity and artistry arising when the discipline of music is cultivated faithfully and diligently within its own sphere of competency and authority, irrespective of cultural context.

Remembering that my intention, as a teacher of music, is to use ideas presented in the Reformed tradition as opportunities to rouse and inspire my students, I have found that presenting music, and all art, as an opportunity to know and engage with God justifies attentiveness to the study of music, as opposed to attentiveness for the purpose of a more satisfying and humane life or for its own sake.

4. The Place of the Artist

These sorts of conversations address the large pedagogical question "What does God intend for art and music in my life personally?" which brings me to the second global question for my core introductory arts class: "What should be the place of the specialized artist in my community?" While affirming that aesthetic considerations are constituent to daily human life and relationships, what do the skills, insights, and training of a vocational artist offer her community?

On this front, beyond the course requirement to attend six on-campus arts events, I ask students to observe musicians at their craft. Students are provided with a list of music ensembles on our campus and asked to attend one rehearsal, take substantive notes, and then prepare an essay addressing the following questions: How is the rehearsal time structured (e.g., time for announcements, musical explanations, run-throughs, drills, reading new music, listening, etc.)? How are authority and freedom exercised by those in the room? What are the attitudes among the musicians? Is there a group spirit or group culture, etc.? Student responses normally emphasize the unifying effect of making music with others and the ways the ensemble director works with the musicians to produce something that is satisfying and meaningful.

Placing students in the musicians' workshop, as it were, where they can observe the practices and offices that are at work behind a recital or recording, demonstrates for them the sorts of competencies that musicians assert in their craft, that those competencies are exercised communally, and that, contrary to what we might assume, seeking a flawless performance is really not the reason musicians practice their art. Excellence is a fine standard to hold before ourselves as we work, but it can easily lead to idolatry and, like all idols, consume us. In this way, music can become just another instance in which humans deny their Creator and look to some component of creation as ultimate.

I prefer to emphasize to my students that, instead of a flawless concert, the *process* of music making, the hours of study, listening, lessons, private rehearsal, and mentorship that culminate in an act of sharing within a larger community, is at the heart of what God intends for the specialized artist. This means that the larger community should show an interest in what its musicians are up to and should support them. It also means that musicians should view their work as service to their communities. Most of my students visiting ensemble rehearsals for the first time express an interest in attending that ensemble's next concert and sharing in the fruits of their labor.

Through specialized training and mentorship, the artist learns the givens of her art—in movement, line and color, resonance, harmony, and form—and she uses these givens to offer her community an expression of reality: the glories of the world around us, the struggle within institutions and every human heart for or against God, and the vision of a universal flourishing with justice and peace for all, as God intends. In the case of music, the sorts of stories she tells are musical, or need only be musical. That is, a composer may construct a musical narrative apart from words or textual associations, using only musical sounds and structures.

For example, in *La Primavera* ("Spring"), Vivaldi's first concerto of *The Four Seasons*, a purely musical narrative is presented that compels and satisfies, even apart from the associated poetic imagery of birds, murmuring brooks, a thunderstorm, and the return of birdsong at the end. The accompanying pictures are fun to point out because they are relatively easy to discern, but students respond most warmly when Vivaldi's underlying ritornello structure is explained to them, with insight into how the story plays out in purely musical ways. The storm is portrayed with virtuosic flashes on the violin, and its effect is felt as the ritornello theme is transposed to a minor key. When the birdsongs resume and the ritornello is returned to the home key, at the end, the listener is relieved and comforted. I tell my students that they are free to substitute in their own storms, as they listen. This music is timeless because the sweep of its musical narrative is timeless. It says something true about the world; there are storms, and there is hope for renewal.

In addition to telling true stories, the musical artist serves the members of her community by cultivating their aesthetic senses, i.e., their abilities to perceive structure, meaning, and harmony, so that they may find pleasure and that their lives know beauty on a deep, satisfying level. But, more importantly, she serves so that the members of her community may find new aesthetic applications in their own work and service. All fields of endeavor have aesthetic considerations, and experiencing art often prompts our creativity. By awakening her audience members to aesthetic living generally, the artist equips them to be creative and to strive with nuance and sensitivity in their own work.

In his lecture "Calvinism and the Arts," Kuyper asserts that God is at work in and through the artist and that the work of the artist should be considered an outpouring of grace in our midst—the sort of grace that restrains our worst impulses and injustices on any given day, that empowers our artists to tell us the truth and shape our sensibilities, and that ever guides creation's unfolding as God intends it:

> Calvinism, on the contrary, has taught us that all liberal arts are gifts which God imparts promiscuously to believers and to unbelievers, yea, that, as history shows, these gifts have flourished even in a larger measure outside the holy circle. "These radiations of Divine Light," [Calvin] wrote, "shone more brilliantly among unbelieving people than among God's saints." And this of course quite reverses the proposed order of things. If you limit the higher enjoyment of art to regeneration, then this gift is exclusively the portion of believers, and must bear an ecclesiastical character. In that case, it is the outcome of particular grace. But if, at the hand of experience and history, you become persuaded that the highest art-instincts are natural gifts, and hence belong to those excellent graces which, in spite of sin, by virtue of common grace, have continued to shine in human nature, it plainly follows that art can inspire both believers and unbelievers, and that God remains Sovereign to impart it, in His good pleasure . . . (Kuyper 1953, pp. 160–61)

In preparation for the final cumulative assignment for my "Introduction to the Arts" class, I require that my students listen to President John F. Kennedy's 1963 remarks at Amherst College, in which he contends for the place of the artist in democratic society. In that address, Kennedy asserts,

> In serving his vision of the truth, the artist best serves his nation. And the nation which disdains the mission of art invites the fate of Robert Frost's hired man, the fate of having nothing to look backward to with pride and nothing to look forward to with hope...I look forward to an America which will reward achievement in the arts as we reward achievement in business or statecraft. (John F. Kennedy Presidential Library and Museum 1963)

In response to Kennedy's remarks, all students submit an essay in which they must present their visions for the place of the artist in their own societies, nationally and locally. Though opinions and emphases vary from person to person, of course, students generally agree that artists should be empowered to pursue their vision, to cultivate their skills, and then to share their labors for the common good. My own conviction, shared by many of my students, is that we need our artists to be free to help us see and hear the world differently from what we assumed it to be. We need artists because they are our visionaries and our teachers.

I should add, quickly, that this does not mean that specialized, professional artists are somehow superhuman and should be treated as a class of people exempt from the struggles of life that are common to all. I do intend that my students realize that we need artists, as much as farmers, accountants, doctors, and pastors, and that we must make room for them in our communities, however that may play out in a given time or place. For example, the presence of arts professionals in educational institutions provides a venue for them to enjoy stable employment, cultivate their art within a community, and develop insights that can be passed on to students. Regional arts councils and music groups engage members in making art locally. And federal support for the National Endowment for the Arts ensures that artistic activity is supported across the nation. My students in the core program may not be artists themselves, but many of them will serve their communities on school boards, volunteer time and resources to arts organizations, and all will vote for leaders articulating a vision for our national life together.

5. Sphere Sovereignty and the Arts

The idea of sphere sovereignty is complex, and it is described variously by different thinkers in the Calvinist tradition. The idea is rooted in John Calvin's own distinguishing between the powers of the church and the state, both free to assert appropriate authority within their own spheres, as well as in Calvin's teaching about the many complex structures of the created universe, which each reflect God's intentions and unfold under God's rule.

At heart, sphere sovereignty is a respect for diversity, an acknowledgement that the different arenas of human endeavor deserve space to do their work well, and that, at any given time, multiple ways of being need a place in our midst. Abraham Kuyper's own elaboration of the idea of sphere sovereignty emphasizes that care must be taken to preserve the integrity of each sphere and that no sphere may impose its principles upon another, i.e., no sphere may exert authority over another sphere, for they all exist directly under the rule of God. As a negative example, Kuyper points to the sort of imposed authority that organized religion may assert over the arts. Referring to artistic endeavor broadly, Kuyper writes,

> She is a plant that grows and blossoms upon her own root, and without denying that this plant may have required the help of a temporary support, and that in early times the Church lent this prop in a very excellent way, yet the Calvinistic principle demanded that this plant of earth should at length acquire strength to stand alone and vigorously to extend its branches in every direction. (Kuyper 1953, p. 163)

Furthermore, for Kuyper, within the sphere of aesthetic cultivation, artists are equipped and responsible to discern God's intentions:

> [T]he world now, as well as in the beginning, is the theater for the mighty works of God and humanity remains a creation of His hand, which, apart from salvation, completes under this present dispensation, here on earth, a mighty process, and in its historical development is to glorify the name of Almighty God. To this end He has ordained for this humanity all sorts of life-utterances, and among these, art occupies a quite independent place. Art reveals ordinances of creation which neither science, nor politics, nor religious life, nor even revelation can bring to light. (Kuyper 1953, pp. 162–63)

Kuyper describes a robust confidence of God's sovereignty, which, in my experience, is a *sine qua non* in Reformed thinking. It would not be impossible, though, for one to be challenged by his describing that sovereignty at work in the sphere of art through "ordinances." To explain his thinking in a productive way, we can say, firstly, that if God has established norms for art, they are surely to be found in the cultivation of art, not in the scientific process or laid out systematically on the pages of the Bible, as Kuyper explains above. And, ideally, when determined, these ordinances or norms are to be studied and cultivated among artists who add encouragement when they are obeyed and who note carefully when they are misdirected. This is another opportunity for the professional artist to serve her community and to promote human flourishing in her own area of responsibility and equipping.

So, what are God's intentions for art? Specifying creational laws, as proposed by Kuyper and other Reformed thinkers, is a major challenge for artists within the Reformed tradition, especially for musicians, and there have been different perspectives. Generally speaking, Kuyper is very generous to the creators of Greek classical art, and he concludes that the Greeks, through their cultivation of arts such as sculpture, unfolded the principles of harmonized beauty which still hold true today. The Greek emphasis on beauty, though, explained as an earthly indication of Plato's world of ideals, implied hierarchies of material and immaterial, matter and spirit, that proved problematic for generations of Reformed thinkers after Kuyper.

For instance, still drawing upon the traditional Greek concept of beauty, though denying its dualism, Herman Dooyeweerd identifies harmony as the nucleus of the aesthetic mode of existence. Similarly, Hans Rookmaaker describes "beautiful harmony" as the nucleus of aesthetic living. So, for Dooyeweerd and Rookmaaker, artistic cultivation is most faithful to God's intentions for art when it addresses problems of unity in variety, proportionality, conciseness of expression, and directness of appeal.

In North America, the lifelong work of Calvin Seerveld offers a more recent development of Reformed thinking applied to aesthetics. Following the ideas of Dooyeweerd, Seerveld's contributions to aesthetics have been to explore the nature of aesthetics as an irreducible mode of existence, to describe how aesthetic considerations interrelate with other modes of living, and to articulate normative principles for aesthetic life:

> Aesthetics is a special science like economics, linguistics, physics, psychology, or whatever body of analysis that can cohere as a systematic investigation of reality brought into focus by some prime structuring feature...Aesthetics is meant to be a basic science with its own kind of integrity because there is an irreducible order of reality that demands special treatment as aesthetic reality, interwoven with all the other features of the universe. (Seerveld 2014, p. 46)

Seerveld's conclusions about creational laws, applied within the sphere of aesthetics, challenge prevailing Western notions that art is the study of harmony and beauty. In this way, Seerveld also challenges (and reforms) Dooyeweerd and Rookmaaker. In place of harmonized beauty as the heart of artistic cultivation and aesthetic living, Seerveld prefers a playful allusiveness or imaginativity:

> My attempt to reform the Western philosophical tradition on BEAUTY as the norm for good living and sound art is to posit instead that the nuclear moment of what has come to be called "aesthetic" is *ludicity*—that is playfulness that assumes vital, sensitive formative ability is at the core of imaginativity. The norm for the imaginative side of experiential life is, "Be allusive!": "fool around" in the connotations of your speech, in the conjectural dimension of your thinking, within the diplomatic element of your just-doing, be a trifle flirtational in keeping troth with your neighbor. (Seerveld 2014, pp. 151–52)

Seerveld's emphasis on allusiveness necessitates meaning in an artistic act, and, for Seerveld, the artist serves her audience members by sharpening and nuancing their ability to draw meaning from the world and their lived experience:

Artwork is an entity or act defined by adequately answering in its very structural formation to God's creational ordinance, "Be imaginative!" An artist is called by God, I believe, to serve the imaginative needs of one's neighbors with artworks. An artful image, constellation of sounds, or staged dramatic conflict, can disclose states of affairs normally unnoticed by people whose habit of daily perception and thought is casual, if not slovenly. (Seerveld 2009, p. 397)

Music and all art can certainly be considered a meaningful text that profitably rewards our sustained attention, proportional to the skill of the artist and the learned ability of the audience. Here, artistry discloses what the artist has seen and understands of the world, its nature, possibilities, dangers, and glories. And, in doing so, art amplifies and embodies the reality of lived experience, thereby shaping our understanding of that reality.[10] Put simply, our lived experience in the world teaches us about God, and the artist specializes in presenting aesthetically nuanced insight into lived experience.

More specifically, though, the Christian artist will use juxtaposition, metaphor, and the cost-conscious application of her resources to orient her audience towards *shalom*. *Shalom*, for Seerveld, is the world as it should be, with justice, peace, and flourishing available to all, and, as a concept, *shalom* prompts two important thoughts: (1) *Shalom* laments things as they are, mired in humanity's apparently limitless capacity to pollute, poison, degrade, and disfigure; (2) *Shalom* asserts that we do not have to live this way. *Shalom* hopes, with good reasons, that God is at work among us, here and now, redeeming, restoring, pulling people together, saying "Yes!" to us, in all our brokenness. Seerveld concludes,

Artist and patron who understand what the LORD God requires of us will be generous stewards of artwork that makes Jesus Christ's call to repentance and offer of grace to forgive known allusively in imaginative deed to those who never darken the insides of art museums or churches. (Seerveld 2009, p. 384)

Thus, for Seerveld, God's intentions for the practices of art are concerned with how art functions, the ends for which it is made, and how we engage it in meaningful ways. The benefit of this approach is that one need not preclude the possibility of artistic givens changing (in contrast to God's command for justice, which always applies). For example, the melodic possibilities offered by tuned strings and the receptive potentials of the human ear defined the development of musical art for centuries. Now, with bone conduction headphones a deaf man can hear a symphony, 3-D printing technology is opening up new worlds of possibility for instrument creation, electronic dance music is redefining the nature of musical creativity, and audiovisual technologies associated with augmented reality promise to enlarge the creative media for artists, far into the future.[11]

In his book *Art Rethought: The Social Practices of Art*, Nicholas Wolterstorff describes the many meaningful ways all humans live aesthetically in the world, in the sort of integrated manner theorized by Seerveld. In contrast, Wolterstorff explains a "grand narrative," once commonly accepted as an account of art in the modern world, which describes the increased prominence of "disinterested contemplation," ideally during periods of leisure, as the normative mode for engaging art (Wolterstorff 2015, p. 7ff.).

---

[10] Consider Rowan Williams's comments about the creative writings of Fyodor Dostoevsky, how, in their construction, they set forth his vision of reality and the place of God in that reality: "The Dostoevskian novel . . . enacts the freedom it discusses by creating a narrative space in which various futures are possible for characters and for readers. And in doing so it seeks—in the author's intention—to represent the ways in which the world's creator exercises 'authorship,' generates dependence without control . . . The fiction is like the world itself—proposed for acceptance and understanding but unable to compel them, since compulsion would make it impossible for the creator to appear as the creator of freedom" (Williams 2011, p. 12). In this instance, Dostoevsky's reader is presented with what Dostoevsky has concluded about the world, and in engaging his vision, the reader's own lived experience is enlarged. Of course, an artist's concept, presented as it is in what she has made, may be astute or wrongheaded. In either case, by engaging the artistic creation, a person has opportunity for his sense of God to be expanded, while experiencing, considering, or challenging the author's account.

[11] Furthermore, advances in artificial intelligence (AI) raise legitimate questions about the possibility of music composed by—and for—AI.

With their eyes on the art world, with its institutions, traditions, and specializations, and in an attempt to reserve art from serving purely utilitarian ends—art *for* something—thinkers like G.W.F. Hegel proposed that art is a means for finding truth and is, therefore, valuable in its own right—art *for art's own sake* (Wolterstorff 2015, p. 40).

The unhappy consequence of this line of thinking was to sideline memorial art, protest songs, hymns, and the like as somehow less worthwhile than high art traditions which created art for disinterested contemplation, e.g., string quartets and sonatas. So, while affirming art as a legitimate area of specialization and vocation, Wolterstorff reminds us that God's intentions for art are not limited to fancy concerts and gallery attendance. If art is another means of knowing God, we must acknowledge the possibility that artistry shines forth in the common things of life, every day.

This impulse to emphasize the integrated nature of human life while also acknowledging essential differences among the diverse spheres is a hallmark of the Reformed tradition. In fact, Kuyper's explanation as to why Calvinism had not produced its own religious art style (aside from what Marilynne Robinson (Robinson 2010) has called a "chaste simplicity") is the result of Calvinism's freeing the artist from overdependence upon the Church and its institutions for creative outlet. In Kuyper's account, Calvinism refused to "embody its religious spirit in monuments of splendor" (Kuyper 1953, p. 147) preferring, rather, a spirituality that pervades all of lived experience. Quoting Eduard von Hartmann, Kuyper included the following in his "Calvinism and Art":

> It is pure spiritual Religion which with one hand deprives the artist of his specifically religious art, but which, with the other, offers him, in exchange, a whole world, to be religiously animated. (Kuyper 1953, p. 159)

6. The God of Materials Things

Generally speaking, the Reformed tradition is resolute in affirming our rootedness in the material world, the physical universe in which we are called to action and accountability. Therefore, artistic endeavor in this tradition is often a wrestling with material reality and our extraordinary existence as physical beings *coram deo*, "before the face of God," rather than a striving after an otherworldly, immaterial ideal. An excellent example of a musical investigation of and wrestling with creation as revelation is heard in Mr. Jonathan Posthuma's recently composed song cycle for singers and orchestra titled *The God of Material Things*.

Posthuma is a graduate of the music program at Dordt College, and *The God of Material Things* was his final thesis project for his master's degree in music composition at the University of Wisconsin-Madison. The song cycle lasts over forty minutes, and it is comprised of eleven poems by Dordt College Emeritus Professor of English, David Schelhaas. *The God of Material Things* can be heard online using the following link: soundcloud.com/jnthnpsthm/sets/the-god-of-material-things.

Overall, Posthuma describes his composition and Schelhaas's poems as sharing a vision for how quotidian events can have deep significance. Drawing upon several recurring themes and musical motives, his work expounds picturesque, though common, events and observations about the world, accompanied by the deep, emotional questions explored in Schelhaas's poetry. Posthuma's music awakens his audience to the fact that grief at the loss of a loved one, for example, finds echoes in the natural world, which contextualizes that suffering within a larger framework. In a public presentation of his song cycle, Posthuma commented,

> The poems share a "narrative voice" that I describe as earnest, but easy-going. There is a gentle wisdom, playful wit, and a deep understanding that describes how material experiences and everyday happenings have a deep spiritual significance. (Posthuma 2015)

The cycle opens with "Prelude: Sky Dance," which includes a read narration describing a cloud of starlings wheeling about the sky in playful choreography. The starlings call to each other as they flit about during the day and as they settle down together for the night. At dawn, their renewed noise fills the air, and Posthuma quotes the familiar hymn "This is My Father's World" with forceful brass instruments, which serves as his shorthand translation of their collective declaration. A brief silence precedes the birds taking off again for a new day of action in the world.

Musical metaphors arise from the text of the poetry, and they find correspondence in Posthuma's score, e.g., "melodies of shape move contrapuntally, weaving a staff of eighth and quarter notes above the trees" (Schelhaas 2007, p. 33). The musical metaphors eventually introduce a paradox for the narrator, who perceives a general order to the birds in their enthusiastic and apparently arbitrary movements: "random yet patterned, harmoniously wild" (Schelhaas 2007, p. 33). The piece concludes with the narrator asking what such glory of energy and excitement could mean ultimately, "Did he who marks the sparrow's fall with care design this choreography for birds and air?" (Schelhaas 2007, p. 33)

In the first sung portion of the cycle, "A Prayer," Posthuma scores a wise "maternal voice," who discovers that her own groundedness in God is mirrored in the flourishing of ash trees on 2nd Ave (Posthuma 2015). The text runs,

> For these bony old ash trees on Second Avenue,
> their tough branches with twisting starts and stops,
> elegant curves,
> sudden juts and turns,
> haphazard as my prayers in the night,
> yet lifted up in the tremulous confidence
> that you have made them beautiful,
> thank you, oh Spirit of God. (Schelhaas 2007, p. 1)

Posthuma describes this piece as "prayerful" and explains how the musical material slowly unfolds over harmonic drones toward a stirring climax of realization. His music aurally depicts "huge tree branches aching and groaning as they are lifted up beautifully as an offering to God" (Posthuma 2015).

Generally, the first half of *The God of Material Things* focuses more on natural experiences within the context of modern urban life, all the while marveling at God's faithfulness in creation. The second song is "Interrupted Message," which begins with the poet ambling down the street in the early morning light with a musical accompaniment of bird calls, imitated playfully in the score. The singer notes that the dance of light on the road, like the whistling birds, seems to declare the coming of Spring:

> The looping swoops of tar that patch the road I walk
> are a golden script with which the just-rising
> sun has scrawled a cheery note. (Schelhaas 2007, p. 13)

Posthuma scores a new section in a jaunty waltz time (marked "With Jollity") to humorously feature the poet's likening one particular tree to a circus calliope and to emphasize the pleasantness of the morning for the singer. Suddenly a woodpecker begins to beat out his own message in Morse Code, and Posthuma includes an emphatic pattern played by woodblock in imitation of the woodpecker. The woodpecker's testimony is cut short, though, and he abandons his message about the arrival of spring for the glory of experiencing its reality for himself:

> He bangs out an S-P-R but then, distracted
> by diving finches scooping up the air,
> flits off to taste and see
> what it was he meant to say. (Schelhaas 2007, p. 13)

In the fourth song, "Morning News," (marked "Smaltzy, with Rubato") human struggles come to the fore. The soloist begins by describing four mourning doves, as if rehearsing a barbershop quartet song, and nostalgically recalls an earlier stage in life, analogous to their pleasant music making. In contrast, though, as the morning news of the singer's adult life seems overwhelmingly negative (more like the squawk of a crow), Posthuma's score turns dark and dissonant for the song's troubling close:

Now, most mornings, I hear crows squawking
the cruel, discordant news of the day:
air strikes, suicide bombings, death counts. (Schelhaas 2007, p. 18)

Whereas these solo songs describe our human experience, the impact of sin, and attest to God's grace mediated to us through creation, Posthuma's intent is that the narrated scores that open and close the cycle engage larger themes concerning creation, as in "Prelude: Sky Dance," and redemption, as in "Conclusion: The God of Material Things." The conclusion features the aged narrator affirming what he has learned through a lifetime of watchfulness, while three hymns are sung beneath his statements ("God Himself Is With Us," "O Jesus I Have Promised," and "Holy, Holy, Holy"), weaving together in a triple counterpoint. On this portion of his cycle, Posthuma says,

> This central thesis of the entire cycle is bound up in the Postlude, to which all of the movements have been building theologically...Throughout the cycle the singers had confessed that although we sometimes struggle to believe in the midst of our human experiences, God's grace—a "spiritual" concept—keeps showing itself and has physical, "material" existence. (Posthuma 2015)

Schelhaas's poetry for this culminating portion is stirring, as it takes on a new power when heard alongside the hymn tunes sounding beneath it, which add their own separate layers of significance:

This I know: as soon as I could see,
I saw God everywhere. He was always hanging around the house.
Never a meal, but there sat God,
smiling and blessing and keeping his elbows off the table.
Sunday morning he was in his holy temple
and all the earth (except the crying children) kept silence before him.
On endless Sunday afternoons he sat with my dad
and grandpa, smoking those terrible cigars that grandpa smoked
and spelling out the mysteries of faith.
In my room at night as I read the fat children's Bible
full of pictures and stories about David, Daniel, and those other giants,
there was God holding the flashlight and reading with me under the covers,
though sometimes as I got older the batteries failed
and darkness filled the room.

. . .

It's true I don't see him everywhere these days
but still, well, like this morning,
I was weeding the perennials,
dew-wet in morning glory light,
the wren singing his perky little heart out,
and suddenly, there was God again,
like a rabbit popping out of the strawberry patch,
God, just for a moment,
Taking my breath away. (Schelhaas 2007, pp. 30–31)

7. Conclusions

In conclusion, I have found helpful resources in the Reformed tradition that have aided me in thinking deeply about music, the art that I practice and which I have the privilege to teach. In an educational setting, I constantly observe students genuinely inspired by the comprehensive vision articulated in the Reformed/Calvinist tradition, a vision that allows believers to be faithfully engaged in every field of human endeavor because it presupposes that Christ is concerned with it all, even music. It is this vision that my colleagues and I share with our students, and, as Jonathan Posthuma's work demonstrates, the result can be very satisfying.

Conflicts of Interest: The author declares no conflict of interest.

References

Calvin, John. 1949. *Institutes of the Christian Religion*. Translated by Henry Beveridge. London: James Clarke and Company.

Hart, David Bently. 2003. *The Beauty of the Infinite: The Aesthetics of Christian Truth*. Grand Rapids: Eerdmans Publishing, pp. 282–83.

John F. Kennedy Presidential Library and Museum. "Remarks at Amherst College, October 26, 1963." Available online: https://www.jfklibrary.org/Asset-Viewer/80308LXB5kOPFEJqkw5hlA.aspx (accessed on 27 January 2017).

Kalinak, Kathryn. 2010. *Film Music: A Very Short Introduction*. New York: Oxford University Press, p. 1ff.

Kuyper, Abraham. 1953. *Lectures on Calvinism*. Grand Rapids: Eerdmans Publishing.

MacInnis, John. 2014. The Arts of War: Reconsidering Conflict through Interdisciplinary Artistic Collaboration. Available online: http://digitalcollections.dordt.edu/faculty_work/58 (accessed on 30 March 2017).

McLuhan, Marshall. 1964. *Understanding Media: The Extensions of Man*. New York: McGraw-Hill.

Plantinga, Alvin. 2000. *Warranted Christian Belief*. New York: Oxford University Press.

Posthuma, Jonathan. 2015. The God of Material Things. Paper presented at Dordt College Kuyper Scholar's Honor Program, Sioux Center, Iowa, IA, USA, 28 September 2015.

Robinson, Marilynne. 2010. Christian Freedom. In Paper presented at Dordt College First Monday Lectures, Dordt College, Sioux Center, Iowa, IA, USA, 7 February 2010.

Schelhaas, David. 2007. *The God of Material Things*. Sioux Center: Dordt College Press.

Seerveld, Calvin. 2009. "How Should Christians Be Stewards of Art?" *Journal of Markets & Morality* 12: 377–85.

Seerveld, Calvin. 2014. *Normative Aesthetics*. Edited by John Kok. Sioux Center: Dordt College Press.

Williams, Rowan. 2011. *Dostoevsky: Language, Faith, and Fiction*. New York: Baylor University Press, p. 12.

Wolterstorff, Nicholas. 2015. *Art Rethought: The Social Practices of Art*. New York: Oxford University Press.

Article

Dirk Philips' Letter and Spirit: An Anabaptist Contribution to Reformation Hermeneutics

Aaron Schubert

Dallas Theological Seminary, Dallas, TX 75204, USA; Agarwaen111@gmail.com

Academic Editor: Christopher Metress
Received: 28 January 2017; Accepted: 13 March 2017; Published: 15 March 2017

Abstract: Dirk Philips provides an explanation of how a Christian should interpret Scripture in his *Enchiridion*. Such chapters as "The Sending of Preachers and Teachers," "The Tabernacle of Moses," and "Of Spiritual Restitution" provide the clearest picture for students of this Anabaptist hermeneutic, a hermeneutic which interprets all of Scripture through the dichotomy of the letter and the Spirit, united in their central theme, Christ and the Church, a reading that can only be found through a hermeneutic of obedience.

Keywords: Dirk Philips; hermeneutic; obedience; interpretation; scripture; Anabaptist

1. Introduction

Dirk Philips remains a lesser known theological figure of the Reformation, overshadowed even within the Anabaptist movement by Menno Simons. This is a pity because Philips provides perhaps the most systematic explication of an Anabaptist hermeneutic of the Scriptures. Becoming an Anabaptist in 1533 at the age of 29, he lived another 35 years preaching and teaching in that tradition in Northern Germany and the Low Countries, a remarkably long time considering the dangers of persecution. In his *Enchiridion*, a compilation of his works collected and edited by him before his death, Philips presents not only a treasure trove of examples of how he uses the Bible to support his arguments, but he goes even further to explain in detail how a Christian should handle the Holy Word. As students can see particularly in his chapters "The Sending of Preachers and Teachers," "The Tabernacle of Moses," and "Of Spiritual Restitution," this hermeneutic reads all of Scripture to center on Christ and the Church, a reading established in the dichotomy of the letter and the Spirit of the text through a hermeneutic of obedience.

2. Letter and Spirit

On the most fundamental level, Dirk Philips argues that the Scriptures can be read for the meaning of the letter, as presented in the Old Testament, and the meaning of the Spirit, as presented in the New Testament. The letter represents what one might call the historical reading. This reading views the events portrayed in the Old Testament as historical events recorded by men through the work of the Holy Spirit. This reading is true, so far as it goes. Philips would be the last to deny that God created the heavens and the earth, that Moses parted the Red Sea, or that Solomon built the temple. However, this reading for the meaning of the letter is insufficient. It sees the types and figures without perceiving their object, the shadow but not the person. According to Philips, "Christ Jesus is the spirit and the substance of all the types and figures that have passed away, the end and fulfillment of the law of types, figures and shadows, but the beginning of the true substance and completeness... and all shadows and figures are fulfilled in him" [1]. "Therefore," Philips concludes, "all things are changed in Christ and are transfigured and made new by him, that is, changed from the letter to the Spirit, from the carnal to the real, from the old to the new, from the figure into the true abiding substance...

from the transitory to the eternal and heavenly" ([1], p. 325). The truth of the letter reading is not denied, but it is not what brings life, and it is not the lasting and eternal. That is only found in the Spirit reading, a reading that sees the symbolic and figurative reality of the Old Testament pointing forward to Christ and the Church.

2.1. The Letter of the Law and the Spirit of Christ

As students of the Reformation will see, Philips is neither the first nor the last to use Paul's words in II Corinthians 3 that the letter kills but the Spirit brings life as a broader framework to interpret Scripture. Philips argues that this division of letter and Spirit is between the Old and New Testaments:

> The Anabaptists approached this expression from II Corinthians 3 in a quite different way. They followed Augustine in assuming that the primary point at issue in the discussion of this chapter was the relation between the Old and New Covenants. Thus when Paul said "the letter kills" he was referring primarily, if not exclusively, to the Old Testament and the letter of the Law there. He cannot have meant the New Testament writings or any literal observance of them because the New Testament letter does not kill but the words of Christ bring life [2].

The letter of the events of the Old Testament, although true, need to be reinterpreted by the Spirit in order to understand their greater meaning in light of Christ and the Church. As Ben Ollenburger points out, this claim is not so much the result of exegetical work as it is a basic hermeneutical assumption: "One of the pre-understandings of the Anabaptists which separated them from their environment was their sharp distinction between the Old and New Testaments. We call this a pre-understanding because it stands as a principle of exegesis, not a result of exegesis" [3]. This divide, and the spiritualizing interpretation that attends it, was fundamental to Philips's hermeneutical work, and it helps to explain how he can sound to students at times like a hyper-literalist (when discussing paedobaptism in the New Testament) and at other moments like an uninhibited allegorist (when portraying Samson and Delilah as a prefiguration of Christ and his bride, the Church). His guiding hermeneutic allowed for both concrete, literal interpretations as well as spiritual allegorizing, as long as the former were interpretations of the New Testament and the latter of the Old [4].

2.2. A Hermeneutic of Obedience

But how does one read not only the letter but the Spirit of the Old Testament so as to understand the spiritual meaning therein? Philips gives a simple answer—you do not, the Spirit reveals it to you: "But now the figures of the old testament [sic] must be carefully examined and be understood, not according to human opinion, but just as they came from, were spoken and given by God through the Holy Spirit, so also must they, by the same Spirit, be revealed, taught and explained (2 Pet. 1:21)" ([1], p. 259). Only the Holy Spirit can teach the spiritual meaning, the deeper, fuller meaning of the Scriptures. The preacher merely passes on what he himself has been taught: "[T]he ministers of Christ, the teachers and leaders of his church, must have the Holy Ghost, by whom they must, first and above all things, be well instructed in the word of God" ([1], p. 180).

This, however, merely raises a new question for many students. How can one know what is taught by the Holy Spirit and what is human opinion, either in one's own reading or in the teaching of others? Philips is again aware of the question and seeks to answer it. The origin of an interpretation, human or divine, is evidenced in the person's life:

> From these and similar passages of holy scripture it is easy to recognize the true teachers, especially so far as the true doctrine is concerned, namely if they teach the word of God rightly, whereby they seek the glory of God and the salvation of men, if they are spiritually minded, if they have renounced all earthly and perishable things . . . if they love God above all else and carry on his work without deceit and hypocrisy ([1], pp. 181–12).

Philips stresses that these external evidences demonstrate that the person is obedient to God and therefore is indwelt by the Holy Spirit. Only in such a case can the Word of God be rightly understood and taught. As he notes later, "The holy scripture shows that a true teacher must bear fruit; for where the word of God is implanted in the human heart and proclaimed in the power of the Spirit, it must, according to its nature, be effective, active and fruitful" ([1], p. 184). The obedient life testifies to the power of the Spirit since it is its natural result, and only with the power of the Spirit can the Scriptures be known in their Spirit as well as their letter.

This behavior is contrasted to those who are not indwelt by the Spirit, and who thus cannot hope to rightly teach the Word:

> Since, then, an ungodly man cannot teach aright, and he is really an ungodly man who transgresses and abideth not in the doctrine of Christ, as John says (2 John 1:9), it follows incontrovertibly that no one can teach God's word aright unless he himself abides in Christ and in his doctrine. But no one may understand the doctrine of Christ, much less abide therein, except through the Holy Ghost; and no one has the Holy Ghost but those who are no longer carnally minded, but spiritually minded... Therefore whoever has not died unto sin, and does not live unto righteousness, has not the Spirit of God. But whoever has not the Spirit of God does not comprehend the word of God, and cannot discern spiritual things ([1], pp. 183–34).

For Philips, the obedient life, which is also the work of the Spirit, is inseparable from a right understanding of the Word of God, which must be understood spiritually, not merely in its letter. The division of letter and Spirit therefore leads to a hermeneutic of obedience, where obedience is a necessary prerequisite to understanding.

3. A Spiritual Reading

Philips does not end his hermeneutical discussion with this prerequisite. He wishes to go further and provide an example of a reading of the Old Testament that reveals the Spirit and not merely the letter of the text. He does so in both the history of the Old Testament as well as through its objects.

3.1. History as Symbol

Philips takes up the history of the Old Testament in order to show that, when read by the Spirit, it symbolically points toward Christ and the Church. He begins with creation, saying, "In the first place, in Christ Jesus has been restored the creation of heaven and earth; for God has made new heavens, namely, the believers, in whom God dwells... [and] the new earth, that is, the hearts of Christians, into which the seed of the word of God has been sown (Matt. 13:8)" ([1], p. 326). The creation story is not denied, but a deeper meaning of the heavens, the sun, and the earth is given for the edification of Christians.

Similarly, the union of Adam and Eve takes on a new spiritual meaning: "Moreover, the symbolical wedlock between Adam and Eve is also spiritually restored in Christ Jesus; for he is the second and new Adam, and his bride who has been taken from his side... is the spiritual Eve, the mother of all believing Christians" ([1], p. 329). As one can see, Philips borrows heavily from New Testament explanations of Old Testament symbols, seeking to maintain an apostolic interpretation.

According to Philips, "Christ is the true, spiritual Noah, the preacher of righteousness, and the members of his household are the children of God (Matt. 12:49)... he has hereby also built an ark, that is, the holy Christian church for the protection and preservation of all believing souls" ([1], p. 330). Obviously, for Philips, a running theme in each of these narratives is Christ, but it is noteworthy to also observe the Church, here explicitly in the ark, but also earlier represented in the obedient children of the second Adam, the second Eve, and the heavens of creation. Philips is presenting a reading that places Christ as symbolically at the center of each story, but Christ is almost always accompanied by his Church.

As he continues his spiritualized reading of Old Testament history, he takes up Abraham, Isaac, and Jacob, the two covenants seen in the two wives, Sarah and Hagar, and of course, the description of Melchisedec. Jesus is also the true Jacob, the true Joseph, the true Moses, the paschal lamb, and the pillar of fire and clouds, David and Solomon. Even less noble figures like Samson are taken up:

> This figure [Samson] is spiritually fulfilled in Christ, for he is the true Nazarene, the holy son of the Most High..., and the Judge of the Israel of God, who took unto himself the heathen and choose therefrom a church and gathered it by the preaching of the gospel... He overcame the young lion, the adversary of Christians, that is, Satan... with the jawbone of an ass, that is, with the uneducated apostles, who in the eyes of the world were as stupid as asses, he vanquished the uncircumcised of heart ([1], pp. 346–47).

Philips even makes an effort to weave in unflattering elements from the Old Testament, like the heathen bride, so as to symbolically foreshadow the spiritual fulfillment of these stories. He concludes by saying:

> From all this it is evident that all things are restored and shall be repeated, spiritually, in Christ Jesus and in the time of his dominion until the time of his coming and appearing, as the apostle says (I Peter 1:5; Acts 3:20). Therefore we need not expect any other restitution or repetition of all things in any other than in a spiritual sense in Christ Jesus who is the Alpha and Omega ([1], p. 362).

The political dimensions of this passage can be made clear to students by pointing out that Philips, in addition to expressing a particular biblical hermeneutic, is also addressing what he perceives to be a contemporary misreading of scripture. In the passage above, Philips is challenging the Anabaptist rebels of Münster, who had in 1534 overthrown their princes in order to bring about a theocracy in the style of the Old Testament. According to Philips, using the Old Testament to justify such behavior fails to appreciate the spiritual meaning of the Old Testament and sees only the letter of the Law. The time for establishing theocracies is over, Philips argues, and we are to understand such happenings in the Old Testament for their spiritual rather than their literal meanings. Thus, he concludes, "All that the prophets have prophesied and declared regarding [...] the restitution of all things must be thus understood and be changed from the letter to the Spirit" ([1], p. 363).

3.2. Objects as Symbol

Philips also takes up the objects contained in these Old Testament histories for spiritual reinterpretation, most notably the tabernacle of Moses. The tabernacle serves Philips' hermeneutical purpose both as a symbol to be spiritually understood in terms of the New Testament as well as a symbolic representation of the division between letter and Spirit embodied in the two testaments. The tabernacle of Moses prefigures the entirety of Scripture, and in its division between Law and gospel, letter and Spirit, it prefigures the whole interpretive work Philips believes is essential to a correct understanding. It is important to note that he does not pit Law against gospel, but explicitly states that they are in agreement when rightly read, just as the letter and the Spirit, which he has identified with them, are also ultimately in agreement. The letter of the Law may end, but its Spirit continues and points to the fullness of the New Testament revelation.

In addition to this larger symbolism, Philips argues that everything within the tabernacle was figurative both for that time and for the future: "All God's dealings with Moses, from the tabernacle or tent and its preparation, equipment and adornment, was figurative, to the time of the Law, which was present, and to the time of grace and truth which was to come and which appeared by Jesus Christ" ([1], p. 344). The repetitive sacrifices symbolized the incompleteness of the Law. The yearly entrance of the high priest into the holy of holies pointed to Christ's once-for-all sacrifice. The Levites typified the Old Testament while the high priest typified Christ. The cherubim which covered the mercy seat represented the two testaments, both pointing to Christ. Every figure eventually results in a Christological foreshadowing, most often with an ecclesiological accompaniment.

3.3. Christ and His Church

Douglas Shantz proposes that as Christ is the central motif in interpretation for Luther, so ecclesiology is for Dirk Philips. According to Schantz, "Gerhard Ebeling and Walter Loewenich have both emphasized the Christocentric focus of Luther's use of Scripture. In contrast, Dirk's central hermeneutic principle was 'ecclesiocentric,' focusing on the Body of Christ, the church. This theme ran through both testaments" [5]. However, a careful reading of Philips's instructions on hermeneutics suggests a more nuanced stance. Christ is so central to the figures and images of the Old Testament in Philips's readings. Every story and every object can be traced to him and is spiritually fulfilled by him. I would agree that Philips does emphasize the Church's place in these images as well, but never outside of the context of the Church's relationship to Christ. They are always paired together, Christ and his bride. Every one of Philips's spiritual readings of the Old Testament include Christ. Many include the Church, but the Church is never symbolized without Christ also being symbolized in the same story or image.

This dual focus is important in that it helps reveal not only how Philips thinks one should read Scripture but also because it reveals his understanding of the close relationship between Christ and the Church. One cannot be a part of the Church without being a follower of Christ, and one cannot follow Christ apart from the Church.

4. Conclusions

Dirk Philips's hermeneutic interprets all of Scripture through the dichotomy of the letter and the Spirit, united in their central theme, Christ and the Church, a reading that can only be found through a hermeneutic of obedience. His entire treatment of Scripture hinges upon the concept of the letter and the Spirit. The Old Testament is the letter, prefiguring what is to come in the Spirit, Christ and the Church as revealed by the New Testament. The Old Testament must therefore be spiritually and allegorically interpreted in light of this higher, fuller, and clearer revelation. The New Testament does not require an allegorical interpretation because it speaks of the spiritual reality plainly in Christ. The Holy Spirit is key to understanding the spiritual realities of both Testaments, whether spoken of plainly, as in the New, or in figures, as in the Old. The necessity of the Spirit in interpretation leads Philips to develop a hermeneutic of obedience, since no one can possess the Spirit if he does not abide in Christ, and to abide in Christ is to obey his commands. Therefore, the life of the interpreter plays a key role in validating his interpretation. While this hermeneutic is unfamiliar to most students, its complexity and power demonstrates the significant, if often forgotten, contribution of the Anabaptist theologians to the study of the Reformation and to later evangelical and pietistic movements.

Conflicts of Interest: The author declares no conflict of interest.

References

1. Philips, Dirk. *Enchiridion*. Translated by Abraham B. Kolb. LaGrange: Pathway Publishers, 1978, p. 325.
2. Klassen, William. "Anabaptist Hermeneutics: The Letter and the Spirit." *The Mennonite Quarterly Review* 40 (1966): 86.
3. Ollenburger, Ben C. "The Hermeneutics of Obedience: A Study of Anabaptist Hermeneutics." *Direction* 6 (1977): 21.
4. Dyck, Cornelius J. "The Place of Tradition in Dutch Anabaptism." *Church History* 43 (1974): 34. [CrossRef]
5. Shantz, Douglas H. "The Ecclesiological Focus of Dirk Philips' Hermeneutical Thought in 1559: A Contextual Study." *The Mennonite Quarterly Review* 60 (1986): 126–27.

Article

Spenser's Blatant Beast: The Thousand Tongues of Elizabethan Religious Polemic

Christopher A. Hill

Department of English and Modern Foreign Languages, University of Tennessee Martin, Martin, TN 38238, USA; chrish@utm.edu

Academic Editor: Christopher Metress
Received: 31 January 2017; Accepted: 28 March 2017; Published: 4 April 2017

Abstract: This article addresses the final two books of the 1596 edition of Spenser's *Faerie Queene*, in which there arises a formidable adversary: the Blatant Beast. This monster, whose presence dominates the end of Book Five and a substantial portion of Book Six, represents the worst excesses of caustic and satirical rhetoric as manifest in the theological and ecclesiastical pamphlet disputes that erupted after Fields and Wilcox's 1572 *Admonition to Parliament*. That these disputes were about serious and far-reaching matters is undeniable; it is also undeniable that the means by which these disputes were waged, especially in notorious cases like those of Martin Marprelate, caused significant intellectual, rhetorical, and religious anxiety among combatants and observers alike. Spenser's heavily allegorized presentation of polemic and pamphleteering in the figure of the Blatant Beast—and the travails of the Knights of Justice and of Courtesy in bringing the beast to heel—can illustrate for students the full extent of that anxiety in Reformation England, as well as articulate Spenser's call for the timely application of "well guided speech" as the solution to these reckless disputes.

Keywords: polemic; allegory; satire; rhetoric

1. Introduction

In the collision of the topical and broadly allegorical modes that mark Spenser's method in his *Faerie Queene*, the student of his work finds many opportunities to read his commentary on features of Elizabethan politics and culture. Instructors can capitalize on Spenser's method and follow his example of illustrating moral and ethical concerns by concretizing them in identifiable fictional figures. One of the more puzzling instances of Spenser's allegorical and narrative strategy arises at the end of Book Five, the Legend of Arthegall. Having defeated the great wrong ("Grantorto") on Irena's behalf, and having restored the commonweal of Irena's island to a form of justice, the Knight of Justice is called back to the court of the Faerie Queene to render Gloriana further service ([1], 5.12.26–27). Upon gaining the "strand" of Faerie Land, he is immediately set upon by two hags and a monster: Envy, Detraction, and the Blatant Beast. This episode, placed at the very end of the twelfth canto of the book, puts the knight and his story in a remarkably unsettled position. There is a surprising amount of discord and even condemnation following what should have been occasion for a triumph. An experienced reader of Spenser would not necessarily find it surprising that any one of the six books of the poem ends with a continuation rather than a conclusion; this is after all the pattern that holds in each of the other books. Arthegall's strange and unaccustomed passivity in response to vicious and even physically disgusting attacks may strike a student as remarkable: he "seem'd of them to take no keepe," wordlessly passing on. What is more, he "forbids" his lethal iron man Talus from administering what would have been an entirely justifiable chastisement, instead keeping on his original course ([1], 5.12.42–43).

Arthegall's inaction here in Canto 12 can be at least partially explained by Spenser's topical political analysis in Book 5, especially its links to the trial and execution of Mary Queen of Scots on the one hand and the ongoing—for Spenser, immediately relevant—permutations of Elizabethan policy toward Ireland. In this closing episode of the book, Arthegall is often linked to Lord Grey, Lord Deputy Governor of Ireland from 1580–1582—for whom Spenser worked as secretary and about whom he writes in *A View of the Present State of Ireland* (published 1633). In the broader allegorical sense, throughout Book 5 we have been repeatedly shown how the operations of sovereign justice are both necessary and precarious. We are also shown how those same operations can be open to criticism, spite, and envy. In the case of Arthegall and the aftermath of his climactic battle with Grantorto, we are invited to see the criticism literally flung at the knight of justice (see [1], 5.12.39) as particularly unjust, especially given what we ourselves have observed in his conduct. In any case, however, we have to grapple with the fact that Arthegall does nothing in response to considerable provocation. His apparent indifference to the necessity of an active response has an effect far beyond himself and this one moment, allowing the Blatant Beast to spread destruction in the following book; the Beast spends eleven cantos eluding the grasp of Calidore, the knight of courtesy who has been tasked with bringing it to heel.

Students of Spenser might rightly ask why it should fall to the knight of courtesy rather than the knight of justice to subdue this monster. Arthegall has already proven his sufficiency against any foe, especially when paired with the rigor and power represented by Talus, so it is not a matter of ability. It may be better interpreted to students as a matter of relevance: Spenser assigns the Beast to Calidore partially because of the larger design of his "dark conceit," but also because the Blatant Beast represents social sins or interpersonal wrongs that fall outside or only liminally within the purview of the formal operations of justice. Accounts of the Blatant Beast, especially as it takes a central role in Book Six, therefore emphasize three points: first, that the Beast manifests its power through its teeth and its voice; second, that the Beast's attacks are aimed at the innocent or the heedless; and third, that the Beast's range carries it through all estates and degrees, leaving no one secure from the threats it represents. The teacher of Elizabethan history and culture can profitably use Spenser's allegorical method to examine the link between these characteristics of the Beast and one of the aforementioned features of Elizabethan popular culture: the burgeoning market for cheaply printed religious polemic, particularly Martin Marprelate's pamphlets and the flood of anti-Marprelate pamphlets that followed in the years 1589–1591. This controversy even in its earliest phases seemed in the eyes of many observers to have gotten out of hand, doing more to regenerate itself than to put theological or ecclesiological questions to rest. Much like Hooker's *Laws of Ecclesiastical Polity*, written to methodically defang the Presbyterian challenge to the Elizabethan settlement, the 1596 Second Part of *The Faerie Queene* comes along far too late to serve as a direct intervention in the specific controversy to which it seems to refer—but it does show that the discursive and rhetorical concerns highlighted by the brief Martinist pamphlet warfare are very much on Spenser's mind, requiring a discursive and allegorical response that highlights the social virtue of courtesy as the surest remedy.

2. Fighting the Blatant Beast

In the several descriptions we are given of the Blatant Beast, we notice that its power comes from or is focused on its mouth. We read that it "barks and bays" in response to the provocations of Envy and Detraction, to the point that all the air "rebellows" from its voice. Its "hundred tongues" bray at Arthegall, reinforcing and amplifying the attacks of the hags (see [1], 5.12.41). When reporting the appearance of the Beast to Calidore at the beginning of the following book ([1], 6.1.9), Arthegall describes its "thousand tongues," and again recounts how it "bayed and loudly barkt," though he also knows that it was not dangerous to him personally ("I knew my selfe from perill free"). In the final canto of Book Six, when the Beast is cornered and finally turns to fight Calidore, we read the description of its "iron teeth in ranges twaine" ([1], 6.12.26), and the horrors of its gaping mouth:

> And therein were a thousand tongs empight,
> Of sundry kindes, and sundry quality,
> Some were of dogs, that barked day and night,

And some of cats, that wrawling still did cry;
And some of Beares, that groynd continually,
And some of Tygres, that did seeme to gren,
And star at all, that ever passed by:
But most of them were tongues of mortall men,
Which spake reprochfully, not caring where nor when.

And them amongst were mingled here and there,
The tongues of Serpents with three forked stings,
That spat out poyson and gore bloudy gere
At all, that came within his ravenings,
And spake licentious words, and hatefull things
Of good and bad alike, of low and hie;
Ne Kesars spared he a whit, nor Kings,
But either blotted them with infamie,
Or bit them with his banefull teeth of iniury. ([1], 6.12.27–28)

Those "teeth" are described by the hermit in Canto Six as being "exceeding venemous and keene,/Made all of rusty yron, rankling sore,/That where they bite, it booteth not to weene/With salue, or antidote, or other mene/It euer to amend" ([1], 6.6.9). The damage done is certainly real enough, sometimes grievously so.

The Blatant Beast is associated with several figures in Book Six, several of whom refer at least glancingly to what the Beast's name means. In his annotated edition of *The Faerie Queene*, A.C. Hamilton identifies "blatant" as deriving from the verb "blatter" [2]. His reference points to the OED, which defines the word as "to speak or prate volubly" and provides an example from Hugh Latimer (1533): "Procuring also certain prechers to blatter agaynst me" [3]. Latimer's use of the term shows what we are supposed to understand, making links to slander, backbiting, nonsense, railing, and generally loose talk. The verb "to rail," like "snarling" or "biting" or "barking," words that show up frequently in the descriptions of the Beast, is explicitly used by Elizabethan satirists in the self-conscious revival of the Juvenalian tradition to describe their own tone; Marston's dedicatory poem "To Detraction" in his satire collection *The Scourge of Villainy* provides the whole gamut:

Foul canker of fair virtuous action,
Vile blaster of the freshest blooms on earth,
Envy's abhorred child, Detraction,
I here expose, to thy all-tainting breath,
The issue of my brain: snarl, rail, bark, bite,
Know that my spirit scorns Detraction's spite. ([4], lines 1–6).

Almost all of Marston's terms here are assigned by Spenser to figures associated with the Blatant Beast: it appears beside Envy and Detraction when Arthegall returns from his defeat of Grantorto. It also collaborates with the three brothers Despetto (spite), Decetto (deceit), and Defetto (blame) in the episode where it attacks and wounds Arthur's squire Timias ([1], 6.5.13–20). Envy, detraction, spite, blame, and deceit all describe malicious uses of language—uses that, significantly, may not be illegal although they would certainly be judged to be wrong by Spenser's usual ethical and moral standpoints.

The Blatant Beast is also associated with several other monstrous figures within and without the poem. Its presence as a questing beast, with reference to the original meaning of that name, is a clear nod to the monster of Arthurian myth [5]. As a fearsome and even ravenous canine creature, it resembles the Hyena sent to chase down Florimell in Book 3. When the hermit in 6.6 points out that the only way to avoid its poison is to avoid the occasion of its attack, we should recall the encounter between Guyon, the Knight of Temperance, and his adversaries Furor and Occasion in Book 2; Guyon has to learn to confront Occasion, lest Furor should become too powerful for him to handle. Though Spenser gives us two sets of parents for the Beast, Cerberus and Chimera in 6.1.8 and Echidna and Typhon in 6.6.11, the tie to the canine monster Cerberus and the three-formed Chimera is particularly important because, according to the *Spenser Encyclopedia*, Natale Conti's *Mythologiae* (1567) glosses Chimaera as a representation of the arts of rhetoric ([6], Book 9, Chapter 4) (Figure 1).

Figure 1. Natale Conti, "Sphinx and Chimaera" [6].

In the first appearance of the Beast, Spenser only has it make noise; Arthegall knows that its voice is a problem but remains confident that he is in no physical danger. As Book 6 carries us along, however, we recognize that the Beast can do far more serious damage, or "injury" , to all estates and degrees of person ([1], 6.12.28). This is indicated among other things by the progression of the descriptions in that particular stanza: from noise to poison to physical wounding. The middle cantos of Book 6 do in fact show examples of the progression described above, especially with the two attacks on Serena and Timias, a beautiful young lady representing tranquility in the first incident, and Arthur's errant squire in the second. These characters reveal how the Blatant Beast causes direct and fairly intimate harm.

Serena and Timias, their names indicating their own innocence and native goodness, are wounded by the Blatant Beast in two separate episodes wherein they, like Arthegall at the end of Book 5, think themselves secure. Their self-assurance of their security means that they remain heedless of the danger it represents. The Beast's attack on Serena—whose name belies how she is made victim in Canto 6—comes after she has been assured of both her own good reputation and her good pleasure; she has been embracing her lover and innocently weaving a garland "without suspect of ill or dangers hidden dred" ([1], 6.3.23). From her wandering the Blatant Beast bears her away in its mouth, piercing both her sides with its iron teeth. The wound proves to be nearly fatal, and would be if not for Calidore's pursuit; it only drops her to better flee from Calidore because it "durst not abide with Calidore to fight" ([1], 6.3.24–27). Its later assault on Timias makes use of similar language. Timias has been restored to the good graces of Belphoebe, his unattainable love, and finds himself "nether of enuy, nor of chaunge afeard/Though many foes did him malign." Finding him on a hunt for "saluage game," the beast both draws him into "danger of defame" and bites him with his "tooth impure" while luring him into the intended ambush by Defetto, Decetto, and Despeto ([1], 6.5.12–20). Though certainly hardy enough to withstand them at first, Timias requires the unlooked-for intervention of his master Arthur before he can put the threat to rest.

In both cases, however, we learn that the wounds caused by the Beast are not easily cured: as both Serena and Timias are caught when least aware of the danger, both of them also begin to suffer from inward corruption thanks to the poison of its "infamy":

> Such were the wounds, the which that Blatant Beast
> Made in the bodies of that Squire and Dame;
> And being such, were now much more increast,
> For want of taking heed unto the same,
> That now corrupt and cureless they became. ([1], 6.6.2)

The hermit who cures them both has to provide "counsell to the minde" to counteract the putrefaction of their "inner parts," using "fit speaches" and the "art of words" to provide the impetus toward healing that ultimately only Timias and Serena can provide to themselves by right thought and right conduct. In other words, the wounds heedlessly earned must be carefully and purposefully healed from within. Experienced readers of Spenser recognize at moments like this that Spenser's allegorical frame is pushing us to make some important connections; the Beast has created wounds we cannot help but associate with harmful uses of language—but language must also be used to heal those very same wounds. Unfortunately, the wounds are created with much greater speed than can possibly be brought to bear on their restoration—the latter is a slower process that even the hermit, with all his counsel, can only begin. The completion of the healing work has to be left up to the wounded figures themselves.

Serena and Timias are hardly alone in their suffering, though they are given a starring role in the middle of the book. As Calidore continues to pursue the Blatant Beast, we see that it has also cut a wide swath of destruction through court, city, town, country, and "priuate farms" ([1], 6.9.3) in an echo of what happens when Cupid runs away from Venus in Book 3 ([1], 3.6.13–16). Those locations illustrate briefly both the magnitude of Calidore's task and the breadth of the Beast's reach—how it affects all people. As this fictional frame expands to encompass more kinds of people, it can provide a teacher with shorthand descriptions of a political and religious issue that appeared to Elizabethan observers of all stripes to affect everyone. This breadth of range is emphasized in the final episode of the book, when Calidore follows the Blatant Beast's path through "all estates" in which it has left "massacres," finding that not even the clergy have been spared. Following this pursuit and its destruction, Calidore is finally able to use his shield to "suppresse, and forcibly subdew" the monster ([1], 6.12.31). Calidore's triumph is widely praised, and is matched with a fitting restoration of the destruction and spoils the Blatant Beast had caused. However, the book is not done before the Beast breaks its chain to cause even "more mischiefe and more scath … to mortall men, than he had done before," and at which point we see that it has broken free of the poem, victimizing the poet himself in addition to every other "degree and state" ([1], 6.12.39–40). Unlike many of Spenser's antagonists, the Blatant Beast is not tied to a particular genre, poem, location or circumstance; Error and Mammon are confined to their caves, Busyrane has his enchanted palace, while the Dragon and Grantorto each oppress a specific nation. The Blatant Beast, on the other hand, ranges freely and even promiscuously. Wherever it ranges, it does its characteristic "barking and biting" and "rends without regard of person or of time" ([1], 6.12.40), revealing the very same characteristics that made it fearsome from its first entry into the poem.

Each major adversary in the six books of The Faerie Queene is given qualities that are calibrated to reveal the crucial elements of each corresponding knight's quest and character. The part the Blatant Beast plays in both the plot and the symbolic development of Book 6 should indicate to students of his work how seriously Spenser, writing as a poet and as a political and social observer, takes the challenges of poetic and social discourse. The Blatant Beast is a monster that strikes with biting voice and biting teeth when its victims are least prepared to defend themselves; it is a monster that cannot be fully subdued either by force or by art; and it is a monster whose wounds are given by words and harm more than the body:

No wound, which warlike hand of enemy
Inflicts with dint of sword, so sore doth light,
As doth the poisonous sting, which infamy
Infixeth in the name of noble wight:
For by no art, nor any leaches might
It euer can recured be againe. ([1], 6.6.1)

And even when subdued by the operations of courtesy, it escapes to cause even greater harm.

Much of why Arthegall is not the man to subdue the Blatant Beast is implicit in these descriptions of the monster; from a strictly symbolic or allegorical standpoint, it is simply not his task. Every knight is given a quest—Grantorto's defeat belonged to Arthegall—the story must move on. But it is also not the case that the Knight of Justice has no reasonable connection to punishing verbal or rhetorical wrongs. In fact, Talus's handling of the revolutionary rhetoric of the Levelling Giant shows that there is a direct way for the rigorous hand of justice to deal with proud and swelling words ([1], 5.2.49—54). So too does the scene where we come upon Malfont, with his tongue nailed to a post as punishment for his "reviling," and "blasphemy," his "bold speeches," "lewd poems," and "rayling rhymes," and for his being a "welhed/Of euill words, and wicked sclaunders" ([1], 5.9.24–26). With his former name, "BON FONT," not quite completely obscured by his new name, "MAL FONT," he has apparently received notoriety for his ability as a poet, but he also chose some of those words carelessly—or with care for the wrong things. The link to Elizabeth's policies regarding spoken and written discourse is crucial for students to grasp because this is the ground from which so much Elizabethan social commentary arises. Utterances that could be construed as disloyal to the monarch, or to her political and—critically in the 1570's and 80's—ecclesiastical settlement, could and would contribute to widespread social disorder. It falls to the mechanisms of justice, then, to protect and reinstitute that order, just as Arthegall helps set the disordered realms under Radigund and Grantorto back into proper frame once he has won victory by his might. Among the many manifestations of how justice operates, these examples show that it can be profitably applied against disordered language. Yet Spenser recognizes, and uses the sixth book of his poem to show, that courtesy, with its foundation in self-control and its orientation toward social union, provides an even surer remedy to those same kinds of disorder.

3. The Blatter of Pamphlets

Spenser uses Calidore to at least provisionally or temporarily solve the discursive problems represented by the Blatant Beast because he is studying carefully the broader rhetorical challenges facing the English ecclesiastical landscape in the decades following the 1572 Admonition Controversy. These challenges exist in two realms at once. On the one hand, there is the problem of unregulated and even promiscuous speech—manifest most glaringly in the burgeoning world of cheap print—and its tendency to cross boundaries of decorum. On the other hand, there is the problematic relationship between religious belief and practice in the context of political and ecclesiastical conformity. In the pamphlet warfare of the late 1580's and 90's—the period during which Spenser was writing the *Faerie Queene*—these problems are dramatically manifest in the unauthorized publications of Martin Marprelate, and also the various writers hired and inspired to write pamphlets against him.

Though the Marprelate tracts are widely regarded as the most dramatic and rhetorically inventive of the pamphlets supporting the presbyterian critique of the Elizabethan church, and while they retain enough energy to merit a recent critical edition [7], they do represent only part of a varied and vigorous combat waged through the cheap press. It is therefore necessary to pair our appreciation of Marprelate's energetic attacks on the Elizabethan bishops with similarly close attention to the pamphlets written in defense of the Elizabethan church, or at least as attacks on the attacker. The pamphlets written from the establishment perspective highlight the rhetorical concerns inherent in pamphlet warfare in a way that Marprelate, going on the attack and with no reputation or establishment to defend, does not.

Many of the official responses to Puritan provocations—Marprelate's most dramatically—spend their energy not attempting to change people's minds about their theological or devotional commitments, but instead linking religious conformity to political order and pursuing remedies along those lines. Thomas Cooper's 1589 *Admonition to the People of England*, and the oft-referenced Paul's Cross sermon delivered by Richard Bancroft in February 1589, both official defenses against the early Marprelate tracts, explicitly reference this idea: to make common cause with Martin Marprelate, they assert, makes one not only an opponent of true religion, but also a common conspirator with Brownists, Anabaptists, Family-of-Loveists, and even Papists—all for the purpose of overturning good government and civil society. Bancroft, taking as his sermon text 1 John 4:1, warns that unless we "test the spirits" of the prophets speaking to us, we are at the mercy of "*Arrians, Donatists, Papists, Libertines, Anabaptists*, the *Familie* of love, and sundry other (I know not of what opinion) so many sectaries and schismaticks, as that in very deed divers do revolt daily to Papistrie, many are become meerly Atheists, and the best do stand in some sort at a gaze" [8]. The result is fearful to contemplate. As Thomas Cooper warns in his *Admonition*, "if this outragious spirit of boldenesse be not stopped speedily, I feare he wil proue himselfe to bee, not onely *Mar-prelate*, but *Mar-prince, Mar-state, Mar-lawe, Mar-magistrate*, and all together, vntil he bring it to an Anabaptisticall equalitie and communitie" [9]. The political, social, and moral disorder can be clearly discerned in the kind of language used to mock, back-bite, and rail:

> For, *Sermo est index animi*, that is, Such as the speeche is, such is the minde. *Ex abundantia cordis os loquitur*. It hath also in all Histories bene obserued, that loose boldenesse of minde toward the Superiours, is ioyned alwayes with contempt: and contemptuous boldenesse is the very roote and spring of discord, dissention, vprore, ciuill warres, and all desperate attemptes, that may breede trouble and danger in the State. [9]

What becomes clear when we read the pamphleteering surrounding and arising from the Marprelate Controversy is that the uproar itself, and its mode of argument by *ad hominem* attack and satirical extravagance, is for many observers more significant than the ecclesiastical matters allegedly under dispute. Cooper's many warnings about Marprelate's tone can be summed up in his comment that "not he that is railed at, but he that raileth, is the wretched man" ([9], p. 41). To return to Bancroft's sermon, his point is the same: when we read the intemperate words, we should recognize the intemperate spirits behind them and beware.

Martin Marprelate is all too aware of the unique possibilities represented by his ability to cause a commotion, and he certainly makes use of his readers' squeamishness as an element of his argument. For example, in one of Marprelate's most famous comments on the notoriety occasioned by his first pamphlet (The *Epistle* of October 1588), he gripes perhaps not entirely seriously that the "Puritans"—the very figures we might assume to be on his side in the ecclesiastical dispute — are angry with him for "jesting":

> The puritans are angry with me, I mean the puritan preachers. And why? Because I am too open. Because I jest. I jested, because I deal against a worshipful jester, D. Bridges, whose writings and sermons tend to no other end than to make men laugh. I did think that Martin should not have been blamed of the puritans, for telling the truth openly. For may I not say that John of Canterbury is a petty pope, seeing he is so? You must then bear with my ingramness. I am plain, I must needs call a spade a spade, a pope a pope. ([7], p. 53)

There is a carefully calibrated vocabulary and appeal to truth here: the jesting for which Marprelate is blamed, by both his enemies and his supposed allies, should be understood as a mode of discourse that is both paradoxically decorous and strenuously truthful. If it violates readers' expectations of how one should deal with such matters, the "indifferent reader" (to whom so many pamphlets are written) might need to examine the reasons for those expectations and whether they are answerable to the requirements of the present moment.

Martin's strategic "jesting" proved to be both incredibly potent for his own purposes and too seductive for many of his adversaries to resist. Having had the institutional heft of Bridges' *Defense of the Government Established* ridiculed in the first two Marprelate pamphlets, and the moral earnestness of Bancroft and Cooper turned to mockery in *Hay Any Work for Cooper* (March 1589), the next steps were for the defenders of the church to answer Martin "after their own vein" in writing [10]. Anti-Marprelate pamphleteers, then, joined playwrights and doggerel poets in counter-mockery of Marprelate's mockery. From the standpoint of policy, this seems like it was a necessity if only for the sake of form. Yet there appears to be deep discomfort with the moral compromises necessary to adopt Marprelate's "jesting" style. In even the most aggressive anti-Marprelate pamphlets, we read the negotiation between the risks of the railing style and the apparent righteousness of the cause of the Elizabethan bishops. In his epistle to "The Indifferent Reader," the writer of *Pappe with an Hatchet* (1589) is quick to provide a defense of the "undecent" characteristics of the style he has adopted. His discomfort is plain, and the defense implicitly admits moral compromise while also asserting that the "lavish" or jesting style is necessary because of the conditions Martin Marprelate has himself created:

> I seldome vse to write, and yet neuer writ anie thing, that in speech might seeme vndecent, or in sense vnhonest; if here I haue vsed bad tearmes, it is because they are not to bee answered with good tearmes: for whatsoeuer shall seeme lauish in this Pamphlet, let it be thought borrowed of Martins language. [11]

Martin in his self-defense, and the writer above in his, both point out that the apparent infelicities of their style are entirely attributable to the deficiencies of their adversaries. What results is a proliferation of the *tu quoque* style of argument, each attempting to out-rail the other.

There are plenty of examples in the anti-Marprelate pamphlets. Thomas Nashe uses three gossipy pamphlets in the persona of Pasquil, a name derived from a Roman statue associated with satire, to expose "Pruritan" foibles like ignorant preaching. He also taunts them with his customary bravado while glancing significantly at allegations of multifarious sins both lurid and banal.[1] Meanwhile, Catholic pamphleteers like the Jesuit Robert Parsons and Richard Verstegan write that the uproar surrounding this controversy reveals an ecclesiastical polity broken beyond recognition. As Parsons writes in his polemical *Advertisement Written to a Secretarie of my L. Treasurers of Ingland* (1592),

> he gathereth together divers particuler, & speciall causes of the troubles, and dangers of her Majestie, and Ingland, whereof the first and principall, and roote of the reste, is (as he saith) the greate and irreconcilable differences, and warres in Religion, not onely with the Catholiques, but especially betweene the protestants, and puritanes them selves, who he saith, are mortall enemies, and would have been longe agoe by the eares together, had not the feare of the Catholique helde them bothe in awe. He toucheth divers of their books written one against the other as *Martin Marprelate, Mar Martin; The Worke for the Cooper. The Countercuffe to Martin Junior; the Owles Almanack; the Pap with a hatchet, or countrycuffe. The Epistle to Huffe Ruffe, and Snuffe*; in which among other things is affirmed, that the Martinistes or Puritans are much more dangerous for domestical broyles, then the Spaniardes for open warres, which this answerer also confirmeth, for that they must needs (as he saith) hate her Majestie, & the protestante Councell most deadly. [12]

The titles he references are not merely Marprelate tracts; most of them are among those we classify as anti-Marprelate pamphlets—and the point he sardonically makes is that the "domestical broils" of the pamphleteers are far more dangerous to the commonwealth than any foreign Papist power.

---

1. Disappointingly, most of Pasquil's allegations were promised in what was sure to be a tremendously popular and (given its authorship) entertaining volume called *The Lives of the Saints*. Despite all of Pasquil's repeated promises, it never appeared.

Small wonder, then, given even this brief sampling, that slightly more removed observers like Ben Jonson and Francis Bacon write disappointed commentaries referencing not only the unlawful presbyterian pamphlets but also the licit, though equally immoderate, responses by the defenders of Whitgift's and Bancroft's policies. Jonson's comment on this ilk appears in his *Discoveries*:

> *Controvers. scriptores.*—Some controverters in divinity are like swaggerers in a tavern that catch that which stands next them, the candlestick or pots; turn everything into a weapon: ofttimes they fight blindfold, and both beat the air. [*More Andabatarum qui clausis oculis pugnant.*] The one milks a he-goat, the other holds under a sieve. Their arguments are as fluxive as liquor spilt upon a table, which with your finger you may drain as you will. Such controversies or disputations (carried with more labour than profit) are odious; where most times the truth is lost in the midst or left untouched. And the fruit of their fight is, that they spit one upon another, and are both defiled. These fencers in religion I like not. [13]

Bacon's firm admonition against treating the matters of the church in the language of the theater is the most famous comment on the controversy by far: "first of all, it is more than time that there were an end and surseance made of this immodest and deformed manner of writing lately entertained, whereby matters of religion are handled in the style of the stage" [14]. Countering Marprelate's assertion that the harsh style is an indicator of truth, Bacon points out that the harsh style is necessarily destructive in its lack of discipline and decorum. The bulk of Bacon's *Advertisement* repeats and expands on that assessment, casting critical blame at length in both directions.

These assessments are not limited to the rarefied judgments of poets laureate and chancellors; writers closer to the level of cheap print show some of the same concerns. Richard Harvey, brother of Spenser's friend and correspondent Gabriel Harvey, tries to offer an evenhanded warning in his pamphlet *Plain Percival the Peace-Maker*:

> Nay no further Martin, thou maist spet in that hole, for ile come no more there: here I pitch my staffe, and stand to vrge thee, with these premises aboue named: thou begannest first, and therefore giue not ouer last. Thy beginning was worst, let thine ending be best. Controuersies be meate and drinke to the people: but doo not cramme them with such gobbets, as may sticke in their throats, least they hang the head on the shoulder, like him that was slaine with an arrow at Tiburn prickes. That is a new kinde of diet, with all my hart. Yet sir, when the steele and the flint be knockde togither, a man may light his match by the sparkle: surely, but I thinke tinder be verie danke now adaies, and though it take fire quickly, yet it takes light by leisure: for there hath been striking and iarring euer since, and a great while before, that a learned man some what on thy side, Martin, seemed to persuade that contention for good matters was good: you should haue his words: but that Græcum est, non potest legi [Car.] and yet I see no more Candles tinded thē wont to be, but a great many Beacons more fired then ought to be. You shall neuer make me belieue, that many Arguments turne soonest to Agreements. [15]

If we look beneath the aggressively jocular tone, we can see that to Harvey, the "striking and jarring" is at the heart of his urgent concern. What is certain is that the firing of beacons and making of arguments puts the entire commonwealth in a precarious position. Even those readers convinced of the need for polemical defenses of truth—or attacks on heresy and disorder—cannot help but recognize a troubling paradox: books of controversy, or pamphlets of invective, accomplish little more than generating more books of controversy, or pamphlets of invective. As Jesse Lander clarifies in his *Inventing Polemic*,

> It is this public quality of "Bookes of Encounter" that guarantees their endlessness, for it becomes common to assume not simply that polemics can be answered but that they *must* be answered. In such a world to have had the final word was considered a victory. Martin Marprelate is not merely engaged in special pleading when he asserts that Cartwright bettered Whitgift in the Admonition Controversy simply because Whitgift failed

to answer Cartwright's last book. A printed book, far more than a circulated manuscript, was perceived to require a printed response, a response required because such a document was immediately seen to be attempting to reach a diverse audience, but also because from its beginnings print conferred a certain authority. [16]

Every printed pamphlet calls forth further printed pamphlets, each attempting to answer the former in tone and notoriety, and the reach of the conflict expands beyond the point of any possible reconciliation or resolution. As Joseph Black quips, "a dignified silence appears not to have been an option" [17]. The Blatant Beast is a vivid and active representation of what Lander and Black detect as features of a bellicose discursive mode, and as such can provide a local habitation and a name to crucial but apparently remote Elizabethan rhetorical concerns.

4. The Remedies of Courtesy

Students both of Spenser and of the cultural moment in which he is writing can find in his poem a rigorous engagement with both the matter and the form of what is described above. Spenser finds himself observing these doctrinal and ecclesiastical conflicts—he in fact had personal contacts with several of the parties involved in the conflict, including Richard Harvey and Thomas Nashe—and undoubtedly arrives at the same conclusion most of them assert: no matter the theological or doctrinal motivation behind it, immoderate language is itself a problem, and forecloses the possibility of any meaningful resolution. The repeated use of harsh invective, satire, and mockery can only break the communal bonds that make a church possible in any sense, regardless of the particularities of theological controversy. In the words of Spenser biographer Andrew Hadfield, "Spenser's religious position is less doctrinal or confessional in emphasis and more based on a commitment to the institution of the church as a means of incorporating the diverse believers who constitute a nation" [18]. Though written as a gloss on the July eclogue of Spenser's *Shepherd's Calender* (1579), an earlier work than *The Faerie Queene*, Hadfield's succinct description of the unifying role of the church does illustrate for us why Spenser's remedy for the rhetorical and discursive destructiveness of the Blatant Beast in Book 6 of the *Faerie Queene* must be the social and sociable value of courtesy, "which of all goodly manners is the ground,/And roote of ciuill conuersation" ([1], 6.1.1–3). Calidore, the knight of courtesy, is

> beloued ouer all,
> In whom it seemes, that gentlenesse of spright
> And manners mylde were planted naturall:
> To which he adding comely guize withall,
> And gracious speach, did steal mens hearts away. ([1], 6.1.2)

He is able to augment his natural gifts through close attention to the finest points of his conduct. This serves as the index to his moral qualities as well:

> he could wisely vse, and well apply,
> To please the best, and th'euill to embase.
> For he loathd leasing, and base flattery
> And loued simple truth and stedfast honesty. ([1], 6.1.3)

Students should not miss the ethical and affective ties here: Calidore's simple truth and steadfast honesty here is tied to gentleness of spirit, mild manners, and gracious speech. Whereas Marprelate claims truth as a kind of license to invent new canons of decorum, and in doing so sets in motion the destruction illustrated by the Blatant Beast, Calidore uses truth in conjunction with his native courtesy to please the best and "embase" the evil. What makes courtesy important in this polemical context is that the courteous man is able to speak and act well, even pleasingly, in any circumstance, no matter the degree or status of the persons involved. Because Calidore's speech is "gracious" and "true," he—like Arthur in Book 1 ([1], 1.7.42)—manifests the "civil conversation" that is the true sign of the courteous mind.[2]

The difference between words that bring healing, like Calidore's or Arthur's, and words that create wounds and division, like Marprelate's or Pasquil's, is reinforced in the person of the hermit in the middle canto of Book 6. The medicine he supplies to Timias and Serena reveals discourse that heals instead of wounding:

> One day, as he was searching of their wounds,
> He found that they had festred privily,
> And ranking inward with unruly stounds,
> The inner parts now gan to putrify
> That quite they seem'd past helpe of surgery,
> And rather needed to be disciplined
> With holesome reede of sad sobriety
> To rule the stubborne rage of passion blinde:
> Give salves to every sore, but counsell to the minde.
>
> So taking them apart into his cell,
> He to that point fit speaches gan to frame,
> As he the art of words knew wondrous well,
> And eke could doe, as well as say the same. ([1], 6.6.5–6)

The hermit is able to apply goodly and civil words to overcome railing and poisonous words and the wounds they have caused. In the context of the hermit and the wounding mouth of the Beast, there is another application to be made to the world of cheaply printed polemic and the risks it seems to pose. The Beast has its thousand tongues and many voices, highlighting more than cacophony and unpleasant noise. The thousand tongues, and the many realms through which the Beast tramples, show that its influence is both on and manifested through the multitude of readers well beyond the control of any authority. Put simply, you may be able silence the barking of the dogs, but not necessarily the "wrawling" of the cats ([1], 6.12.27).

One more example can help reinforce for students of Spenser how Calidore's courtesy provides a better solution to the discursive and social problems posed by the Beast. In the end of Book 6, when the Beast is nearing the end of its rampage through all the degrees and estates, it turns to the Church:

> Through all estates he found that he had past,
> In which he many massacres had left,
> And to the Clergy now was come at last,
> In which such spoile, such havocke, and such theft
> He wrought, that thence all goodnesse he bereft,
> That endless were to tell.
> . . .
> From thence into the sacred Church he broke,
> And robd the Chancell, and the deskes downe threw,
> And Altars fouled, and blasphemy spoke,
> And th'Images for all their goodly hew,
> Did cast to ground, whilest none was them to rew;
> So all confounded and disordered there. ([1], 6.12.23–25)

---

[2] It seems likely that Spenser is influenced in this phrase by Stephano Guazzo's four volume handbook of *Civil Conversation*, translated into English by George Pettie and Bartholomew Young in 1581 (the first three books) and 1586 (the fourth book). Guazzo's dialogue places "civil" conversation at the center and as the realization of all of the proper social virtues.

The church and the clergy stand defiled and defaced, even blasphemed—Spenser provides the latter as an inescapably verbal offense. In the end of the combat between the Beast and Calidore, we even see the beast compared to the Hydra, both many-headed and yet again many voiced. In an echo of the warnings voiced by Richard Bancroft, Thomas Cooper, and even Ben Jonson, the cacophony increases in intensity and scope to encompass physical wounding of people, and then increases even more to the ruin of church and commonwealth. In each case, the destruction of social amity is the precursor and symptom of more severe trouble. The social virtue of courtesy, showing as it does the combination of so many other virtues, is called on to fix the problems, hence Calidore's conditional victory. His victory echoes the remedy proposed by many who saw the controversies of the church and wished, regardless of their doctrinal positions, that moderate and apt speech might more profitably counter and even overcome the grievous proliferation of vain and destructive speech.

Conflicts of Interest: The author declares no conflict of interest.

References

1. Spenser, Edmund. *The Faerie Queene*. London: Printed for William Ponsonbie, 1596.
2. Spenser, Edmund. *The Faerie Queene*. Edited by A. C. Hamilton, Hiroshi Yamashita, Toshiyuki Suzuki and Shohachi Fukuda. Longman Annotated Poets. London: Longman, 2001, p. 599n.
3. "Blatant, adj and n." *OED Online*, December 2016. Oxford University Press. Available online: http://www.oed.com/view/Entry/19969?redirectedFrom=blatant (accessed on 28 January 2017).
4. Marston, John. "To Detraction I Present my Poesie." Available online: http://poetrynook.com/poem/detraction-i-present-my-poesie (accessed on 28 January 2017).
5. Hamilton, A.C., ed. "s.v. 'Blatant Beast'." In *The Spenser Encyclopedia*. Toronto: University of Toronto Press, 1990.
6. Conti, Natale. *Natalis Comitis mythologiae, sive explicationum fabularum. Libri decem in quibus omnia prope naturalis & moralis philosophie dogmata sub antiquorum fabulis contenta suisse demonstratur.* Venetiis: n.p., 1568, Available online: https://archive.org/details/image62A47MiscellaneaOpal (accessed 28 January 2017).
7. Joseph Black, ed. *The Martin Marprelate Tracts: A Modernized and Annotated Edition.* Cambridge: Cambridge University Press, 2008.
8. "A Sermon Preached at Paules Crosse the 9 of Februarie, being the First Sunday in the Paleament, Anno 1588 by Richard Bancroft D. of Divinitie, and Chaplane to the Honorable Sir Christopher Hatton Knight L. Chancelor of England." Available online: http://www.anglican.net/works/richard-bancroft-sermon-preached-at-pauls-cross-1588/ (accessed on 28 January 2017).
9. Cooper, Thomas. *An Admonition to the People of England. 1589.* Edited by Edward Arber. London: The English Scholar's Library, 1882, p. 31.
10. Peel, Albert, ed. *Tracts Ascribed to Richard Bancroft.* Cambridge: At the University Press, 1953, p. xviii.
11. John Lyly. "Pap with a Hatchet." In *Elizabethan and Jacobean Pamphlets.* Edited by George Saintsbury. Freeport and New York: Books for Libraries Press, 1970, p. 49.
12. Parsons, Robert. "Advertisement Written to a Secretarie of My L. Treasurers of Ingland." 1592. Available online: http://tei.it.ox.ac.uk/tcp/Texts-HTML/free/A09/A09610.html (accessed on 29 March 2017).
13. Jonson, Ben. "Timber: Or, Discoveries." In *Ben Jonson.* Edited by C. H. Herford, Percy Simpson and Evelyn Simpson. Oxford: Clarendon, 1947, vol. VIII, pp. 595–96.
14. Bacon, Francis. "An Advertisement Touching the Controversies of the Church of England." In *Francis Bacon.* Edited by Brian Vickers. Oxford: Oxford University Press, 1996, p. 3.
15. Harvey, Richard. *Plaine Percevall the Peace-Maker of Englande.* London, 1589, pp. 19–20.
16. Jesse Lander. *Inventing Polemic: Religion, Print, and Literary Culture in Early Modern England.* Cambridge: Cambridge University Press, 2006, p. 15.

17. Black, Joseph. "The Rhetoric of Reaction: The Martin Marprelate Tracts (1588–1589), Anti-Martinism, and the Uses of Print in Early Modern England." *Sixteenth Century Journal* 28 (1997): 707–25. [CrossRef]

18. Hadfield, Andrew. *Edmund Spenser: A Life*. Oxford: Oxford University Press, 2012, p. 138.

Article

Reformation Leads to Self-Reliance:
The Protestantism of Transcendentalism

Rachel B. Griffis

Department of Language and Literature, Sterling College, 125 W Cooper Ave, Sterling, KS 67579, USA;
rachel.griffis@sterling.edu; Tel.: +1-620-278-4326

Academic Editor: Christopher Metress
Received: 27 December 2016; Accepted: 14 February 2017; Published: 21 February 2017

Abstract: This article examines connections between the Protestant Reformation and American literature and argues that Protestantism's best expression exists in contemporary iterations of self-reliance. The first part focuses on William Ellery Channing's and Ralph Waldo Emerson's literary criticism of John Milton, a poet who represents the Protestant ideals these writers combine with American principles to develop the literary tradition. The second part discusses the trajectory of American literature in the nineteenth century and extends this discussion to current assumptions regarding teaching and learning.

Keywords: Protestantism; transcendentalism; self-reliance; Milton; Channing; Emerson

---

In 1775 when the British conservative Edmund Burke commented on revolutionary and religious zeal in America, he drew attention to the unique relationship between the Protestant Reformation and the identity of America, the site for what he called "the protestantism of the Protestant religion" ([1], p. 71). When the American transcendentalist literary movement emerged in the next century, the writers of this period also drew upon the Protestant Reformation to express the tenets of their own age. American literary critic and Catholic convert Orestes Brownson's aptly titled article "Protestantism ends in Transcendentalism" (1846) describes transcendentalism as "nothing but the fundamental principle of the Protestant reformation itself" ([2], p. 115). Similarly, Ralph Waldo Emerson, the quintessential transcendentalist, suggests the Protestant Reformation produced Calvinism, which "rushes to be Unitarianism, as Unitarianism rushes to be pure Theism" ([3], p. 117). Like Burke, Brownson and Emerson locate America as a place where the Reformation manifested itself, although they point to the movements of the nineteenth century, and not the founding of the country, as the furthest reaches of Protestant thought.

Historians, theologians, and literary scholars have long noted the complementary relationship between Protestantism and nineteenth century print culture in America. However, scholars have tended to discuss this relationship in terms of the eventual secularization of American culture rather than to consider literature as a significant medium for the continuation and development of American Protestantism, which may be most visible today in the cultural virtues of self-reliance.[1] This article will demonstrate the importance of teaching nineteenth American literature as a powerful agent for Protestantism as well as connect this century's literary and religious developments to current assumptions about learning and education. In the first part, I will suggest that the role many

---

[1] For example, Brad S. Gregory, whom I will reference in the body of the article, connects Protestantism to secularization when he argues that "the expansion of rights inaugurated by the right to religious liberty would eventually include the right to religious unbelief and the right to live in ways antithetical to Christian morality" ([4], p. 188). While I agree with Gregory that Protestantism set in motion the option of unbelief, my article focuses on the ways in which the culture of self-reliance, wrought from individual rights, is itself an expression of Protestantism and evidence of religiosity in America.

writers, specifically William Ellery Channing and Ralph Waldo Emerson, expected literature to play in American life is indicative of Protestantism's legacy in the United States. By examining Channing's and Emerson's criticism on John Milton, this section will highlight how they idealized literature as the conduit for the values and concepts of individualism, freedom, and self-government. The second part traces the role of literature in the moral lives of Americans through trends in the latter half of the nineteenth century and concludes with a discussion of education in light of the Reformation through an aspect of Protestantism that inspired many American writers: what Brownson describes as "the right of private judgment" ([2], p. 125).[2] Overall, I hope to show that the development of the American literary tradition reflects the far-reaching effects of the sixteenth century European Reformation, which distantly yet significantly inspired the literature of the United States to function as a moral voice in the lives of the people.

1. Protestantism Gives Way to Transcendentalism: Milton, Channing, and Emerson

In the first few decades of the nineteenth century, American writers became increasingly concerned with developing a literary tradition that was uniquely American and equal to England's. In 1815, Walter Channing lamented the absence of "a literature of our own" as he speculates whether,

> our venerable fathers, when they deserted their own country, bring with them a thread of that literary tissue, so varied, so rich, and so beautiful, which had been the result of the dignified and delightful labour of England through so many ages of its history? Have we, their descendants, united our industry to theirs? ([5], pp. 35–36)

Channing's desire for a specifically "American" literature demonstrates his concern that the nation's writers produce works exemplifying the lives and values of American people in a way that equals, if not rivals, creative works by the British. In 1820, the British writer Sydney Smith fanned the fires when he taunted Americans regarding their literature. "In the four quarters of the globe," he writes, "who reads an American book? Or goes to an American play? Or looks at an American picture or statue?" ([6], p. 79). The nation's writers in the first half of the nineteenth century responded to remarks such as Channing's and Smith's by building a national literature, of which the transcendentalists were a vital part.

The transcendentalists' vision for a national literature was inspired by their moral, Protestant-inflected ideals as much as their patriotism, an important point for teachers and students of the Reformation and the American literary tradition. F.O. Matthiessen acknowledges the moral undertones of this literary movement when he writes, "the transcendent theory of art is a theory of knowledge and religion as well" ([7], p. 31). More pointedly, Perry Miller asserts "that the Transcendental movement is most accurately to be defined as a religious demonstration," and, "Neither Emerson nor Thoreau conceived of himself as an artist, but each of them came close—perilously close perhaps—to imagining himself a prophet" ([8], pp. 8–9). As Matthiessen's and Miller's comments show, many of the transcendentalists studied today by undergraduates and included in anthologies believed their objectives were religious ones and that they furthered the efforts of the sixteenth century reformers. For example, Margaret Fuller, hoping to renew what she calls the Protestants' "great principle," writes to support what she understands as the reformers' original mission: "respect for the right of private judgment and the decision of conscience in the individual" ([9], p. 93). The novelist Catharine Maria Sedgwick celebrates "the great principle achieved and fixed by the Protestant battle—the right of private judgment" as she berates the Calvinists for obstructing

---

2   Many other nineteenth century authors used this phrase to refer to the accomplishments of the Protestant Reformation, including Catharine Maria Sedgwick and Margaret Fuller, who will be cited in this article.

this principle ([10], p. 338).[3] The Unitarian minister William Ellery Channing, the older brother of Walter, calls for the continuation of the Reformation in his promotion of Unitarianism because "a Papal dominion is perpetuated in the Protestant church" ([12], p. 101). These statements, which express the common goals of the European reformers and the transcendentalists, demonstrate how many American writers in the nineteenth century viewed themselves as stewards of Protestantism in the New World and not necessarily apostates who sought to liberate others from religion. They were instead seeking the fulfillment of freedom promised by the Reformation.[4]

Emerson, perhaps the most studied and influential of the transcendentalists, writes about movements such as the Protestant Reformation and the American Revolution as steps in the path to self-reliance, the ultimate form of human freedom. He suggests that Protestantism progresses into such movements as "Calvinism into Old and New schools; Quakerism into Old and New," as a result of one "key" phenomenon: "the mind had become aware of itself" ([3], pp. 325–26). Emerson goes on to describe and celebrate the progress of human culture toward his self-reliant ideals:

> Men grew reflective and intellectual. There was a new consciousness. The former generations acted under the belief that a shining social prosperity was the beatitude of man, and sacrificed uniformly the citizen to the State. The modern mind believed that the nation existed for the individual, for the guardianship and education of every man. This idea, roughly written in revolutions and national movements, in the mind of the philosopher had far more precision; the individual is the world. ([3], p. 326)

The sixteenth century European Reformers and the eighteenth century American Revolutionaries, Emerson suggests, had conceived of new religions and nations while unwittingly grasping at the realization of the individual, to which the transcendentalists gave release with works like "Self-Reliance" (1841) and *Walden* (1854). In answering the call for a national literary tradition and furthering the work of the Protestant Reformation, Emerson argues that both government and religion should serve the individual, whom he proclaims, "is the world" ([3], p. 326). Or, as Henry David Thoreau states, "Now that the republic—the *res-publica*—has been settled, it is time to look after the *res-privata*—the private state" ([14], p. 174). The Protestant Reformation and the founding of the United States were, in the transcendentalists' view, events that would culminate in their own movement. As Thoreau writes, they then turned to "the private state" to advance inner freedom, as they believed Americans needed to be liberated from tradition and authority, and that literature was a particularly well-suited medium for their message of freedom ([14], p. 174).[5]

Emerson and Channing both produced essays in the 1820s and 1830s that reveal the influence of Protestantism in the American literary tradition, and these works help students to understand better the ideas expressed in more familiar transcendentalist texts such as "Self-Reliance" and *Walden*. In his "Remarks on National Literature" (1830), Channing conveys aspirations for a literature that accomplishes work nearly indistinguishable from that of religion and the clergy. He hopes literature can "produc[e] superior men," and he states, "We want a literature, in which genius will pay supreme, if not undivided homage, to truth and virtue" and which "will give place to a wise moral judgment; which will breathe reverence for the mind, and elevating thoughts of God" ([12], pp. 168, 185). Moreover, Channing's vision that the nation's literature "will pay supreme, if not undivided" attention

---

[3] Catharine Maria Sedgwick also positively refers to Burke's description of religion in America in *The Linwoods* (1835), a reference that indicates American writers' interest in promoting the principles of Protestantism in literature and culture ([11], p. 41).

[4] Alexis de Tocqueville, a French writer who visited America in the 1830s, affirms how the Americans understand their Protestant heritage. He writes that Americans, "after having shaken off the authority of the pope, acknowledged no other religious supremacy: they brought with them into the New World a form of Christianity, which I cannot better describe, than by styling it a democratic and republican religion" ([13], p. 245).

[5] It is important to note that the transcendentalists' preoccupation with freedom did not exclude the question of slavery, though they held that inner liberty was the highest form of freedom. They were indeed aware of the contradictions in American thought that allowed the Declaration of Independence and the institution of slavery to co-exist.

to a morality that results in "reverence for the mind" along with "elevating thoughts of God" reveals the particularly Protestant declensions of religion in nineteenth century America, which focused on elevating both humanity and God ([12], p. 185). Channing's and Emerson's literary criticism also provides further insights into the transcendentalists' expectations for literature. Their admiration for John Milton, the British, Puritan poet of *Paradise Lost* (1667), specifically expresses how they envision a literature that celebrates their Protestant ideals and values, including individualism, freedom, self-government, and the elevation of humanity.[6] As Brad S. Gregory explains, Milton is a "radical Protestant" who "simply spelled out what was implicit in Luther, Calvin, and every other sixteenth-century Protestant reformer," an explanation that sheds light on the transcendentalists' regard for this poet and their decision to draw upon him as they created their literary movement ([4], p. 215).

Respectively written in 1826 and 1838, Channing's and Emerson's essays on Milton depict the poet as a progressive Protestant with ideas that anticipate and resemble the transcendentalists' views in nineteenth century America. Channing's essay on Milton emphasizes the poet's commitment to freedom by highlighting the ways in which the poet interacts with civic and religious issues, a commitment he argues is motivated by Milton's elevation of freedom of the mind. Channing states,

> Freedom, in all its forms, and branches, was dear to him, but especially freedom of thought and speech, of conscience and worship, freedom to seek, profess, and propagate truth [. . .] The tyranny which he hated most was that which broke the intellectual and moral power of the community. The worst feature of the institutions which he assailed was, that they fettered the mind. ([16], p. 508)

Writing against the institutional "fetter[ing] of the mind," and the inhibition of people's "moral" and "intellectual" "power[s]," Channing emphasizes the incorporeal aspects of freedom with his references to "thought" and "conscience" ([16], p. 508). Like Channing, Emerson considers Milton "an apostle of freedom," especially highlighting him as an individualist ([17], p. 271). For example, writes Emerson, "he is never lost in a party. His private opinions and conscience always distinguish him" ([17], p. 270). Emerson also praises Milton's rejection of spiritual authority by his absence from church, noting, "The most devout man of his time, he frequented no church" ([17], p. 273). Emerson admires Milton for his spiritual autonomy, for the independence of heart and mind to eschew church authority and to take responsibility for his own spirituality, tendencies Emerson himself also possessed.[7]

Milton's role as "an apostle of freedom" also gives both Emerson and Channing a way to express their high view of human nature, a view they believed had its roots in the Protestant cause, but had been obstructed by Calvinism in America ([17], p. 271). For example, as he writes about Milton's elevation of humanity, Channing suggests that Milton's contribution to theology is an emphasis on the human aspects of God. He argues that Milton "is more disposed than Christians in general to conceive of the Supreme Being under the forms and affections of human nature," adding, "He thought, not so much what man is, as of what he might become" ([16], pp. 511, 509). Emerson, similarly, counts among Milton's great achievements his resolve "to raise the idea of Man in the minds of his contemporaries and of posterity" ([17], p. 254). Taking his characteristic shots at Calvinism, Emerson also praises Milton for *Paradise Lost*, a work he interprets as glorifying the first man. Writing unabashedly about the glories of this first man, Emerson suggests, allows the poet to "reascend to the height from which

---

6   Milton was very popular among Americans in both the eighteenth and nineteenth century. Twenty-eight editions of Milton's poetry were published by American printers between 1787 and 1815 (Sensabaugh [15], p. 17).

7   The Milton presented in this article is as Channing and Emerson interpret him, and I am interested in that interpretation for what it reveals about Channing and Emerson. Many Miltonists indeed read the poet as more Puritan than transcendentalist. For example, regarding *Paradise Lost*, Stanley Fish has argued in *Surprised by Sin* that Milton tricks the reader into indulging his or her disorderly sympathies, wherein "he places himself in a compromising situation," which is that "He has taken his eyes from its proper object—the glory of God and the state of his own soul" ([18], p. 12). In doing so, Milton reinforces the concept of original sin, a concept which Channing and Emerson found repugnant and wanted to minimize in their reading of Milton.

our nature is supposed to have descended," a position the transcendentalists believed Americans encumbered with Calvinism had forgotten or perhaps deliberately ignored ([17], p. 274).[8]

Channing's and Emerson's aspirations for American literature in their essays point to the Protestant roots of their ideas and how morality was promoted through literature in the nineteenth century. Furthermore, connecting the Reformation and transcendentalism shows that the Protestants' contentions and causes, such as their distrust of authority and their elevation of the individual, lead to the kind of thinking eventually articulated by Emerson. Like Milton, Emerson expresses such radically Protestant sentiments in "Self-Reliance" as "To believe your own thought, to believe that what is true for you in your private heart is true for all men,–that is genius" ([19], p. 29). In agreement with Burke's and Brownson's statements which began this article, Gregory's theological genealogy suggests that the United States was the place where "formally [...] individuals, their rights secured by the state, would choose their own goods as they chose their own beliefs" ([4], p. 217). This assertion effectively articulates in political terms what Emerson claims for the inner lives of individual Americans. Joe B. Fulton more directly establishes a lineage between the reformers and transcendentalists when he writes that "New England's new theological and literary movement [was] the logical outcome of Luther nailing his ninety-five theses to the church door in Wittenberg and Calvin penning his *Institutes* while exiled in Switzerland" ([20], pp. 404–5). These genealogies point to the possibility that literature was not only the medium through which Americans received the cultural virtues of self-reliance, but also the most effective conduit for the growth of Protestantism, from which self-reliance originates.

2. American Literature's Moral Purpose: Individual Interpretation and Learning

Protestantism continued to influence American literature in the movements that followed transcendentalism, a lineage particularly evident in the ways literature participated in the moral lives of Americans during and after the Civil War. In his call for a national literary tradition, Channing states that poetry takes on salvific proportions, a role that will become more evident as the nineteenth century progresses. Poetry, Channing writes, "the divinest of all arts," "has the same tendency and aim with Christianity: that is, to spiritualize our nature" ([16], p. 498). Miller explains such statements as a result of the "precommitment" of the transcendentalists "to making literature a substitute for religion" ([8], p. 14). One of the results of poetry having "the same tendency and aim with Christianity," as Channing puts it, is that literature becomes a source for moral questions and answers and the nation's writers become the clergy ([16], p. 498). For example, a character in one of William Dean Howells's novels, *The Rise of Silas Lapham* (1884–1885), asks a minister at a dinner party if he is "envious" of the power of novels in people's lives ([21], p. 175). Similarly, in one of Mark Twain's sketches, he writes,

> nine-tenths of all kindness and forbearance and Christian charity and generosity in the hearts of the American people to-day, got there by being filtered down from their fountain-head, the gospel of Christ, *through dramas and tragedies and comedies on the stage, and through the despised novel* [...] and NOT from the drowsy pulpit! ([22], p. 53)

These developments in American literature point to the deepening moral imperatives of the nation's writers in the nineteenth century and the waning authority of the very sources of oppression Emerson had warned his readers about, such as the church and tradition. In my classroom, I ask my students to identify Protestant and Emersonian sentiments in works from and after the Civil War period not only to help them make connections between sixteenth century Europe and American literature but also to encourage them eventually to recognize the prevalence of Emersonian Protestantism in contemporary culture.

---

[8] Given Milton's association with Calvinism, a branch of Christianity the transcendentalists eschewed, Emerson and Channing thus worked to curtail this tradition's impact on Milton's thinking. Channing, for example, writes, "Swayed as Milton was by the age in which he lived, his spirit could not be subdued to the heart-withering faith of the Genevan school" ([16], p. 517).

Other historical and cultural phenomena in the nineteenth century contributed to the elevation of literature in the moral lives of Americans, and several are useful for helping students to trace the links between the Reformation and American literature and culture. Two are worth mentioning here for their relationship to reading and learning: Protestant print culture and skepticism regarding the authority of the Bible. Protestant print culture, with its emphasis on individual Bible reading and the narrative testimonies of believers, promoted the dissemination of morals through literary texts. David S. Reynolds suggests that clergy adapted their work according to the literary market, "knowing they had to compete with novels for the public's attention," thus creating their own publications ([23], p. 15). In *The Word in the World* (2004), Candy Gunther Brown studies evangelical print culture specifically, showing how literature was a fundamental aspect of this branch of Protestantism. Although many of the writers Brown highlights would not endorse the cynical attitudes of Howells and Twain regarding the role of clergy and sermons in the Christian life, her research nevertheless shows that literature was essential to the success of evangelicalism. She explains, "Readers and writers made progress in a spiritual journey through textual practices, giving and receiving encouragement from other readers and writers, by placing themselves within the story of the church's communal pilgrimage" ([24], p. 11). Although these evangelical communities did not follow, at least directly, Emerson's enjoinder, "Nothing can bring you peace but yourself," they expressed self-reliant ideals in their high view of literature's ability to augment the individual's moral life ([19], p. 52). They also had similar, non-aesthetic goals. As Brown asserts, "Usefulness, rather than genre or form, was the primary characteristic that marked texts as evangelical" ([24], p. 7). Moreover, as Channing's and Emerson's criticism of Milton indicates, evangelical print culture was preoccupied with conveying certain ideas rather than developing pristine literary forms.[9]

Additionally, the authority of the Bible strenuously came under question during the Civil War, a conflict this holy book failed to solve. Mark A. Noll argues that this conflict "revealed a significant theological crisis," which perhaps suggests how and why, for many Americans, literature replaced the sermon as the conduit for morals ([27], p. 6). Harriet Beecher Stowe's *Uncle Tom's Cabin* (1854), for example, depicts the opposing views of Bible-readers in relation to slavery while employing the sentimental formula to show her readers which interpretation is most moral. Furthermore, in her concluding remarks, she describes the Protestant, self-reliant way an American can grow in morality and thus function as a responsible and compassionate member of a community. She famously states, "every individual can judge," and "they can see to it that *they feel right*" ([28], p. 624). Stowe's vision for advancing a moral view of slavery and human rights assumes, as Gregory points out, that people "would choose their own goods as they chose their own beliefs," and so she undertook a persuasive writing project that would convict individuals through their feelings to support the abolition of slavery ([4], p. 217). Outsold only by the Bible in the nineteenth century, *Uncle Tom's Cabin* reveals, perhaps unwittingly, that Scripture was not reliable for answering the slavery question. Instead, this novel suggests that individual sentiments, albeit Christian inflected ones, would restore order and morality in the country, a suggestion that points to the effects of the Protestant Reformation on the development of American literature. As Gregory suggests,

> From the outset of the Reformation to the present day, the insistence on *sola scriptura* and its adjuncts has produced and continues to yield an open-ended range of incompatible interpretations of the Bible, with centrifugal social and wide-ranging substantive implications for morality. ([4], p. 205)

---

[9] As Anne C. Rose points out, "the Transcendentalists began their careers as reformers of religious philosophy," and as a result, the literature tends to have a moral purpose over an aesthetic one ([25], p. 39). A focus on content over form is a characteristic of the transcendentalists, and this focus is evident in their criticism of Milton, which emphasizes "the ethical and didactic excellences in Milton" while overlooking "a technical examination of the stylistic features" (Pettigrew [26], p. 58).

The American literary tradition, though making no claims to function as the sacred word of God, encourages the self-reliant protesters and descendants from the sixteenth century to interrogate texts, to arrive at their own interpretations and thus their own beliefs.

Gregory's observation regarding the "adjuncts" of *"sola scriptura"* is evident in Emerson's statement at the outset of "Self-Reliance" quoted above: "To believe your own thought, to believe that what is true for you in your private heart is true for all men,–that is genius" (Gregory [4], p. 205; Emerson [19], p. 29). The elevation of believing for oneself and thinking for oneself are concepts to which the Reformation gave rise, concepts which Emerson expressed explicitly, and which American education often takes for granted. It is cliché among educators to state that one's goals for a particular course are for students "to think for themselves," as such goals are assumed. In *Why Read?* (2004), Professor Mark Edmundson expresses the heritage of Emersonian self-reliance in the academy when he argues that students must decide for themselves which goods they will pursue on their intellectual journeys "through encounters of the best that has been known and thought" ([29], p. 86). He continues,

> We all have promise in us; it is up to education to reveal that promise, and to help it unfold. The power that is in you, says Emerson, is new in nature. And the best way to release that power is to let students confront viable versions of experience and take their choices. ([29], p. 86)

David Foster Wallace also articulates these educational principles in his famous commencement address when he asserts, "'Learning how to think' really means learning how to exercise some control over *how* and *what* you think" ([30], p. 53). Edmundson's and Wallace's lofty expressions are what Brownson describes pejoratively as the natural consequences of "the right of private judgment," though Edmundson's vision in which students seriously consider "the best that has been known and thought" and "take their choices" is entirely sincere (Brownson [2], p. 125; Edmundson [29], p. 86).

On the other hand, what Brownson perhaps anticipates in his critique of Protestantism and transcendentalism is that American students will resist learning because of the Emersonian platitudes they have internalized, often without having read Emerson himself. Emerson's statements—"imitation is suicide," "Trust thyself," and "Whoso would be a man must be a nonconformist"—inform many students' perspectives on education ([19], pp. 29–31). Or, they echo Thoreau, who criticizes formal schooling and suggests that students "should not *play* life, or *study* it merely, while the community supports them at this expensive game, but earnestly *live* it from beginning to end" ([31], p. 38). As Edmundson concedes, students often protect themselves from learning that requires them to "reveal and risk [themselves]," only tolerating the kind of knowledge that "allow[s] [them] to keep [their] cool" ([29], p. 13). They choose the least demanding goods which require minimal change and growth. Alluding to the transcendentalists' ideals, R.R. Reno explains Edmundson's concession by drawing attention to the shortcomings of current and prevalent American assumptions about education. For Reno, learners lack a disposition of "docility," or, "the capacity to be guided or led" ([32], p. 98). More pointedly, he states,

> neither students nor teachers are disposed to accept the instruction of the wise, whose voices continue to live in the great books of the past. We will not allow ourselves to be taught about spiritual, moral, and political realities. We are indocile to tradition. ([32], p. 100)

Reno's observation that students and teachers alike are "indocile to tradition" recalls the individualism of the transcendentalists, which they inherited from the Protestants who empowered the individual with the right of private judgment. This indocility is why Brownson, according to Carl F. Krummel, believed that Catholicism would "[balance] the democratic tendency with respect for authority" ([33], p. 24).

Gregory's account of the Protestant perspective on authority, specifically that "in the end one was one's own sovereign authority, answerable only to God," is also an apt description of the transcendentalists' views which persist in the "indocility" that has become commonplace in contemporary American culture ([4], p. 215). In Brownson's words, "Protestantism, then, necessarily lays down the principle, that each and every man is in himself the exact measure of truth and goodness,—the very fundamental proposition of transcendentalism" ([2], p. 127). Gregory argues that this high view of the individual and the subsequent impoverished view of authority "undermined the importance of counsel that shaped one's moral formation in a moral community" ([4], p. 215). Its current impact on educational communities is that the virtue of docility, as Reno notes, is neither practiced nor recognized. The great literary critic R.W.B. Lewis also makes the connection between transcendentalism and extreme individualism when he aptly suggests, in *The American Adam* (1955) that "The dismissal of the past has been only too effective: America, since the age of Emerson, has been persistently a one-generation culture" ([34], p. 9).

Teaching students who have internalized Emerson thus presents its own challenges, as few of us have the audacity of Stanley Hauerwas, who, as one student reports, dismantles Emersonian assumptions by announcing in his classroom, "I don't want you to think for yourselves. I want you to think like me" ([35], p. 26). Furthermore, as Edmundson and Wallace demonstrate, the American ideal for Protestant-inflected, democratic education has worthwhile and moral ends. Edmundson argues that American education has the potential to influence students to become "wiser, more vital, kinder, sadder, more thoughtful, more worth the admiration of their children [. . .] because they are free to become who they aspire to be after their own peculiar fashions" ([29], p. 142). On the other hand, Gregory's argument about the Reformation questions whether liberating students, in Edmundson's words, "to become who they aspire to be after their own peculiar fashions" can possibly produce the virtuous results Edmundson lists because of the radical individualism it encourages ([29], p. 142). Alasdair MacIntyre, in *After Virtue* (1981), a project similar to Gregory's, suggests more directly that Edmundson's aspirations are impossible given the "grave disorder" of "the language of morality" in our culture ([36], p. 2).

Gregory's and MacIntyre's critiques of post-Reformation culture demonstrate how many educators are indeed working against cultural assumptions regarding the individual and the purpose of learning, assumptions wrought from Protestantism and self-reliance. For such teachers, both Protestant and Catholic, it may be helpful to consider seriously not only Brownson's assertion that "transcendentalism is the strict logical termination of Protestantism," but the history of transcendentalism, which is recognized as the first major literary movement in the United States ([2], p. 127). In this history, Miller states that transcendentalism itself was "no longer visible" by 1850, concluding that "it had won its point" when "America adopted it and made it orthodox" ([8], pp. 13–14). Given how deeply Americans internalized its principles, the school of transcendentalism was, according to Miller, no longer needed. As many educators today will affirm, students tend to step into our classrooms with "Trust thyself" at their fingertips and with internal barriers fully constructed against docility ([19], p. 30). If, as the nation's writers have suggested, transcendentalism is the progression and outgrowth of the Reformation, educators should consider the possibility that Protestantism is indeed most alive in self-reliance. Emersonian perspectives on teaching, learning, and the individual are therefore religious issues educators must engage as such in order to communicate with their students about the moral traditions to which they may be indocile.

Conflicts of Interest: The author declares no conflict of interest.

References

1. Edmund Burke. *Burke's Politics: Selected Writings and Speeches of Edmund Burke on Reform, Revolution, and War.* Edited by Ross J. S. Hoffman and Paul Levack. New York: Alfred A. Knopf, 1949.
2. Orestes Brownson. *The Works of Orestes A. Brownson.* Edited by Henry F. Brownson. Detroit: Thorndike Nourse Publisher, 1884, vol. VI.

3.   Ralph Waldo Emerson. *The Complete Works of Ralph Waldo Emerson*. Boston: Houghton Mifflin Co., 1883, vol. X.

4.   Brad S. Gregory. *The Unintended Reformation: How a Religious Revolution Secularized Society*. Cambridge: Belknap Press, 2012.

5.   Walter Channing. "Reflections on the Literary Delinquency of America." *North American Review* 2 (1815): 33–43.

6.   Sydney Smith. "Statistical Annals of the United States of America." *Edinburgh Review* 33 (1820): 69–80.

7.   Francis Otto Matthiessen. *American Renaissance: Art and Expression in the Age of Emerson and Whitman*. New York: Oxford University Press, 1941.

8.   Perry Miller. *The Transcendentalists: An Anthology*. Cambridge: Harvard University Press, 1950.

9.   Margaret Fuller. *Margaret Fuller, Critic: Writings from the New-York Tribune 1844–1846*. Edited by Judith Mattson Bean and Joel Myerson. New York: Columbia University Press, 2000.

10. Catharine Maria Sedgwick. *The Life and Letters of Catharine M. Sedgwick*. Edited by Mary E. Dewey. New York: Harper & Brothers Publishers, 1871.

11. Catharine Maria Sedgwick. *The Linwoods, or, "Sixty Years Since" in America*. Edited by Maria Karafilis. Hanover: University Press of New England, 2002.

12. William Ellery Channing. *Selected Writings*. Edited by David Robinson. New York: Paulist Press, 1985.

13. Alexis de Tocqueville. *Democracy in America*. Translated by Henry Reeve. Edited by Isaac Kramnick. New York: W. W. Norton & Company, 2007.

14. Henry David Thoreau. *Reform Papers*. Edited by Wendell Glick. Princeton: Princeton University Press, 1973.

15. George F. Sensabaugh. *Milton in Early America*. Princeton: Princeton University Press, 1964.

16. William Ellery Channing. *The Works of William E. Channing*. Boston: American Unitarian Association, 1901.

17. Ralph Waldo Emerson. *The Conduct of Life and Natural History of Intellect and Other Papers*. Boston: Houghton Mifflin Company, 1929.

18. Stanley Fish. *Surprised by Sin: The Reader in Paradise Lost*, 2nd ed. Cambridge: Harvard University Press, 1997.

19. Ralph Waldo Emerson. *Essays: First and Second Series*. New York: Library of America, 1991.

20. Joe B. Fulton. "Reason for a Renaissance: The Rhetoric of Reformation and Rebirth in the Age of Transcendentalism." *The New England Quarterly* 80 (2007): 383–407. [CrossRef]

21. William Dean Howells. *The Rise of Silas Lapham*. New York: W. W. Norton & Company, 1982.

22. Mark Twain. *What is Man? and Other Philosophical Writings*. Edited by Paul Baender. Berkeley: University of California Press, 1973.

23. David S. Reynolds. *Beneath the American Renaissance: The Subversive Imagination in the Age of Emerson and Melville*. New York: Oxford University Press, 1988.

24. Candy Gunther Brown. *The Word in the World: Evangelical Writing, Publishing, and Reading in America, 1789–1880*. Chapel Hill: University of North Carolina Press, 2004.

25. Anne C. Rose. *Transcendentalism as a Social Movement, 1830–1850*. New Haven: Yale University Press, 1981.

26. Richard C. Pettigrew. "Emerson and Milton." *American Literature* 3 (1930): 45–59. [CrossRef]

27. Mark A. Noll. *The Civil War as a Theological Crisis*. Chapel Hill: University of North Carolina Press, 2006.

28. Harriet Beecher Stowe. *Uncle Tom's Cabin, or, Life Among the Lowly*. Edited by Ann Douglas. New York: Penguin Books, 1981.

29. Mark Edmundson. *Why Read?* New York: Bloomsbury, 2004.

30. David Foster Wallace. *This is Water: Some Thoughts, Delivered on a Significant Occasion, about Living a Compassionate Life*. New York: Little, Brown and Co., 2009.

31. Henry David Thoreau. *Walden, Civil Disobedience, and Other Writings*. Edited by William Rossi. New York: W.W. Norton & Company, 2008.

32. Russell Ronald Reno. *Fighting the Noonday Devil and Other Essays Personal and Theological*. Grand Rapids: William B. Eerdmans Publishing Company, 2011.

33. Carl F. Krummel. "Catholicism, Americanism, Democracy, and Orestes Brownson." *American Quarterly* 6 (1954): 19–31.

34. Richard Warrington Baldwin Lewis. *The American Adam: Innocence, Tragedy, and Tradition in the Nineteenth Century*. Chicago: University of Chicago Press, 1955.

35. William Cavanaugh. "Stan the Man: A Thoroughly Biased Account of a Completely Unobjective Person." In *The Hauerwas Reader*. Edited by John Berkman and Michael Cartwright. Durham: Duke University Press, 2001, pp. 17–32.

36. Alasdair MacIntyre. *After Virtue: A Study in Moral Theory*, 3rd ed. Notre Dame: University of Notre Dame Press, 2007.

Article

How Not to Link the Reformation and Science: Reflections on Brad Gregory's *The Unintended Reformation*

Josh A. Reeves

Samford University, Samford Center for Science and Religion, 800 Lakeshore Drive, Birmingham, AL 35229, USA; jareeves@samford.edu; Tel.: +1-205-726-2940

Academic Editor: Christopher Metress
Received: 3 February 2017; Accepted: 1 May 2017; Published: 4 May 2017

Abstract: This article evaluates Brad Gregory's argument in *The Unintended Reformation* that links the Reformation with the rise of secular science. I provide an overview of Gregory's claims and make two criticisms, arguing that Gregory's thesis lacks historical evidence to support it and mistakenly implies that retaining the framework of premodern metaphysics would have prevented the rise of scientific naturalism. The paper concludes by pointing to more positive accounts on the connection between the Reformation and science by recent historians.

Keywords: Reformation and Science; science and Christianity; history of science and Christianity; Brad Gregory; Unintended Reformation

1. Introduction

This article will evaluate the first chapter of Brad Gregory's *The Unintended Reformation*, critiquing the connections that he draws between the Reformation and modern secular science. As I will outline below, Gregory draws a direct line from the Reformation to the rise of the "new atheists" such as Richard Dawkins or Daniel Dennett. This assertion might seem puzzling at first. Yes, the Reformation may have made the individual the supreme authority for deciding truth, undercutting traditional authorities, but what does this have to do with science? What do the theological and institutional changes initiated by the Reformers have to do with the study of nature, especially since the Scientific Revolution occurred over a century later?

Gregory places his account of science and Christianity in the first chapter because it most strikingly confirms his overall thesis: the Reformation, from at least a Christian point-of-view, has had catastrophic effects on Western culture. Whereas the Reformers wanted to reform and purify society in light of the gospel message, they sowed the seeds of a post-Christian society. Science is now perceived as conflicting with Christian belief because it provides a naturalistic framework that disenchants the natural world, leaving no room for the providentialist God of Christianity. If the Reformers are ultimately responsible for godless science, then the consequences of the Reformation are far more severe than commonly assumed.

2. Teaching the Christian Intellectual Tradition

In what follows, I will argue that the links between the Reformation and science are not as clear as Gregory suggests. Before I criticize Gregory's account, let me first give some positive comments about the book. Read any of the numerous reviews, and one will see consensus on this point: *The Unintended Reformation* is a work of enormous scope and scholarship. Like many reviewers, I found the work impressive for the footnotes alone, covering some 150 pages. More importantly, Gregory's arguments and criticisms seemed to be often on target. One can object to his account of the relationship between the Reformation and science, while still accepting most of the analysis he sets forth in the rest of the book.

There is also much to appreciate in Gregory's work for instructors teaching the Christian intellectual tradition. Specifically, Gregory provides a helpful historical background to the questions we wrestle with today: "How should I live?" and "How can I know what is true? He provides a narrative that helps both scholars and students to make connections between debates 500 years ago and our modern culture. As Gregory says, "the Western world today [is] an extraordinary complex, tangled product of rejections, retentions, and transformations of medieval Western Christianity, in which the Reformation era constitutes the critical watershed" (6, p. 2). In short, Gregory argues for why we all, secular and religious alike, should study the Christian intellectual tradition.

To explain the emergence of modern culture, Gregory is not hesitant to address questions of metaphysics, philosophy, and morality, topics outside the normal purview of modern historians. As he says, "A different approach is needed if we are to avoid being overwhelmed by specialized scholarship...which tends to reinforce ingrained assumptions about historical periodization that in turn hamper an adequate understanding of change over time" (6, p. 3). His willingness to go beyond normal disciplinary boundaries allows him to offer a larger narrative, a schema for connecting debates in the Reformation to modern beliefs and attitudes. I find his ambition and critique of disciplinary specialization to be exactly right. From a teaching perspective, it is difficult to teach the "Christian intellectual tradition" if we cannot provide larger frameworks for connecting diverse thinkers and topics. Our students need stories which allow them to see the big picture and integrate new information.

3. Gregory's Argument

The big-picture perspective is well and good, of course, but our narratives need to explain history, instead of imposing a narrative upon it. So how does Gregory connect the Reformation and science? When one reads Gregory's account, one sees that despite the title, the real blame for the rise of secular science lies with medieval philosophy. He argues that the philosophers Duns Scotus and William of Ockham bear responsibility for the rise of secularism, for they introduced ideas about God and nature that would later culminate in secular science.

For Gregory, the Christian doctrine that God created the world *ex nihilo* contains certain metaphysical commitments shared by the Christian tradition up until Scotus. Thomas Aquinas, for example, believed in an "analogical metaphysics of creaturely participation in God," meaning Aquinas "presupposed and sought to preserve a view of God so 'otherly other' that God shares no genus in common with creatures" (6, p. 30). In other words, the transcendent God of Christianity is, by this definition, unlike any other thing in the universe, because of the infinite distance between creator and creature.

Gregory claims that Scotus, by contrast, believed in a univocal conception of being, a metaphysical move that predicates in conceptually equivalent terms of everything that exists, including God. Scotus's move made it much easier to talk of God, because God, in Robert Barron's phrase, is "mappable on the same set of coordinates as creatures" (6, p. 37). By shifting away from Aquinas's metaphysical position, the logical and historical outcome of Scotus' philosophy is an "antisacramental" view of nature, because the natural and supernatural cannot be active at the same time in the same event. Scotus brings God down to the same ontological order as the created world, making it easy to exclude God from explanations of the natural world. Scotist metaphysics makes it easier to picture, as Descartes did, the cosmos as a closed mechanical universe. For Gregory, this mechanistic view of nature was a catastrophic move, for it assumes that nature operates according to its own intrinsic principles, independent from God.

What role do the Reformers play in this story? They inherited from Scotus these inferior metaphysical beliefs about God, but Gregory says the Reformers matter for the emergence of modern science in another way: only after the intractable theological disputes of the Reformation did the view of Scotus start to have toxic effects. Christian views about God and the world were sidelined because of unsolvable theological disagreements, leaving alone univocal assumptions. Unable to conceive of God as working through natural causes, disenchantment became the only option when empirical science was unable to discover God's action in the world.

Gregory's account of Scotus and Ockham is popular in theological circles. As the historical theologian Michael Horton skeptically says, "Once you know the Scotus Story, everything else falls into place. The Reformation is the carrier of modern 'disenchantment.' Tearing the fabric of the sacramental tapestry, the reformers pushed the logic of metaphysical univocity, voluntarism, and individualism to its obvious conclusions" (10). Unfortunately for Gregory, I do not think he makes a convincing case that the emergence of an obscure metaphysical doctrine in the Middle Ages is either necessary or sufficient to explain the rise of secular science. I will give two reasons for my skepticism, and then conclude by pointing to more positive, and more evidentially supported, accounts about the Reformation and the rise of science.

4. Criticism: Lack of Historical Basis

One problem for Gregory and other advocates of the Scotus story is that specialists in Scotus—scholars like Richard Cross, Thomas Williams, and Marilyn McCord Adams—find no basis in Scotus's own writings for the theological error attributed to him (14; 1; 5). Scotus' theory of univocity is better seen as a theory about language rather than metaphysics and "is wholly consistent with the view that creatures somehow participate in divine attributes," the view that Gregory says was lost (1, p. 16).

Gregory's misreading of Scotus is not fatal if he can show how Scotus's philosophy was received by later interpreters. The real difficulty with Gregory's narrative is how little historical evidence he gives for it, relying upon secondary sources for his argument. As one reviewer said: "There isn't a single primary source (or even a reference to secondary specialists) to justify this central thesis of his book" (10). Historical studies of the medieval and Reformation period do not find the widespread influence of Scotus' metaphysics. In a recent article, for example, Richard Muller concludes: "A significant sampling of philosophers writing in the Reformed context confirms...a Scotist language of the univocity of being is not at all characteristic of Reformed orthodox thought. The absence of such language from what is arguably the majority of Reformed formulations...stands against the facile characterization of early modern Reformed thought as 'Scotist'" (11, p. 144).

Moreover, it is not clear that a mechanistic philosophy of nature should be equated with excluding God from the natural world, as Gregory asserts. While the mechanical philosophy introduced a strong emphasis on causal reductionism into Western science, many of its early advocates had strong theological reasons for supporting it. As the historian John Hedley Brooke argues, " ... those seventeenth-century scholars who did most to usher in the mechanical metaphors were those who felt that, in so doing, they were enriching rather than emasculating conceptions of divine activity" (4, p. 118). According to thinkers such as Pierre Gassendi, the proof of God's existence is an empirical inference from the nature of matter (12). Because matter is inert, it does not have the ability for self-motion, much less to organize in the complex ways displayed in the natural world. Just as a watch exhibits no purpose except that of the artisan who constructed it, so too nature only reveals the purpose and perfection of the divine watchmaker. Rather than picturing nature as having its own intrinsic principles, as Gregory asserts, the mechanical philosophy encouraged natural philosophers to see the world as filled with inert matter and thus entirely dependent upon God's will.

I thus do not find persuasive the case that Gregory makes which links the philosophy of Duns Scotus to the rise of secular science. For all the historical material that Gregory packs into *The Unintended Reformation*, the chapter itself just repackages a traditional Catholic metanarrative which blames Christianity's problems on a deviation from the metaphysical scheme of Thomas Aquinas.

5. Criticism: Thomist Metaphysics Does Not Avoid the Problems Bequeathed by Science

There are attractive aspects to Thomist metaphysics, especially the idea that God is not to be understood as another object in the furniture of the universe, competing with physical objects to accomplish his will. But Gregory is overly optimistic to think this could have resolved major tensions between science and Christianity, or could have headed off the rise of naturalism. Gregory suggests that whenever one reasons from the physical world about the nature of God, one has committed a metaphysical error. He says, for example, "It is self-evident that a God who by definition is radically distinct from the natural world could never be shown to be unreal via empirical inquiry that by definition can only investigate the natural world" (6, p. 32).

To see why this is not sufficient, consider the fact that "methodological naturalism"—where God is not considered as an explanation for natural events—only became the norm of scientific discourse at the end of the nineteenth century, much later than Gregory seems to assume. After 1870, scientists increasingly avoided invoking the supernatural as an explanation for phenomena within the natural world, thus severing the link between science and natural theology (13). This move toward naturalism helps to explain why the work of Charles Darwin was considered significant. Darwin's hypothesis represented a general approach to scientific explanation, though many scientists disagreed with the details.

Does this confirm Gregory's claim about univocity, where moderns are presented a false choice between whether God intervened to create biological organisms or it was natural process, but not both? It is not clear to me that this metaphysical move alone would solve the challenge of Darwinism. The core of the challenge of Darwinian evolution is how to reconcile the providentialist God—who in the Biblical tradition cares for us, down to the very hairs on our head—and the seeming role of chance in natural selection. Can the same event be both unintentional and specifically intended by God? Can a genetic mutation be both random, as biologists claim, and providentially determined? In the human realm, it makes little sense to claim that I can specifically choose the particular outcome of a random coin flip. Even if we use Thomist metaphysics to claim that a transcendent God can choose the outcome of chance events, it still suggests that poorly designed aspects of nature (or at least 'poorly designed' from a human perspective) are still divinely determined. Why would a gambler lose vast sums of money at the casino table if he or she could determine the outcome of each roll of the dice? Why would God use this process for creation and not others?

I am not suggesting that there are not answers to these questions. My point simply is Thomist metaphysics will not magically make this and other problems go away. I see no reason why the history of science after Darwin would have ended up differently if Duns Scotus had never entered the realm of philosophy.

6. Conclusions: Telling a Better Story about the Reformation and Science

I conclude with better ways to tell the story of the Reformation and Science. In the end, *The Unintended Reformation* is a deeply pessimistic book, attributing most of modern ills to the Reformation. If Gregory had been interested in a more positive account of the way Christianity encouraged the rise of science, there are many alternative accounts from historians of science upon which to draw.

Thus, for example, Peter Harrison argues in *The Bible, Protestantism, and the Rise of Natural Science* that the Reformers' literalism denied the symbolic capacity of objects to refer beyond themselves, which became a necessary ingredient of the Scientific Revolution (7). The outlook of natural historians during the period of the Renaissance is often referred to as the "emblematic world view," because it was "a world where animals are just one aspect of an intricate language of metaphor, symbols, and emblems" (2, p. 305). If one were to consult the *History of Animals* (1551–58) by Conrad Gesner for information on the peacock, one would find not a collection of empirical generalizations, but rather a concordance of materials culled from ancient sources. One would find, for example, peacock recipes, proverbs, and legends (such as the fact that the bird's flesh does not decay after death), as well as other curiosities (that, for instance, it is ashamed of its feet). Thus, to quote the historian William Ashworth, "Gesner believed that to know the peacock, you must know its associations—its affinities, similitudes, and sympathies with the rest of the created order" (2, p. 306). When the Reformers began to emphasize the literal sense of Scripture, it naturally suggested a new way of ordering nature, where it was no longer filled "with signs and symbols of transcendental truths" (8, p. 500).

There are many other ways to draw positive connections between the Reformation and the rise of science. For example, Francis Bacon provided an important theological rationale for the study of nature because it would lead to an increased appreciation of God's power and glory. Science should be judged by the "good fruits" it produced, as Scripture commanded of the believer (3). Reformed presuppositions can also be detected in the advocacy of experimental approaches to natural knowledge, where persons like Bacon and Robert Boyle argued that the effects of original sin required a cautious, experimental approach to nature (9). Instead of speculating about general principles of nature, as philosophers tended to do, it would be far more useful to focus on what happened during particular experiments. Christian assumptions about God and nature helped lay the foundations for the emergence of science, which for some historians explains why modern science began in European culture.

In the end, I conclude that Gregory's aim to pin the errors of the modern world unto the Reformation pushes him to read too much of our modern conflict between science and Christianity back onto the early modern period. As inheritors and teachers of the Christian intellectual tradition, we can tell a far richer and more accurate story about the history of science and Christianity.

Conflicts of Interest: The author declares no conflict of interest.

References

1. Adams, Marilyn McCord. 2014. What's Wrong with the Ontotheological Error? *Journal of Analytic Theology* 2: 1–12.
2. Ashworth, William Jr. 1990. Natural History and the Emblematic Worldview. In *Reappraisals of the Scientific Revolution*. Edited by David C. Lindberg and Robert S. Westman. Cambridge: Cambridge University Press, pp. 303–32.
3. Briggs, John Channing. 1996. Bacon's Science and Religion. In *The Cambridge Companion to Bacon*. Edited by Markku Peltonen. Cambridge: Cambridge University Press, pp. 172–99.
4. Brooke, John Hedley. 1991. *Science and Religion: Some Historical Perspectives*. Cambridge: Cambridge University Press.
5. Cross, Richard. 2001. Where the Angels Fear to Tread: Duns Scotus and Radical Orthodoxy. *Antonianum* 76: 7–41.
6. Gregory, Brad S. 2015. *The Unintended Reformation: How a Religious Revolution Secularized Society*. Cambridge: Belknap Press.
7. Harrison, Peter. 2001. *The Bible, Protestantism, and the Rise of Natural Science*. Cambridge: Cambridge University Press.
8. Harrison, Peter. 2006. Miracles, Early Modern Science, and Rational Religion. *Church History* 75: 493–510. [CrossRef]
9. Harrison, Peter. 2009. *The Fall of Man and the Foundations of Science*. Cambridge: Cambridge University Press.
10. Horton, Michael. 2016. Reviews, Bible & Theology: The Unintended Reformation. *The Gospel Coalition*, February 15. Available online: http://www.thegospelcoalition.org/article/book-reviews-the-unintended-reformation (accessed on 2 February 2016).
11. Muller, Richard A. 2012. Not Scotist. *Reformation & Renaissance Review* 14: 127–50.
12. Osler, Margaret J. 2004. *Divine Will and the Mechanical Philosophy: Gassendi and Descartes on Contingency and Necessity in the Created World*. Cambridge: Cambridge University Press.

13. Reeves, Josh A. 2008. The Field of Science and Religion as Natural Philosophy. *Theology and Science* 6: 403–19. [CrossRef]
14. Williams, Thomas. 2005. The Doctrine of Univocity Is True and Salutary. *Modern Theology* 21: 575–85. [CrossRef]

MDPI AG

St. Alban-Anlage 66

4052 Basel, Switzerland

Tel. +41 61 683 77 34

Fax +41 61 302 89 18

http://www.mdpi.com

Religions Editorial Office

E-mail: religions@mdpi.com

http://www.mdpi.com/journal/religions